FIGHTING FOR GIRLS

SUNY SERIES IN WOMEN, CRIME, AND CRIMINOLOGY

———————

Meda Chesney-Lind and Russ Immarigeon, editors

FIGHTING FOR GIRLS

New Perspectives on Gender and Violence

Edited by

MEDA CHESNEY-LIND

and

NIKKI JONES

STATE UNIVERSITY OF NEW YORK PRESS

Published by
STATE UNIVERSITY OF NEW YORK PRESS, ALBANY

© 2010 State University of New York

For information, contact
State University of New York Press, Albany, NY
www.sunypress.edu

Production, Laurie Searl
Marketing, Anne M. Valentine

Library of Congress Cataloging-in-Publication Data

Fighting for girls : new perspectives on gender and violence / edited by Meda Chesney-Lind and Nikki Jones.
    p. cm. — (SUNY series in women, crime, and criminology)
  Includes bibliographical references and index.
  ISBN 978-1-4384-3293-9 (hardcover : alk. paper)
  ISBN 978-1-4384-3294-6 (pbk. : alk. paper)
  1. Female juvenile delinquents—United States. 2. Teenage girls—United
States. 3. Violence—United States. 4. Juvenile justice, Administration of—United
States. 5. Discrimination in criminal justice administration—United States.
I. Chesney-Lind, Meda. II. Jones, Nikki, 1975–

HV9104.F54 2010
364.36082'0973—dc22   2010007180

10 9 8 7 6 5 4 3 2 1

CONTENTS

TABLES AND FIGURES

ACKNOWLEDGMENTS

We began working on this book after a set of conversations at the American Society of Criminology Meetings in the fall of 2006, as we both struggled to find ways to respond to the racism we saw in the contemporary framing of the moral panic around girls' violence. Meda had come at the topic from one direction, specifically, through the critical deconstruction of media images of hyperviolent girls of color, and Nikki was coming at the topic from the ground up, as she was completing a book on the strategies African American inner-city girls use to navigate dangerous neighborhoods and the gendered consequences of their doing so. The two conversations fit together well: both respond in critical ways to the massive media and scholarly attention given to mean girls; both position girls of color at the center of the analysis; and both emphasized the importance of thinking about context and settings when it came to thinking about girls, gender, and violence at the beginning of the twenty-first century. It was Meda's idea to transform these early conversations into an edited volume. Our hope was—and still is—that this book will cut through the media hype on girls and violence and will refocus our scholarly attention on the circumstances and settings that encourage or discourage girls' use of aggression or violence. Yes, girls fight, but what are they fighting for, exactly? And how can we use the best available data to fight for girls who are trapped in correctional facilities, group homes, or distressed urban neighborhoods? The chapters in this book help us to think about girls' use of violence in new ways, and will hopefully inspire new conversations about how to improve the conditions in which girls, especially poor girls of color, come of age.

We'd like to thank the original panelists and each of the contributing authors for their commitment to this project. We'd also like to thank our editors at State University of New York Press, Larin McLaughlin and Laurie Searl. We are grateful for the diligent assistance in preparing the manuscript provided by Syeda Tonima Hadi and Brian Bilsky. Our home departments have also provided the necessary intellectual space and institutional support to complete this project.

Chapter 3 was published earlier in *Youth Violence and Juvenile Justice* 5.3 (2007): 328–345, and appears here with the permission of Sage Publications. Chapter 9 is drawn from material that appears in Nikki's book,

Between Good and Ghetto: African American Girls and Inner City Violence. Many of the following chapters feature the voices and experiences of adolescent girls. We are deeply grateful for their participation in the various research projects that inform these chapters. We hope that this book helps to reframe discussions of girls' violence in ways that will bring more attention to how policymakers, scholars, and practitioners can work to improve the lives of girls, especially those girls who are most vulnerable to increasingly punitive practices in their schools, neighborhoods, and the juvenile and criminal justice systems.

INTRODUCTION

Meda Chesney-Lind and Nikki Jones

A decade into the twenty-first century, it seems like the news about girls is increasingly alarming. Of course, we've always had "bad" girls. Longfellow, no less, penned, that "when she was good she was very good indeed, and when she was bad, she was horrid" (Longfellow, 2004). In the waning decades of the twentieth century, though, the public was jolted by media images of "gangster" girls, every bit as menacing as their urban male counterparts, often pictured glaring at the world over the barrel of a gun. The new century also introduced us to suburban "mean" girls, manipulating and backstabbing their way to popularity, and now, only a few years later, it seems as though our mean girls have suddenly turned violent. YouTube videos of brawling cheerleaders make local and national news and "go viral" on the Web where they are viewed by thousands. Do we really need to worry about girls causing "savagery in the suburbs" (Meadows & Johnson, 2003: 37), as a 2003 headline in *Newsweek* warned? It would certainly seem so if you picked up recent trade books like *See Jane Hit* (Garbarino, 2006) and *Sugar and Spice and No Longer Nice* (Prothrow-Stith & Spivak, 2005), which purport to advise parents and teachers on what to do about girls' violence while also fueling public unease about modern girlhood.

Given the high level of public and academic interest in girls' use of violence and aggression, it is actually remarkable that so little careful academic work has been made available to those concerned with the facts and not the hype. This book fills this void by making two major contributions to the discussion of girls' aggression and violence. One is to challenge the widely accepted notion that girls are "more violent" than in the past—a perception that has largely fueled the media panic about "girls gone wild." These panics about girls' violence are not only ungrounded, but are also potentially quite harmful for poor girls of color. The most punitive consequences of this twenty-first-century crackdown on violent girls is likely to be felt most by girls who live in heavily policed urban neighborhoods and attend troubled inner-city schools that enforce "zero-tolerance" policies. Using a wide variety of empirical sources, this book lays out data that demonstrates how changes in the policing of girlhood and changes in girls' structural and situational

1

circumstances, rather than essential changes in girls' behavior, largely explains the significant increases in girls arrests, particularly for simple assault.

This book challenges the simplistic and somewhat contradictory notion that girls use of violence is somehow inherent in their personalities and a product of them becoming "more like boys" in the new millennium. We offer a number of chapters that challenge the notion that supporting girls' efforts to seek equality in sports or in the classroom—that is, encouraging their efforts to seek and maintain equality with men and boys—will somehow produce unintended consequences like equity in crime. We present cutting-edge research on the contexts that encourage violent behavior among girls, and we show that addressing the unique problems that confront girls in various settings, such as in dating relationships, in damaged families, in school hallways and classrooms, and in distressed urban neighborhoods could go a long way to reducing girls' use of violence. Thus, rather than framing girls and their behavior as "the problem," the chapters in this book focus on how social settings shape girls' responses to potential threats of violence and victimization and the often punitive institutional response to girls' actions. The chapters also highlight the importance of the backgrounds of girls who have used violence. Often using girls' own voices, the authors discuss how and why girls came to use violence in certain situations. These chapters encourage us to pay attention to the degree of trauma found in girls' pasts, as well as the high levels of violence in their families, neighborhoods, and schools, all of which combine to produce girls who use violence in these settings. Many of the poor, young women of color whose voices are featured in the pages of this volume explain very powerfully how the situations they found themselves in encouraged their use of violence; their stories stand in contrast to popular media images that repeatedly construct female victims as white, middle-class suburban girls who have "gone wild."

In pulling this book together, we, as the editors, have drawn on a number of distinct theoretical traditions, but two predominate. The first tradition is that of feminist criminology, particularly that strand of feminist criminology that insists on the importance of "intersectionality" (Morash & Chesney-Lind, 2006; Burgess-Proctor, 2006; Potter, 2006). This phrase foregrounds the ways that race, gender, and class intersect in the lives of all women, but particularly the lives of criminalized girls and women. Such a perspective reminds us that all women have a race, gender, and class position (among others) that informs their actions and the various institutional and interpersonal responses to their actions. This tradition is central to understanding both the contexts that give rise to girls' violence as well as the use of violence itself. The second key theme is that of "voice" (Brown & Gilligan, 1992; Brown, 2003). This is the notion that creating a space for girls to be heard is a central part of the enterprise of good feminist scholarship. The importance of hearing girls' voices directs feminist scholars in the area of girls' studies to rely on methods that showcase and capture, in girls' own words and to the greatest degree possible, perspectives on issues of violence, relationships, victimization, and resistance. A number of chapters in this book do this quite powerfully. Finally, the book relies on constructionist and critical criminologies that focus attention on the importance of the media not only in constructing images of crime, but also in creating moral panics that encourage a harshly punitive response to crime (Cohen, 1972; Hall et al., 1978; Jenkins, 1998).

HOW THIS BOOK IS ORGANIZED

The first aim of this book is to review, using the best data available, trends in girls' violence. In the book's opening two chapters, authors Mike Males, Eve Buzawa, and David Hirschel explore this important issue in different ways. These chapters provide new ways of understanding girls' use of violence by using sophisticated arrest data that gives us specific information on both the context of the offense and the characteristics of victims. Chapter 1 by Mike Males entitled "Have 'Girls Gone Wild'?" sets the stage by reviewing key data presented on the actual trends in girls' violence. Males notes that at a time in which every reliable measure of crime and victimization shows girls are less violent and victimized today, we see a massive campaign by professionals, scholars, institutions, and the media to brand girls as "wild," "mean," and violent. Males explores the "pop psychology" and "pop culture" dimensions of this contemporary anti-girl campaign, and explains how today's "girls' violence" hoax, and the rush by major interests to embrace it, reflects a major breakdown in our society's capacity to analyze and design rational policies for young people, particularly adolescent girls.

In chapter 2, "Criminalizing Assault," Eve Buzawa and David Hirschel present new research on the impact of mandatory arrests in the area of domestic violence, particularly focusing on police bias and its role in the arrests of young people. For the first time, and with considerably more precision regarding what arrests for crimes of violence actually entail, the authors examine the question of whether or not assaults on adults by youth are particularly criminalized. The authors' profile of arrest trends clearly demonstrates that girls are far more likely to be arrested for simple assaults in these incidents, as opposed to more serious assaults. Buzawa and Hirschel also find that girls' assaults are less likely to involve injury or weapons than boys' assaults, and that girls (and boys) who are suspected of hitting their parents are far more likely to be arrested than their adult counterparts. Taken together, these two studies document how changes in criminal justice policies, namely, mandatory arrests for domestic violence, have increased youth exposure to criminal justice sanctions.

The next chapter by Chesney-Lind on the jailing of girls focuses on the sobering fact that we are now arguably in the self-fulfilling-prophecy stage of the hype about "violent" girls detailed in Males' chapter. Here we see a split in the popular treatment of girls violence: we care deeply about saving middle-class "mean" girls from themselves and their peers while shrugging off the consequences of harshly punitive juvenile and criminal justice policies that target poor girls of color and their families. These changing policies have led to increases in the arrests and incarceration of African American girls for violent offenses. A look at the data reveals that not only have girls' arrests for crimes of violence increased, while the number for boys stayed level or dropped, we are also seeing dramatic increases in referrals to court of girls charged with "person" offenses. This increased incarceration is deeply racialized, with African American and Native American girls disproportionately incarcerated for person offenses. This is just one consequence of the present-day panic about violent girls. Resources are funneled into suburban schools for gender-based conflict resolution sessions, while poor girls of color in urban settings continue to be arrested and incarcerated for their use of aggression or violence. Imagine in what rational world would more girls than boys be in court populations charged with violent offenses, and yet that was precisely the case in 2003, the last year for which we have data, when 26% of girls were in court populations charged with person offenses, compared to 23% of boys (Snyder & Sickmund, 2006). Similar trends are observed in sentencing, with dramatic increases in the detention and imprisonment of girls, again with no similar increase in boys' imprisonment. Of course, popular debates about increasingly violent girls make no mention of either the conditions that led to violence or the disparate criminal consequences experienced by girls in different settings.

In short, these chapters document that a careful reading of the best available data does not support arguments that girls today are far more violent than their counterparts in earlier decades. Instead, all the available evidence points to policy changes, most specifically the dramatic shift in the treatment of domestic violence incidents, but also other policy shifts such as "zero-tolerance" policies toward fighting in schools that are producing increasing arrests of girls. The most severe consequences of these shifts are felt most by poor girls of color, since data clearly indicate that such girls, particularly African American girls, are dramatically overrepresented in detention centers and training schools. Once these girls enter the system, they tend to stay in the system, despite fairly clear evidence that in previous decades their behavior would not have warranted a criminal justice response, much less an arrest. The popular concern regarding girls distracts our attention from these important policy shifts and the resulting consequences. Though we are not seeing a dramatic increase in girls' violence, we are witnessing a dramatic shift in criminal justice responses to girls' behavior. We are not seeing the emergence of the new violent girl, but we are seeing dramatic increases in the arrest, detention, and incarceration of girls for person offenses. In essence, the nation is embarking on a massive and unnecessary increase in the incarceration of girls—one with enormous racial and gender consequences, based largely on an increase in girls' arrests that are fueled by policy changes rather than a real increase in girls' violence.

Having established this empirical reality, we turn to a consideration of the context of girls' violence. These chapters reveal how girls' violence is inextricably tied to the contexts and settings within which girls live out their lives. Girls have not become more violent, but for some girls, the conditions in which they come of age are, in many cases, more distressed, more isolated, and, in turn, more violent than is commonly understood. Girls who live in distressed urban areas witness and experience far more violence in their everyday lives than their suburban, middle-class counterparts. Girls who come of age in isolated inner-city neighborhoods share an increased vulnerability to gender-specific violence, including dating violence, harassment, and sexual assault. Adolescent girls who come of age within these structural-cultural contexts, which are deeply influenced by race, gender, and class, are pressured to make choices about how to "survive" in settings where their survival is not guaranteed. These girls face serious dilemmas that most of their middle-class counterparts—white or African American—rarely encounter. In the next section of this book, Girls' Violence: Institutional Contexts and Concerns, we highlight the social and psychological consequences of girls' exposure to violence in various settings, as well as their responses to their increased vulnerability in these settings.

Thus, after effectively critiquing the myths about "violent girls," part 2, "Contextualizing Girls' Violence and Aggression," shifts our attention to the specific contexts within which girls are likely to encounter violence, including schools, neighborhoods, and intimate relationships. Each of the authors in this section challenge simplistic notions of girls' violence and reveal the racialized, gendered, and classed dimensions of girls' experiences with violence along with the cultural, institutional, and individual responses to "violent" girls.

In the first chapter in the section, chapter 4, "The Gendering of Violence and Sexuality in Intimate Relationships: How Violence Makes Sex Less Safe for Girls," Melissa E. Dichter, Julie A. Cederbaum, and Anne M. Teitelman explore the often-hidden experiences of girls in violent dating relationships. Specifically, they push back against notions that boys and girls are equally "violent" as some studies contend. They argue that one must examine how the threat of physical and psychological violence and unequal gendered power dynamics in girls' intimate relationships may increase girls' risk of violence and potential for contracting serious sexually transmitted diseases, including HIV. The authors argue powerfully that the "normal" dating script disempowers girls vis-à-vis boys, and exposes them to forms of partner violence and sexual coercion that most measures of dating violence have never considered.

In chapter 5, Chesney-Lind, Morash, and Irwin critically review the literature on relational aggression, which has been the key literature that produced the "mean girl" imagery and hype. They argue that research to date does not necessarily support the notion that such aggression is the exclusive province of girls; indeed, they find rather convincing evidence that while girls' display the behavior earlier than boys (who are as children more likely to engage in physical aggression or violence), that changes by late adolescence when boys close the gap. More importantly, they argue that those who engage in non-violent, social aggression do not necessarily have other social problems (meaning that they do not also experience problems in school or at home). Finally, they argue that since relational aggression is not predictive of physical aggression or violence, it should not be folded into notions of "bullying," which many schools have done.

The next chapter in this section illuminates the meanings of violence in the lives of girls whose behavior is more likely to be sanctioned by police officers than school counselors. In " 'I don't know if you consider that as violence . . . ': Using Attachment Theory to Understand Girls' Perspectives on Violence," Judith A. Ryder uses the narratives of 24 adolescent girls adjudicated for an assault or robbery to examine the interpersonal and context-dependent nature of their violence. Ryder uses an "attachment perspective" to explain how young women's physical violence develops under adverse conditions as an attempt to coerce others into meeting attachment needs; later developing the use of aggression or violence as an adaptive response in harsh social environments.

Chapter 7, "Reducing Aggressive Behavior in Adolescent Girls by Attending to School Climate," by Sibylle Artz and Diana Nicholson, examines how interactions in institutional settings can produce cultural contexts that inhibit the use of aggression or violence. The authors use thematic and statistical analysis of data from a five-year, longitudinal research project to demonstrate how group dynamics influence positive connections and engagement in school settings. Specifically, their analysis shows that smaller groupings in single-sex settings that support positive values, a sense of connection, and engagement with one's school and one's fellow students, where one need not fear attack or sexual harassment and has confidence that one will be supported and assisted with problem solving and the resolution of conflict, produce positive outcomes even for girls who are identified as high risk, aggressive, and violent.

Still staying in key settings for girls, in chapter 8 Marion Brown considers the effectiveness of "group homes," a ubiquitous and somewhat under-researched setting within which girls who have problems at home and on the streets often find themselves "placed." Brown notes that these settings, far from offering girls a safe haven from dangerous families and streets, instead often encourage the very violence they seek to extinguish. Particularly problematic for the girls whose voices Brown lets us hear is their frustration with the constant and petty surveillance of their bodies and interactions in these settings, as well as the often arbitrary and demeaning rules that characterize many of these facilities. Ultimately, even though she worked in these facilities herself, Brown is very concerned that the cumulative effect of the "micro-technologies" of surveillance, along with "pathologizing" and "individualizing" discourses, end up short changing and even harming the very girls the facilities are intended to help.

In the final section of the book, Girls' Violence: Explanations and Implications, we shift our attention to how neighborhood settings influence girls' use of violence. In "It's about being a survivor . . .": African American Girls, Gender, and the Context of Inner-City Violence," Nikki Jones draws on data collected over years of ethnographic research in two urban settings—Philadelphia and San Francisco—to reflect on the strategies that African American, inner-city girls develop to navigate distressed urban neighborhoods and the gendered consequences of their doing so. Jones reveals that boys and girls who come of age in distressed urban neighborhoods develop a preoccupation with survival. Over time, girls come to recognize the three Rs of "the code of the street"—respect, reputation, and retaliation—which governs much of the violence in their neighborhoods. As Jones illustrates, inner-city girls understand at an early age that stray bullets do not discriminate between young and old, guilt and innocence, or boys and girls. Girls know that the settings of inner-city life, whether school buildings or row houses, neighborhood street corners or porch stoops, do not come with a special girls-only pass to live beyond the reach of violence. The need to avoid or overcome dangers throughout their adolescence presents a unique dilemma for girls who grow up in these neighborhoods. Jones situates African American, inner-city girls' experiences at the center of her research in order to explain how girls reconcile the gendered dilemmas of inner-city adolescence, including how they develop situated survival strategies in between the competing and contradictory expectations of "good" and "ghetto" girls, and the limitations of these strategies when it comes to girls' vulnerability to gender-specific violence, which remains a prevalent threat for adolescent girls who grow up in distressed urban neighborhoods.

In the penultimate chapter, "The Importance of Context in the Production of Older Girls' Violence: Implications for the Focus of Intervention," Merry Morash, Suyeon Park, and Jung-mi Kim use quantitative, longitudinal analysis to examine the relationship of the degree of violence in the community, school, and family contexts to subsequent violence by girls and their reported levels of hopelessness and depression. Finally, Walter DeKeseredy provides an important service to readers in his epilogue, by returning us to the ten-thousand-foot level, if you will, and discussing again core theoretical notions that undergird this collection. There is, first and foremost, the notion of a moral panic that fuels many crime waves, including the girl crime wave that has characterized entry into the new millennium. He also reminds us of the crucial role played by the criminal justice system in both creating and re-creating patriarchal control over girls and women, and, finally, he reminds of us of the importance of context when discussing girls' and women's violence.

BEYOND DENIAL AND DEMONIZATION

Together, the chapters in this book demonstrate that the media hype about the problem of violent girls considerably exaggerates the situation we confront, and it misidentifies the source of the problem (often using misogynistic and racist arguments like the "masculinization" of African American girls). This book challenges media images of girls' violence that relies on both racialized and masculinized images to heighten racial stereotyping and gender trouble rather than exploring the empirical dimensions of the problem. The book also provides powerful evidence about the settings and situational contexts that encourage girls' use of violence. A review of these chapters provides very clear evidence that living in abusive families, attending dysfunctional schools, dating abusive men or boys, living in dangerous neighborhoods, and being housed in controlling group homes all combine to create girls' violence. Turning our attention to girls' "choices" in these contexts provides a clear roadmap in going forward. If we want to reduce girls' violence we have to challenge our cultural obsession with producing "good" girls who meet our cultural expectations of proper femininity. We must expand our attention beyond girls' aggressive or violent behaviors to include a deep concern about the families, schools, and neighborhoods in which girls find themselves. Serious efforts to change those settings are more likely to produce less violence, even among girls with long histories of delinquency.

As we reflect on the dramatic increases in the policing and ultimate incarceration of girls, particularly poor girls of color and often for less serious forms of violence (for example, simple assault), we are drawn to the conditions in the facilities in which girls are punished, which are themselves horrifically violent. As the numbers of girls in these institutions soar, we call for a wholesale reappraisal of those poorly crafted polices, such as mandatory arrest and zero tolerance, which have brought us to this place. Girls do not need more policing and punishment; instead they need polices that create and support safe families, positive and nurturing relationships, schools that teach rather than punish, and neighborhoods that do not traumatize and terrorize. We would all benefit from such an investment.

REFERENCES

Brown, L. M. (2003). *Girlfighting*. New York: New York University Press.
Brown, L. M., & Gilligan, C. (1992). *Meeting at the crossroads: Women's psychology and girls' development*. New York: Ballantine.
Burgess-Proctor, A. (2006). Intersections of race, class, gender, and crime: Future directions for feminist criminology. *Feminist Criminology* 1(1): 6–26.

Cohen, S. (1972). *Folk devils and moral panics*. London: MacGibbon and Kee.

Federal Bureau of Investigation. (1996). *Crime in the United States 1995*. Washington, DC: Government Printing Office.

Federal Bureau of Investigation. (2000). *Crime in the United States 1999*. Washington, DC: Government Printing Office.

Federal Bureau of Investigation. (2006). *Crime in the United States 1999*. Washington, DC: Government Printing Office.

Garbarino, J. (2006). *See Jane hit: Why girls are growing more violent and what we can do about it*. New York: Penguin Press.

Hall, S., Critcher, C., Jefferson, T., Clark, J., & Roberts, B. (1978). *Policing the crisis: Mugging, the state, and law and order*. London: Macmillan.

Jenkins, P. (1998). *Changing concepts of the child molester in modern America*. New Haven and London: Yale University Press.

Longfellow, H. W. (2004). "There was a little girl." In *Poetry X* 27 September 2004, http://poetry.poetryx.com/poems/6357/ (accessed 8 January 2009).

Meadows, S., & Johnson, D. (2003). Girl fight: Savagery in the Chicago suburbs. *Newsweek*, 37.

Morash, M., & Chesney-Lind, M. (2006). *Girls' violence in context*. Office of Juvenile Justice and Delinquency Prevention Girls Study Group Volume. Margaret Zahn, editor. Philadelphia: Temple University Press.

Potter, H. (2006). An argument for black feminist criminology: Understanding African American women's experiences with intimate partner abuse using an integrated approach. *Feminist Criminology* 1(2): 106–124.

Prothrow-Stith, D., & Spivak, H. R. (2005). *Sugar and spice and no longer nice: How we can stop girls' violence*. San Francisco: Jossey-Bass.

Snyder, H. N., & Sickmund, M. (2006). *Juvenile offenders and victims: 2006 national report* (NCJ 178257). Washington, DC: U.S. Department of Justice, Office of Justice Programs, Office of Juvenile Justice and Delinquency Prevention.

PART I

REAL TRENDS IN FEMALE VIOLENCE: GETTING TOUGH ON GIRLS

ONE

HAVE "GIRLS GONE WILD"?

Mike Males

Britney, Paris, Lindsay . . . poster girls-gone-wild for "the new normalcy of addiction for young women" and "the dwindling state of young women's mental health," as one progressive author declares (Martin, 2007, 2007a)? Drunken driving, hard drugs, crazed standoffs, wild hookup sex, even beatings and guns—are pop starlets run amuck the new American Everygirl?

The modern young woman is "a bubbling, acid pit of guilt and shame and jealousy and restlessness and anxiety," announces feminist Courtney Martin (*Perfect Girls, Starving Daughters*, 2007: 4). "We are more diseased and more addicted than any generation of young women that has come before . . . succumbing to dangerous emotional numbs—eating disorders, binge drinking, and even harder drugs" (Martin, 2007a). Worse, adds Loyola University Chicago psychologist James Garbarino, shocked Americans are witnessing a "recent, dramatic increase in violence by troubled girls" (*See Jane Hit*, 2006: 15). Harvard School of Public Health professors Deborah Prothrow-Stith and Howard Spivak warn of "increased rates of girls' arrests for violent crime, including homicide" (*Sugar and Spice and No Longer Nice*, 2005: 48).

So, what else is new? Every older generation recycles the same panics about girls—perpetually shocking sexual precocity, drinking, muggings, insanity—decade after decade. The 1940s and '50s, for example, brought a barrage of government-sponsored docudramas featuring lusty teen girls seducing and robbing innocent men, laughingly gunning down motorists, dying in gunfights with cops. "They start with stealing lipstick, finish with a slaying!" blared "frank truth" films like *Girls Under 21*, *Girls of the Night*, *So Young So Bad*, *Delinquent Daughters*, and *Girls in the Night*. Best-selling early-1950s books blazoned busty, fist-clenched, gun-brandishing teen girls and titles like *The Young and Violent*, *Jailbait*, *Juvenile Jungle*, *Teenage Crime*

Wave, Live Fast Die Young, and (my favorite) *I'll Fix You.* Major magazines like *Life, Reader's Digest,* and *Ladies Home Journal* warned that hundreds of teenage "pickup" girls as young as twelve were making "the sex delinquency of young girls" the worst problem cities faced. "Are These Our Children?" (*Look,* 21 September 1942) and "Boston's Bad Girls" (*Pic,* 17 August 1943) clarioned "Everytown, USA," terrorized by girls gone berserk: "Arrests for drunkenness of girls are up 40 percent . . . prostitution, 64 percent . . . truancy cases are up 400 percent . . . sex offenses involving teen-age girls, up 200 percent . . . the average age of offenders is fifteen . . ." (Barson & Heller, 1998: 35, 38). Everything, in short, but Debbie Does Nukes.

Still, the attacks on girls today, reflecting the same bizarre combination of sympathy for girls' presumed female delicateness and fury at girls' assumed aggressiveness, appear to be setting new records for ferocity. Popular psychologist-author Mary Pipher's *Reviving Ophelia* (1995, 1998) brands girls "moody, demanding, and distant . . . sullen and secretive . . . depressed . . . overwhelmed . . . anorexic . . . alcoholic . . . traumatized . . ." and "fragile . . . saplings in a hurricane" of "eating disorders, school phobias, self-inflicted injuries . . . great unhappiness . . . anxiety . . ." (all that before we're halfway through her first chapter!). In *Queen Bees and Wannabes'* first 15 pages, Rachel Wiseman (2002) calls girls "confused," "insecure," "lashing out," "totally obnoxious," "moody," "cruel," "sneaky," "lying," "mean," "exclusive," and "catty." "GIRLS ARE MEAN," emphasizes *Girl Wars* coauthor Cheryl Dellasega (referring to those who haven't gone through her "relational aggression" program), and "the seriousness of these behaviors is reaching new proportions, resulting in criminal charges, school shootings, and suicides" (Dellasega & Nixon, 2003: 4).

Books by scholarly and professional authors, pundits' commentaries, and mass-media splashes on girls' "new" pathologies have adopted the same sensationalism, titillation, and stereotyping that can only be termed poisonous. The detail that none of the commentators knew the Gloucester, Massachusetts, high school girls they falsely accused of forging a "teen pregnancy pact" did not temper the media's factless disparagements (Kingsbury, 2008), repeated in commentators' later vilifications of the pregnancy of 2008 Republican vice presidential candidate Sarah Palin's 17-year-old daughter. *CBS Evening News'* crusade against girls, including inflammatory reports on binge drinking (6 May 2007), Internet "dangers" (19–22 November 2007), and violence (19 January 2007), typified the mind-numbingly identical girl-bashing reports. All featured dire alarms by self-interested sources and zero genuine evidence (unless staged videos of a minor scuffles, a girl's slap in a *Harry Potter* movie, and "Powerpuff Girls" cartoons are "evidence"). But when Pennsylvania State University criminologist Darrell Steffensmeier (et al., 2005) and the Department of Juvenile Justice and Delinquency Prevention's Girls Study Group (Zahn, 2007) released comprehensive compilations of decades of solid measures showing that girls' violence had not risen, commentators and the major media couldn't get interested.

What are we to make of today's seemingly irrational fear and hostility toward girls? An important factor driving modern girl-fearing may be racial change. Four in 10 girls and young women under age 25 today are black, Latina, Asian, or otherwise of color, dramatically larger percentages than in older generations. Most girl-fearing commentators are white, but they have been joined by some prominent, older African Americans such as entertainer Bill Cosby (2004; see also Dyson, 2005) and pundits Juan Williams (2007), Earl Ofari Hutchinson (2007), and Bob Herbert (see Males, 2004) who also echo racist stereotypes that characterize black girls as increasingly promiscuous and violent (see sidebar).

SAN FRANCISCO'S SHAME

Crude racial and sexual stereotypes toward girls have real consequences, even in the modern era and the most liberal of cities. In San Francisco, the press, police, and interest groups obsessively ignited inflamed panics toward "girl gangs" and crime, ballooning minor assaults into unheard-of crises. Perhaps it's no surprise, then, that African American girls, who comprised just 13% of the city's girls in 2007, suffered four-fifths of girls' drug arrests and 70% of girls' incarcerations. Astoundingly, San Francisco black girls suffer more drug arrests numerically than black girls in Los Angeles (a city whose black population is 20 times larger) and are 15 times more likely to be arrested for drugs than black girls elsewhere in California.

Do San Francisco's black girls suffer extraordinary drug problems, then? Other than arrest, no. California Department of Health Services and Drug Abuse Warning Network reports show that African American females under age 20 accounted for none of San Francisco's 5,000 overdose deaths and fewer than one-half of 1% of hospital emergency cases involving illicit drugs over the last decade. In contrast, two-thirds involved whites, 61% involved males, and 60% were over age 35 (San Francisco Juvenile Probation Department, 2007).

Repeated efforts by the author on behalf of the Center on Juvenile and Criminal Justice to obtain explanations from San Francisco human rights, police, and political agencies for the city's drastically excessive arrests of black girls brought only evasion and indifference. In a progressive city whose burgeoning drug abuse crisis is inconveniently centered in white middle-aged men—a wealthy, powerful constituency politicians, interests, and press covet—the usefulness of scapegoating black girls clearly underlies authorities' continuing refusal to confront either outrage. Rather, interests have united to exploit the so-called "girl trouble" consisting largely of young black women with manufactured criminal records that city policies themselves created.

A related factor is the plunging scholarship and rising emotion characterizing modern books on youth. Anyone can assemble a book, news story, column, or report from personal stories, press clippings, therapy cases (Pipher: "what I see in my practice"), messed-up pals (Martin: "my friends and my friends' friends, and sometimes even my friends' friends' friends"), and similarly selective anecdotes to fashion whatever image of whatever group most pleases and sells. Such works can even be valuable when they illuminate problems afflicting small segments.

However, commentators repeatedly insist they are describing *all* girls and young women as a generation gone tragically rotten. They don't seem to see the irony in inflicting their own demeaning stereotypes on girls en route to denouncing girls' "relational aggression"—that is, bullying by females higher in the "hierarchical order" who spread cruel insinuations about females with less power (Dellasega & Nixon, 2003).

As we'll see, these authors' books and commentaries on girls amount to little more than gossip and name-calling. They claim to speak for girls—or, at least, the white, middle-class suburban girls with whom they seem to be concerned—yet they ignore what girls and young women actually say about themselves as a class and generation. They propagate atrociously wrong "statistics." They ignore solid public health, crime, and other trends that confirm girls' self-descriptions that this is not a female generation of misery, mayhem, addiction, or otherwise diseased by success. They employ sexist, anti-youth stereotypes and sloppy methods that would not be acceptable to apply to other groups in society.

So, let's reverse the lens: Why are authors and commentators slandering today's girls, often in harshly demeaning terms? The troubling statements and popularity of girl-fearing authors suggest that even as we move into the twenty-first century, antiquated prejudices concerning girls' and young women's supposed fragility, irrationality, masochism, and racial diversity are returning with a vengeance.

WHAT GIRLS SAY ABOUT THEMSELVES

Who knows what thirty million girls and young women ages ten to twenty-four think? Not me, a 59-year-old man with a suspect name. Nor any individual, especially not authors like Pipher (1998), who profiles a few troubled cases and condescends, "it's totally simple what teenage girls think."

If we want to know what girls think, we ask them in carefully designed, long-term, large-scale, nonideological surveys of samples scientifically chosen to represent young women as a cohort, such as *Monitoring the Future* (of 500,000 high school seniors from 1975 through 2005) and *The American Freshman* (16,000,000 first-year college students, from 1966 through 2006). Then, we examine the best social and health statistics to assess whether girls' self-reported attitudes are consistent with real-life outcomes.

Do girls—allowed to speak for themselves rather than through commentators presuming to speak for them—report being more depressed, fashion obsessed, threatened, passive, alienated from parents and friends, self-absorbed, violent, or victimized? *No.* Today, 70% of high school senior girls report being happy with themselves, 86% are happy with their friends, 66% are having fun, and 77% are happy with their lives (table 1.1). These totals are somewhat higher than in the past. Girls' general happiness and well-being must be terrible news, since no commentators I can find mention it.

Table 1.1. Monitoring Female High School Seniors

Percentages of Female High School Seniors Responding to *Monitoring the Future*:	1975–76	1980	1990	2000	2005
Happiness					
I'm "very happy"	21%	18%	18%	23%	23%
Satisfied with life as a whole	63%	66%	65%	64%	66%
Having fun	64%	67%	68%	65%	66%
Enjoys fast pace and changes of today's world	45%	42%	58%	56%	50%
Daily participation in active sports/ exercising	36%	38%	34%	35%	36%
Satisfaction with (percent agreeing)					
Yourself?	66%	71%	69%	71%	70%
Your friends?	85%	85%	87%	83%	86%
Your parents?	65%	69%	65%	68%	67%
Your material possessions?	75%	75%	71%	73%	75%
Your personal safety?	68%	67%	66%	69%	71%
Your education?	56%	64%	64%	64%	70%
Your job?	56%	54%	60%	56%	60%
Values (percent agreeing)					
Important to be a leader in my community	19%	20%	33%	40%	46%
Important to make a contribution to society	55%	52%	62%	65%	70%
Important to have latest music, fashions, etc.	77%	78%	70%	59%	51%
Important to have latest-style clothes	42%	47%	57%	42%	39%
Wants to have lots of money	35%	41%	63%	57%	59%
Wants job with status and prestige	52%	60%	69%	65%	67%
Wants job that provides lots of money	84%	89%	86%	86%	86%
Wants job with opportunity to help others	92%	91%	92%	88%	90%

continued on next page

Table 1.1 (*Continued*)

Percentages of Female High School Seniors Responding to *Monitoring the Future*:	1975–76	1980	1990	2000	2005
Values (percent agreeing)					
Women should have equal job opportunity	82%	88%	96%	97%	95%
Wants to correct social/economic inequality	37%	35%	44%	39%	39%
Happier to accept things than create change	37%	39%	36%	39%	35%
Depression/pessimism					
Dissatisfied with self	12%	10%	13%	10%	12%
Sometimes thinks "I am no good at all"	28%	27%	28%	25%	24%
I'm "not too happy"	13%	17%	12%	14%	13%
Feels I am "not a person of worth"	5%	5%	6%	7%	8%
Often feels "left out of things"	33%	34%	36%	34%	29%
Feels there's usually no one I can talk to	6%	5%	6%	6%	5%
Feels "I can't do anything right"	10%	11%	12%	14%	14%
Wishes "I had more good friends"	50%	46%	50%	52%	44%
Not having fun	19%	13%	16%	20%	17%
Can't get ahead because others stop me	22%	21%	26%	26%	20%
Thinks "things change too quickly" today	54%	56%	44%	44%	46%
Thinks "times ahead of me will be tougher"	47%	54%	45%	42%	41%
Don't participate in sports/exercise (<1/month)	22%	20%	25%	22%	22%
Feels "people like me don't have a chance"	6%	5%	5%	5%	5%

Source: Monitoring the Future (1975–2005).

A few attitudes show fairly large changes. Many more girls today report being happy with their education and jobs and optimistic about the future. There are also large increases in percentages of girls supporting women's equality, seeking leadership roles and jobs with status and high pay, and wanting to make a contribution to society. While many commentators have selectively chastised girls' interest in making money as evidence of materialism (curiously, they don't cite the fact that a generation of older Americans is the richest in world history as evidence of our materialism), there may be more practical reasons for that trend, as we'll see. Perhaps most surprising, given commentators' incessant assertions that girls today are obsessed with being trendy (see especially Quart, 2002), fewer girls report obsession with the latest fashions.

Are girls and young women suffering supposedly record levels of tobacco, alcohol, and drug abuse at younger ages? Again, just the opposite. High school girls report drinking and using drugs less today and at older ages (table 1.2). Even "binge drinking," a misleading term in any case (five drinks in five hours have considerably different effect than in five minutes), peaked back in 1980 and now is rarer among girls than in the past. Fewer girls are prescribed mood-altering stimulants or use them on their own. The use of prescription narcotics has held steady, but all other drug, tobacco, and alcohol use has dropped, often substantially. Again, this must be terrible news, since commentators and authors strive mightily to lend the opposite impression.

But even if girls and young women *say* they aren't more miserable, alienated, and addicted today, isn't it a fact that they're more prone to promiscuity, emotionally unattached "hooking up," and sexual consequences such as early pregnancy and sexually transmitted infections (STIs)? Here

Table 1.2. Monitoring Female High School Seniors

Percentages of Female High School Seniors Telling *Monitoring the Future* They:	1977	1980	1990	2000	2005
Smoked cigarettes daily	45%	41%	30%	32%	20%
Smoked daily before 9th grade	12%	17%	10%	13%	4%
Drank alcohol (more than a few sips)	91%	92%	89%	78%	74%
Drank alcohol before 9th grade	21%	24%	32%	28%	19%
Binge drinking (5+ drinks in a row, past 2 weeks)	26%	30%	24%	24%	23%
Binge drinking more than 1 time	16%	20%	14%	14%	13%
Used amphetamines	16%	17%	9%	8%	5%
By physician's prescription	15%	11%	5%	6%	5%
Without a prescription	22%	25%	13%	11%	9%
Used amphetamines before 9th grade	1.0%	1.0%	2.6%	1.2%	0.6%
Used marijuana/LSD/other psychedelics*	60%	64%	44%	58%	45%
Used sedatives/barbiturates/ tranquilizers*	26%	19%	8%	10%	10%
Used heroin/other narcotics/cocaine*	11%	14%	8%	13%	11%

*Treats those who used more than one drug as a single user of each drug.
Source: *Monitoring the Future* (1975–2005).

again, widespread claims by commentators (i.e., Stepp, 2007; Garbarino, 2006; Ponton, 2002) of female sexual apocalypse are not borne out. As far as I can determine, the damning term invented to label modern girls' relationships—"hooking up"—is meaningless ("it isn't exactly anything," Stepp admits), ranging from a casual email to an orgy.

None of these authors present evidence other than fevered anecdotes and openly derogatory stereotypes to justify their claims that modern young women are more sexually compromised. The reason becomes apparent once real trends are investigated: whatever girls today are allegedly thinking or doing, serious outcomes are declining. If girls today are having random, unsafe sex by rising legions, we'd expect pregnancies and STIs to be rising as well. Again, just the opposite is the case (table 1.3).

Further, given Martin's, Quart's, Pipher's, and other culture-warriors' claims of pornographic, misogynist imagery pervading popular culture and corrupting young people of both sexes, surely rape and other sexual violence against young women has skyrocketed in recent years? The best measure of

Table 1.3. Pregnancies per 1,000 Teens

But Aren't Teens Getting Pregnant and Having Babies and Abortions at Younger Ages Today? No!

| | Pregnancies per 1,000 teenage females by age group | | | | | |
| | Pregnancies | | Births | | Fetal loss/abortion | |
Year	10–14	15–19	10–14	15–19	10–14	15–19
1950	*	*	0.9	80.6	*	*
1955	*	*	0.9	89.9	*	*
1960	*	*	0.8	89.1	*	*
1965	*	*	0.8	70.4	*	*
1970	*	*	1.2	68.0	*	*
1976	3.2	101.4	1.3	53.5	1.9	47.9
1980	3.2	110.0	1.1	53.0	2.1	57.0
1985	3.6	106.9	1.2	51.3	2.4	55.6
1990	3.5	116.3	1.4	59.9	2.1	56.4
1995	3.0	101.1	1.3	56.8	1.7	44.3
2000	2.1	84.5	0.8	47.7	1.3	36.8
2005	1.6	70.6	0.7	40.5	0.9	30.1
2008	*	*	0.6	41.5	*	*
Change, 2005 v 1976	–50%	–30%	–54%	–21%	–53%	–37%

*Indicates no data are available yet for that year. Miscarriage rates were higher in earlier years, and illegal abortions were estimated by public health authorities at 750,000 to 2 million per year prior to legalization in 1972.

Source: National Center for Health Statistics (2008).

Table 1.4. Rapes per 1,000 Female Teens

	Rape Victimization Has Declined Dramatically among Young Women		
	Rapes per 1,000 females ages:		
Annual average	12–19	20–24	All 12–24
1973–74	3.4	5.2	4.1
1975–79	3.6	4.1	3.8
1980–84	3.4	3.7	3.5
1985–89	2.9	3.1	2.9
1990–94	3.0	3.3	3.1
1995–99	2.9	2.2	2.6
2000–04	1.9	1.8	1.9
2005–07	1.9	1.3	1.7
Change	–44%	–75%	–58%

*Adjusted for female proportions of total rapes, 1993–2007.
Source: Bureau of Justice Statistics (1973–2007).

crime, the Bureau of Justice Statistics' National Crime Victimization Survey, tells exactly the opposite story. Rape and other violence against females have declined sharply over the last 35 years, and especially in the last decade (tables 1.4 and 1.5).

Sex crimes and other violence have been surveyed in more detail beginning in 1993. In the last 14 years, girls and young women report plummeting rates of completed rape; all other sexual violence including assaults, attempts, and threats; and all other violent crimes. FBI and vital statistics also show sharp drops in murder, sex, and other violent offenses during this

Table 1.5. Sex and Violent Crimes against Women

	All Sex and Violent Crimes against Young Women Have Declined Sharply							
	Rapes and sexual assaults* per 1,000 females				Other violent crime rates, females age 12–24			
Year	age 12–15	16–19	20–24	all 12–24	Robbery	Assault	Homicide	All violent
1993	9.2	12.2	10.4	10.6	7.8	74.2	5.8	98.4
2007	2.0	4.9	5.9	4.4	2.0	32.4	2.8	38.7
Change	–78%	–60%	–43%	–58%	–74%	–56%	–52%	–61%

*Includes all rapes and other sexual assaults, completed, attempted, and threatened, first tabulated in 1993.
Sources: Bureau of Justice Statistics (1993–2008); National Center for Health Statistics (2008).

Table 1.6. Female High School Seniors Reporting One Incident

Percentages of High School Senior Females Reporting at Least One Incident in the Previous 12 Months:	1975– 76	1980	1990	2000	2005
Got into serious fight at work or school	10%	11%	13%	8%	9%
Got into a group fight	12%	11%	15%	15%	16%
Used weapon to commit robbery	1%	1%	1%	1%	1%
Hit instructor/supervisor	1%	1%	1%	0%	2%
Injured by someone with weapon	2%	2%	2%	2%	4%
Injured by someone without weapon	12%	13%	17%	11%	15%

*Source: Monitoring the Future (1975–2005).

period, which is exactly the time girl-violence authors insist "toxic culture" was endangering young women.

What about other crimes and victimization? The general trend was toward slightly more violence from the mid-1970s to the early 1990s, then declines or mixed trends for the largest categories (table 1.6). Unfortunately, the questions don't distinguish between family, acquaintance, and stranger violence, nor between aggressive and defensive behaviors.

Girls' generally healthier trends are persisting past high school. Female first-year college students averaging eighteen to nineteen years old report drinking and smoking less and feeling considerably less depressed, *The American Freshman* survey reports (table 1.7). Unfortunately, interest groups, led by authors and college counseling lobbies, have misrepresented this trend to imply an "epidemic of depression on campus" (Stepp, 2007: 116) to boost their own agendas.

However, there has been an increase in the percentage of women students who feel overwhelmed by all they have to do. Rather than some

Table 1.7. Trends among First-Year College Women

Percentages of First-Year College Women Who Say They (Are) . . .	1970	1990	2006
Aiming to obtain high degree (PhD, EdD, MD, JD, etc.)	12%	32%	32%
Financing education through loans (first asked 1978)	27%	42%	64%
Planning to work off campus to pay for education	23%	21%	31%
Drank beer in the last year	43%	51%	37%
Smoked cigarettes in the last year	11%	8%	5%
Agree an individual can't change society	34%	24%	24%
Think married women should stay home	33%	18%	16%
Agree it's important to be community leader	12%	34%	35%
Agree it's important to be well off financially	25%	68%	72%

Source: Higher Education Research Institute (1966–2006).

Table 1.8. Depressed or Overwhelmed First-Year College Women

	Percentage of First-Year College Women Saying They Feel . . .	
Years	Depressed	Overwhelmed by all I have to do
1985–89	11.4%	25.8
1990–94	11.0%	30.9
1995–99	10.4%	37.7
2000–04	9.3%	35.9
2005–06	8.7%	36.8
Change	–24%	+43%

Source: Higher Education Research Institute (1985–2006) (questions first asked in 1985).

breakdown in girls' mental health, this latter trend may reflect the reality that more women are seeking higher degrees and are working more to pay off larger student loans than in the past (table 1.8). Likewise, girls' desire to earn more money and be well-off financially doesn't necessarily mean greater greed and materialism, as commentators insist; it may simply reflect young women's rational assessment of the fact that women, in particular, need to make more money to pay off college debts and achieve financial independence. Would we be happier if young women reported accepting lower pay?

However, even though a large and rising majority of girls and young women seem well-adjusted and coping with their successes with increasingly healthy behaviors and attitudes, there does remain a troubled fraction (table 1.9). Unlike most young women, Courtney Martin describes herself

Table 1.9. Female High School Senior Dissatisfaction

Percentages of High School Senior Females Telling *Monitoring the Future* They Are Completely or Mostly Dissatisfied with:	1975–76	1980	1990	2000	2005
Yourself?	5%	4%	6%	6%	7%
Your friends?	3%	2%	2%	3%	2%
Your parents?	12%	10%	12%	11%	11%
Your material possessions?	6%	5%	8%	7%	5%
Your personal safety?	8%	7%	9%	7%	5%
Your education?	12%	7%	7%	7%	6%
Your job?	12%	10%	12%	9%	9%
Your life as a whole?	7%	7%	7%	8%	7%
In last year, did you feel depressed*	na	na	11%	10%	8%

Sources: *Monitoring the Future* (1975–2005) (high school senior girls); *Higher Education Research Institute (1966–2006) (first-year college women, question first asked in 1985).

as deeply and constantly unhappy due (in her case) to an all-consuming "hatred" of her body that she imagines all young women must *"wake up in the morning to . . . walk around all day resisting . . . go to bed sad and hopeless about"* (2007: 3, emphasis hers). She's not entirely alone; Monitoring the Future, like other studies, finds around 5% to 10% of young women rate themselves as unhappy and suffering difficulties, and *The American Freshman* finds 8% to 9% of female students describing themselves as depressed in the past year. Martin, like the clients psychologist-authors in particular misrepresent as typical of all girls, clearly belongs to a fraction of troubled young women requiring greater societal attention.

WHAT'S HAPPENING TO GIRLS?

With a few exceptions, girls' and young women's behaviors and attitudes have improved along with their racial diversification and successes in academic and professional life. Still, anyone can say anything to an anonymous survey. Do girls' self-reports translate into lower rates of violence and other troubled behaviors in real life?

In virtually all cases, *yes*. It's simply not true that "the rates for violent crimes perpetrated by girls and young women rose" while "nationally, rates of violent crime have been dropping since the mid-1990s," as Prothrow-Stith and Spivak (2005: 44, 48) declare. These authors' even scarier allegation that "girls are beginning to show up in a new role, a new behavior—the ones doing the killing" is ludicrously false; in fact, girls' arrests for murder have consistently fallen. Between 1998 and 2007, as an example, they fell by 40%).

Far from girls becoming more criminal like boys, boys have become less criminal like girls, especially in the last ten to fifteen years. After large declines in the last decade, both males and females show *lower* rates of the larger category of Part I offenses (felony violent and property crimes considered an index of offending by the FBI) than thirty years ago (table 1.10). It's strange that the fact that today's girls show the lowest arrest rates for serious offenses in at least three decades is depicted as a crisis.

Table 1.10 also shows trends in two factors strongly influencing youth crime—the percentages of youth living in poverty and the arrest rates of adults of the ages to be their parents (30 to 54 in this example). Note that while girls' arrest rates rose from the 1970s to the 1990s, their parents' arrest rates rose even more. The overall trend (with some notable exceptions; see sidebar) is that youths of both sexes have become less prone to arrest over the last three decades while their parents (even with recent declines) have become substantially more so. This is a highly unexpected trend, given that adults ages 30 to 54 are much less likely to be impoverished than youths are and would not be expected to show rising arrest rates.

Table 1.10. Youth Index Crime Arrests

| | Youth Index Crime Arrests per 100,000 Population | | Factors Influencing Youth Crime | |
Years	Female youth	Male youth	Adult arrest rate	Youth poverty rate
1975–79	1,067.9	4,719.1	527.8	16.3%
1980–84	1,032.7	4,329.4	683.0	20.8%
1985–89	1,160.5	4,499.9	831.1	20.1%
1990–94	1,340.7	4,670.2	939.9	21.8%
1995–99	1,361.5	3,731.9	864.7	19.4%
2000–04	1,069.4	2,422.4	718.7	16.9%
2005–07	968.3	2,107.7	727.2	17.7%
Change, 1975–2007	–9%	–55%	+38%	+9%
Change, 1995–2007	–29%	–44%	–16%	–9%

Note: Index offenses designated by the FBI are murder, rape, robbery, aggravated assault, burglary, theft, motor vehicle theft, and arson. Youth arrest rates are arrests of persons under age 18 per 100,0000 population ages 10–17 by sex; adult arrest rates are arrests of persons ages 30–54 per 100,000 population that age.

Source: FBI (1975–2007). Each year's arrest totals for each population group are adjusted for the proportion of the national population covered by the report and are divided by the population of that group for the year to produce rates, averaged for five-year periods shown.

Youth poverty rates also rose from the mid-1970s to the mid-1990s, then fell. Does poverty matter? It certainly does. California's detailed crime and socioeconomic tabulations show violent crime arrest rates are five to six times higher for girls who live in areas with youth poverty levels averaging more than 30% compared to those in areas with average poverty rates of less than 10% (see Males, 2008). Yet, none of the commentators on girls' crime mention these crucial, troubling social trends.

Table 1.11 (next page) compares girls' violent crime arrest rates to trends among boys and among adults of ages to be their parents (again, 30 to 54). There were large increases in arrests for violent crimes from 1985 to 1995 among *both sexes and all ages*. In fact, the increase among their mothers' generation was greater than for the daughters, and the declines in crime over the last decade were more impressive for youths than for adults.

At worst, then, the violence increases being deplored in books are not recent, but occurred from 10 to 20 years ago and affected *all of society, not just girls*. Further, the increase in arrests from 1985 to 1995 may not reflect a real increase in violence. Table 1.12 breaks down the trends by type of crime. It is disturbingly clear that Prothrow-Stith, Spivak, and Garbarino, who brand girls more murderous today, either are woefully ignorant of girls' trends or are willfully misrepresenting obvious facts. By the early 2000s,

Table 1.11. Violent Crime Arrests by Age, Sex

| | Violent Crime Arrests per 100,000 Population by Age, Sex | | | |
| | Youth age 10–17 | | Adult age 30–54 | |
Year	Female	Male	Female	Male
1981	65.1	532.0	40.9	341.4
1985	67.4	526.3	44.1	353.4
1990	104.2	742.1	65.9	488.4
1995	152.9	845.9	103.9	538.7
2000	117.3	497.6	91.5	401.9
2007	104.4	474.5	107.0	314.5
Change:				
2007 v 1981	+60%	–11%	+161%	+3%
2007 v 1995	–32%	–44%	+3%	–42%

Source: FBI Uniform Crime Reports, 1981–2007. Statistics by detailed age and gender were first

girls' arrests for homicide had dropped to their lowest levels in 35 years and, by 2007, to their lowest level since girls' statistics were first reliably compiled in 1964.

Girl-violence authors have failed to mention that *girls' arrest rates now are lower than in 1975* for *murder* (down 50%), *robbery* (down 23%), and *rape* (down 8%, an extremely rare offense for girls). In addition, girls' arrest rates for *property crimes* dropped by 18% and for all serious offenses by 15% over the last three decades. Most intriguing, from 1995 through 2007, when the cultural images girl-violence authors deplore proliferated, girls' rates of arrest for murder, robbery, rape, and felony assault fell sharply; only misdemeanor assault arrests rose.

In fact, the only violent offense to show an increase—and the only reason violence arrests increased overall since 1975—is assault. Felony assault arrest rates rose through 1995, then fell; misdemeanor assaults rose throughout. This trend is evident for both sexes and all age groups, which makes it peculiar that girls' trends are being singled out.

What could explain this pattern of girls' arrests for murder, robbery, and other serious crime *declining* sharply, while the only offense to increase is assault? If girls are becoming more violent, wouldn't we expect all types of violent crime by girls to increase? And if girls' assaults are rising dramatically, wouldn't we expect homicide to increase as well simply as a result of more attacks causing more deaths? It's odd that 90% of the supposed increase in girls' violence has been for simple assault, the *least serious offense.*

As Anne Teitelman and Meda Chesney-Lind detail elsewhere in these pages, this pattern is best explained by new law enforcement initiatives authorized by stronger laws beginning in the 1980s to make arrests for

Table 1.12. Violence Arrests, Girls 10–17

Violence Arrest Rates per 100,000 Girls Ages 10–17 by Type of Offense

		Part I violent felonies				
Years	All violent	Homicide	Rape	Robbery	Assault	Misdemeanor Assault
1975–79	62.9	1.1	0.5	21.1	40.2	115.7
1980–84	66.4	1.1	0.6	19.9	44.9	138.4
1985–89	80.6	1.1	0.9	20.1	58.4	210.9
1990–94	124.0	1.4	0.8	31.3	90.6	314.1
1995–99	135.4	1.1	0.7	26.4	107.2	453.8
2000–04	108.5	0.8	0.6	14.6	92.5	479.5
2005–07	106.8	0.6	0.5	19.5	86.3	505.6
Change:						
2005–07 v 1975–79	+70%	–46%	–1%	–8%	+115%	+336%
2005–07 v 1995–99	–21%	–46%	–29%	–26%	–19%	+11%

Source: FBI (1975–2008).

street, school, workplace, and (especially) domestic violence in cases that once brought warnings or informal discipline. Increased policing of domestic and workplace violence also explains some of the increase in violent-crime arrests among older age groups.

WHAT EXPLAINS TODAY'S ATTACK ON GIRLS?

Virtually all major trends affirm that modern girls represent an impressive success story. Consistent with their dramatic gains in education, employment, and leadership, girls' self-reports reveal greater happiness and confidence. Solid outcome measures confirm that in virtually all respects, girls are healthier, safer, and avoiding the consequences we would expect if they were becoming crazier, wilder, sadder, drunker, sluttier, or meaner.

Evidently, girls doing better is frightening. The most evident pathology surrounding young women is the avalanche of unwarranted fear spread by authors and commentators—some representing august academic institutions—whose vilification of girls borders on a mean-spirited hoax. What visceral fear could be provoking today's irrational public attacks against girls and young women?

To address this mystery, let's suppose for the moment that serious violence and other troubles actually had risen among modern girls, as many commentators proclaim. What might be causing such a trend? It would be logical to analyze proven causal factors that a large body of research strongly connects to girls' troubles. Histories of physical and sexual abuse; family violence and mental illness; and unstable, troubled, addicted parents strongly correlate with girls' delinquency, drug and alcohol abuse, suicidal behavior, school dropout, victimization, early pregnancy, anger, and other problems commentators lament (see Administration on Children, Youth and Families, 2009; Males, 2008; National Victim Center, 1992).

Further, poverty is powerfully correlated with more serious outcomes such as violent crime, victimization, HIV infection, early pregnancy, school dropout, and conditions connected with more dangerous environments. For example, compared to their white, non-Hispanic counterparts, African American girls and young women are four times more likely to live in poverty, five times more likely to be murdered, five times more likely to be arrested for murder, nine times more likely to be arrested for a violent crime, seven times more likely to contract sexually transmitted diseases, and 3.5 times more likely to get pregnant before age 18 (see Males, 2008). One would think, then, that authors concerned about girls would dedicate most of their books to poverty, racial disadvantage, and abusive family environments.

Curiously, however, commentators who brand today's girls more troubled seem largely indifferent to these real-life causal factors. Few mention the tangible realities girls face every day, such as the facts that three million girls under age 18 live in severe poverty (household incomes below $17,000 for a family of three), including one million in destitution (incomes less than half poverty thresholds); 80,000 girls were confirmed victims of physical and sexual abuses at home in 2006; and several million have parents who are addicted and/or imprisoned. When authors reference these vital factors at all, they bury them in a few paragraphs or a list.

Nor can I find any commentators who discuss the salient fact that violent crime arrests among adult women of age to be mothers to adolescent girls rocketed from 33,000 in 1981 to 163,000 in 2007, and for men of age to be fathers, from 229,000 to a staggering 589,000—increases far outpacing the 60% rise in middle-aged populations. Nor have those portraying girls as more messed up cited the explosions in drug abuse and imprisonments among grownups in their parents' generation. Those who brand Britney Spears and Lindsay Lohan as typical modern young women have not similarly dubbed their addicted, imprisoned fathers, suicidal grandparents, and unstable mothers as typical of older generations.

Instead of talking about real problems, Pipher dedicates dozens of pages to "cultural pressures" on girls, such as the Swedish Bikini Team in beer ads. Garbarino spends whole chapters blaming "The Powerpuff Girls" and Harry Potter's Hermione. Prothrow-Stith and Spivak exhaustively denounce celluloid heroines, led by "Lara Croft, Tomb Raider." Other authors likewise fixate on ads, movies, music, Internet social sites, and video games.

When scholars ignore real-life crises shown to cause massive pain, injury, and even death among girls in order to blame Blossom, Bubbles, and

Buttercup, something is badly wrong. Behind authors' and commentators' disturbingly irrational attacks on girls lies their real fear: that girls' supposedly rising pathologies result from females moving outward from protected home environments and into the larger world where, equally unsettlingly, girls are succeeding beyond all expectations. As young women increasingly dominate higher education, major professions such as law and medicine, and even leadership positions, cries that young women are (*must* be!) more vicious, violent, and mentally disturbed have risen to a deafening crescendo.

Authors' deep discomfort with worldly, successful young women, couched in contradictory declarations of sympathy for the unprotected female psyche (much as nineteenth-century anti-suffragettes worried equal rights would corrupt women's weak natures) and anger at modern girls' unladylike assertiveness emerges in their books' first pages and dominates their anxieties throughout. Pipher (1995: 28) juxtaposes girls' supposedly new endangerment and desensitization with the purported fragility and vulnerability of girls venturing out of their once "protected place in space and time" into today's "toxic culture." Likewise, Prothrow-Stith and Spivak (2006: 5–6, 48) blame girls' supposedly increased violence on the fact that boys' and girls' "socialization differences are lessening, as illustrated by girls' participation in sports, enhanced academic opportunities, and expanded job possibilities" and equalized media treatments. "It used to be competitive aspects were not emphasized for young women, but now we're in a totally different world where they are actually encouraged to be aggressive," laments a minister approvingly quoted by Dellasega and Nixon (2003: 35). "Girls becoming more assertive" has produced "the good news of liberation and the bad news of increased aggression [that] is the New American Girl," warns Garbarino (2006: 4). "Underneath the Pollyanna story of our high achievement is an ugly underbelly" of rising mental illness, addiction, and self-destructiveness, writes Martin (2007a).

Many authors go to ludicrous extremes to manufacture "evidence" that it is really *girls' new freedoms and successes that are making them sicker*. "From 1977 to 2000, there was a 13 percent increase in the number of women drivers involved in fatal, alcohol-related crashes," Martin (2007a) declared, citing a notoriously unreliable lobby. (In fact, the numbers of women driving increased by 49% over that period; thus, women's drunken driving *rates* actually dropped significantly.) "Girls are having more trouble now than thirty years ago, when I was a girl," says Pipher (1995: 28), blaming "cultural changes" that leave girls unprotected. (In fact, in Nebraska of the mid-1960s when Pipher was growing up, girls were in much more danger of violent death and early pregnancy than in the 1990s or 2000s.) "As guns become more permissible and available to girls, that will unleash more aggression in them . . . This may already be happening," warns Garbarino (2006: 57). (In fact, as National Center for Injury Prevention and Control [2008] tabulations show, the murder arrest rate for girls has plunged to an all-time low, as have girls' fatalities from firearms.)

But girls' encouraging attitudes and realities don't seem to matter; these authors and commentators clearly *need* for girls to be getting worse. Spreading fear of girls is their vehicle for expressing offense at modern popular culture and advertising images they see as promoting violence, unhealthy sexualization, thinness, addiction, and consumerism. Of course, offended commentators could just as effectively make their points by declaring, "modern ads and cultural images negatively affect *me*" without pathologizing girls.

Interestingly, girls themselves don't rank these culture-war nemeses as terribly troubling. When asked what they see as their most important problems, most girls cite issues such as education, economic concerns, family breakdown, war and violence around the world, poverty, global warming, anti-immigrant sentiment, government failures, drug abuse, environmental issues, racism, and discrimination—that is, *real* problems. Virtually none cite MySpace, Internet threats, advertising images, fashion ads, beer commercials, MTV videos, Powerpuff Girls, or any of the fictional menaces authors insist are driving girls to misery and mayhem.

Even so, we would expect feminist and progressive authors to vigorously defend young women's modern achievements against conservatives' antipathy toward racial diversity, charges that venturing too far into the male world corrupts female morals and sensibilities, and demands for more supervision of young females. We would expect those favoring progressive politics to be delighted at trends among young women, who in the 2004 and 2008 presidential elections not only voted in record numbers but (unlike older men and women) overwhelmingly supported progressive candidates and ideals (see Edison/Mitovsky, 2007; Civic Youth, 2008).

That's not happening. Instead, the eagerness of twenty-first-century authors and commentators of both sexes, white and black, across the political spectrum to demonize girls with groundless panics *specifically linked to girls' rising success and externality* suggests how deeply threatening the traditional, gut-level fear of and for "girls out in the world" remains.

The harsh, analytical lens has been trained on girls long enough; it's time to refocus it on those who fear and condemn them. It's strange enough that in the rich, dynamic diversity of modern American girls, girl-fearing authors and commentators see only desolation, brutality, and helplessness. Stranger still that they cast every standard of modern research and ethics aside in a monomaniacal stampede to deny girls' optimistic generational voices, active agencies, and tangible gains. But it is truly alarming that in this exciting time when manifest realities and societal evolution demand forceful, innovative reevaluation of traditional gender notions, fearful authors and commentators dominating public discussion are retreating back to antiquated little-red-riding-hood dogmas of girls and young women as eternally passive, irrationally masochistic victims of the big, mean, "toxic" world (corporate-ad temptation, mass-culture corruption, Internet porn, lurking cyberwolves . . .) because they've strayed too far from home.

REFERENCES

Administration on Children, Youth and Families (2009). *Child maltreatment, 2007.* Washington, DC: U.S. Department of Health and Human Services. http://www.acf.hhs.gov/programs/cb/pubs/cm07/index.htm (accessed 10 April 2009).

Barson, M., & Heller, S. (1998). *Teenage confidential: An illustrated history of the American teen.* San Francisco: Chronicle Books.

Bureau of Justice Statistics. (1973–2007). *Criminal victimization in the United States, 2007.* Washington, DC: U.S. Department of Justice. http://www.ojp.usdoj.gov/bjs/abstract/cvusst.htm (accessed 10 October 2008)

Civic Youth. (2008). Trends by race, ethnicity, and gender. http://www.civicyouth.org/?page_id=235 (accessed 10 April 2009).

Cosby, B. (2004). Speech, the 50th Anniversary commemoration of the Brown v. Topeka Board of Education Supreme Court Decision. NAACP, Howard University, 17 May 2004.

Dellasega, C., & Nixon, C. (2003). *Girl wars: 12 strategies that will end female bullying.* New York: Simon and Schuster.

Dyson, M. E. (2005). *Is Bill Cosby right? Or has the black middle class lost its mind?* New York: Basic Books.

Edison/Mitofsky (2007). *Exit poll, Nov 7, 2004, presidential election.* CNN. http://www.cnn.com/ELECTION/2004/pages/results/ (accessed 30 March 2008).

Federal Bureau of Investigation (1975–2006). *Uniform crime reports for the United States, 2005.* U.S. Department of Justice (1964–2006). http://www.fbi.gov/ucr/ucr.htm#cius (accessed 30 March 2009).

Federal Bureau of Investigation (1975–2007). *Table 40. Arrests, females by age.* http://www.fbi.gov/ucr/05cius/data/table_40.html (accessed 30 March 2009)

Garbarino, J. (2006). *See Jane hit: Why girls are growing more violent and what we can do about it.* New York: Penguin Press.

Higher Education Research Institute. (1966–2006). *The American freshman: Forty year trends, 1966–2006.* Los Angeles: University of California, Los Angeles.

Hutchinson, E. O. (2007). 'B****** fighting' the troubling trend among some young women. *Huffington Post,* 13 November 2007.

Kingsbury, K. (2008). Pregnancy boom at Gloucester High. *Time,* 18 June 2008. Gloucester pregnancy plot thickens. *Time,* 23 June 2008.

Males, M. (2008). *Girl myths.* http://www.youthfacts.org/girlphob.html (accessed 30 March 2009).

Males, M. (2004). With friends like these. *Extra!* January/February 2004.

Martin, C. E. (2007). *Perfect girls, starving daughters: The frightening new normalcy of hating your body.* New York: Free Press.

Martin, C. E. (2007a). Underneath pop star scandals is a serious message about young women and addiction. *Huffington Post,* 7 June 2007.

Johnson, L. D., Bachman, J. G., & O'Malley, P. M. (1975–2005). *Monitoring the future: Questionnaire responses from the nation's high school seniors. Annual, 1975–2005.* Ann Arbor: University of Michigan, Institute for Social Research. http://www.monitoringthefuture.org/pubs.html (accessed 30 March 2009).

National Center for Health Statistics (2007). *Trends in pregnancies and pregnancy rates by outcome: Estimates for the United States, 1976–2000, 2004. Births: Preliminary Data, 2007.* Atlanta, GA: Centers for Disease Control. http://www.

cdc.gov/nchs/births.htm, http://www.cdc.gov/nchs/pressroom/04news/lowbirths. htm (accessed 10 April 2009).

National Center for Injury Prevention and Control. (2008). *WISQARS injury mortality reports, 1999–2005*. Atlanta, GA: Centers for Disease Control. http://webappa. cdc.gov/sasweb/ncipc/mortrate10_sy.html (accessed 10 October 2008).

National Victim Center. (1992). *Rape in America*. Washington, DC (23 April 1992).

Pipher, M. (1995). *Reviving Ophelia: Saving the selves of adolescent girls*. New York: Ballantine Books.

Pipher, M. (1998). *Reviving Ophelia* (video). Media Education Foundation. http://www. mediaed.org/ (accessed 29 October 2008).

Ponton, L. (2000). *The sex lives of teenagers: Revealing the secret world of adolescent boys and girls*. New York: Dutton.

Prothrow-Stith, D., & Spivak, H. (2005). *Sugar and spice and no longer nice: How we can stop girls' violence*. San Francisco: Jossey-Bass.

Quart, A. (2003). *Branded: The buying and selling of teenagers*. Cambridge, MA: Perseus Publishing.

San Francisco Juvenile Probation Department. (2007). **[[AU: add reference from sidebar text]].**

Steffensmeier, D., Schwartz, J., Zhong, H., & Ackerman, J. (2005). An assessment of recent trends in girls' violence using diverse longitudinal sources: Is the gender gap closing? *Criminology* 43(2):355–405.

Stepp, L. S. (2007). *Unhooked: How young women pursue sex, delay love, and lose at both*. New York: Riverhead Books.

Williams, Juan. (2007). *Enough: The phony leaders, dead-end movements, and culture of failure that are undermining black America—and what we can do about it*. New York: Three Rivers Press.

Wiseman, R. (2002). *Queen bees and wannabes: Helping your daughter survive cliques, gossip, boyfriends, and other realities of adolescence*. New York: Three River Press.

Zahn, M. (Ed.) (2007). *Delinquent girls: Findings from the girls study group*. Philadelphia: Temple University Press.

TWO

CRIMINALIZING ASSAULT

Do Age and Gender Matter?

Eve S. Buzawa
David Hirschel

Waves of unprecedented statutory changes beginning in the 1970s have altered how police respond to domestic violence. Due to the interplay of activist pressure, research, and political imperatives, legislators have enacted legislation and police departments have implemented policies that have produced a marked increase in 'arrest rates (see, e.g., Chaney & Saltzstein, 1998; Lawrenz, Lembo & Schade, 1988; Zorza & Woods, 1994: 12; Wanless, 1996: 58–59; Office of the A.G. California, 1999; Municipality of Anchorage, 2000: 8–9; Hirschel et al., 2007: 6–7).

While domestic violence statutes were initiated primarily to address the needs of female victims of spousal partner violence, these statutes initiated a subsequent wave of revised legislation that included an expansion of the relationships included (Buzawa & Buzawa, 2003). Police are now required by statute to respond aggressively to relationships as varied as heterosexual and same-sex intimate partners regardless of marital status, siblings, parents and adult children, parents and teenagers, grandparents and grandchildren, and teenaged and adult daters and ex-daters.

To date, there has been limited detailed empirical examination of how the increase in domestic assault arrests may disproportionately impact specific subpopulations. Research has primarily used broad categorical relationships to compare arrest rates for intimate partner assault to assaults by acquaintances and strangers (Buzawa & Austin, 1993; Buzawa, Austin, & Buzawa,

1995; Eigenberg, 2001; Elliott, 1989; Felson & Ackerman, 2001; Felson & Paré, 2005; Fyfe, Klinger, & Flavin, 1997; Hirschel et al., 2007; Hotaling & Buzawa, 2001; Smith, 1986; Oppenlander, 1982; Sheptycki, 1993). Some researchers have used these findings to conclude that apparent similarities in domestic and non-domestic assault rates suggest that police treat these assault offenders similarly (Felson & Ackerman, 2001).

However, such broad comparisons are problematic because domestic assault statutes, unlike those governing stranger or acquaintance assaults, have far more explicit requirements for police intervention. In most jurisdictions, officers are now required by statute or department policy to arrest domestic violence offenders on a presumptive, if not a mandatory, basis. Further, officers are authorized by law to make warrantless misdemeanor arrests in domestic violence cases, a power does not exist for other misdemeanor assaults. Therefore, contrasting general arrest practices and determining that police practices may be equally applied across categories may mask significant within-category variations.

A further key limitation of previous research is that studies limited to domestic assault usually only examine the police response to domestic violence in cases of adult domestic violence relationships, that is, "spouse," "ex-spouse," or "dating partner," and typically focus only on male-against-female intimate partner violence (Bachman & Coker, 1995; Buzawa et al., 1999; Feder, 1999). These studies have provided significant contributions regarding the impact of such legislation on the initially targeted population of victims. However, the exclusion of other significant relationships, as well as the failure to examine the differential effect of the variety of socio-demographic characteristics encompassed under domestic violence statutes, have been the source of considerable concern.

First, we believe there is a need to examine in greater depth more specific categories of relationships included under domestic violence statutes and how they vary in the types of offenses committed. Second, there is a need to investigate more closely the factors that impact the decision by police to arrest. Specifically, we believe it is important to provide a more detailed analysis of how the increase in arrests for domestic assault may disproportionately impact two groups who have historically been underserved when victims of domestic assault: females and juveniles.

As we will discuss in the next section, there is a theoretical basis for assuming that police will differentially respond to incidents involving juvenile and/or female offenders. Since cases involving the abuse of children under the age of 13 are handled through existing child protection laws, whereas incidents involving adolescent and young adult children and their caretakers do qualify under domestic violence statutes, we are excluding from our analyses cases with children under the age of 13. For purposes of this study, juveniles will hereinafter encompass victims and offenders aged 13 through 17.

THE DIVERSITY OF DOMESTIC ASSAULT RELATIONSHIPS

As stated earlier, studying the effects of domestic violence statutes by merely examining pro-typical male-against-female intimate partner violence presents a limited perspective as these relationships are not the only relationships subject to police intervention under domestic violence statutes. Indeed, considerable data exist suggesting that these "other" forms of family violence constitute a large portion of domestic violence incidents reported to law enforcement. For the last 25 years, national surveys have consistently found that each year up to 33 million siblings inflict severe violence on their brothers or sisters (Straus & Gelles, 1990). In addition, over a million parents a year are victims of severe violence by their 15- to 17-year-old children. Parents themselves inflict severe violence on adolescent sons and daughters at almost the same rate (Straus & Gelles, 1990). Indeed, it has been suggested that about 25% of young adults grow up witnessing what Zimring and Hawkins (1973) call "everyday violence," including domestic disputes, child abuse, and other forms of non-lethal fights and assaults.

Moreover, data collected since the early 1990s show an increase in the volume of domestic violence cases reported to law enforcement involving relationships other than intimate partners. National Incident-Based Reporting System (NIBRS) data from nine states in 1995 indicated that about 44% of violent crime in families involved relationships other than adult partners, while in 1998, data from 14 states indicated that this proportion constituted 48% of violent household incidents known to and recorded by the police (Federal Bureau of Investigation [FBI], 1999). Between 1998 and 2002, 49% were crimes against spouses, 11% were crimes by parents against children, and 41% were crimes against other family members (Dunrose, Harlow, Langan, Motivans, Rantala, & Smith, 2005). Other data more directly suggest a substantial increase in the proportion of non-adult partner violence seen by the police during the period corresponding with the expansion in pro-arrest domestic violence policies. For example, a random sample of domestic violence incidents drawn from two towns in Massachusetts across three time periods (1990–1991, 1994–1995, and 1997–1998) showed that the proportion of domestic violence calls for assistance involving relationships other than adult partner violence (which definition included current and former daters) increased from 24.2% in 1990–1991 to 29.4% in 1994–1995 to 39.6% in 1997–1998, representing a 63% increase across the decade (Hotaling & Buzawa, 2001).[1]

THE INCREASED LIKELIHOOD OF ARREST FOR ASSAULT

It is now generally acknowledged that recent years have not only seen an overall increase in the rate of domestic assault reaching police attention, but an increase in the likelihood of arrest as well. The impact on overall arrest rates can be documented by estimates of arrest rates during the 1970s and 1980s, which hovered in the 7% to 15% range as compared to current rates that on average are estimated to be higher than 30% (Buzawa & Buzawa, 2003; Hirschel & Buzawa; 2002; Hirschel et al., 2007).

It has been suggested that the statutes mandating more aggressive arrest practices and decreasing police discretion have created sufficient pressure to ensure that officers give primary consideration to legal factors in the arrest decision (Mastrofski et al., 2000). This has been supported by researchers reporting a much greater likelihood of arrest in cases of domestic assault (Bourg & Stock, 1994; Feder, 1998; Jones & Belknap, 1999; Klinger, 1996; Mignon & Holmes, 1995; Municipality of Anchorage, 2000; Office of the Attorney General, State of California, 1999; Peng & Mitchell, 2001; 1967; Robinson & Chandek, 2000; Wanless, 1996; Zorza & Woods, 1994).

Even more significant support for this premise are findings from a large-scale study that contrasted mandatory, presumptive, and discretionary legislative frameworks for domestic violence with arrest rates for assaults (Hirschel et al., 2007). Not only did the researchers report that arrest was more likely for domestic assault in states based on these legislative mandates, but that there was a "spillover effect" for other types of assaults as well. Police officers in states with mandatory or presumptive arrest statutes were more likely than officers in states with discretionary arrest statutes to arrest offenders in incidents of non-domestic assault as well as domestic violence (Hirschel et al., 2007). Thus, it can be surmised that the increase in the likelihood for arrest in cases of domestic assault is paralleled in cases of non-domestic assault resulting in a wider net of people identified as offenders.

This situation gives rise to the question of whether the wider net of arrestees is disproportionately impacting any particular subgroup of offenders. Existing data indicate that there has been a disproportionate increase in overall juvenile arrest rates over the past decade (FBI, 2006). With regard to domestic assault in particular, Buzawa and Hotaling (2000) have reported that juvenile offenders are significantly more likely to be arrested than adults, regardless of victim injury, threat, or protective order violation. In addition, there is a growing body of research suggesting that aggressive domestic violence policies have a greater impact upon juvenile female offenders since females acts of violence are far more likely to be minor compared to male acts of violence (Chesney-Lind, 2002).

DEFINING A CRIMINAL OFFENSE

In making any decision, police must first decide whether an incident qualifies as a criminal offense. Only then will one or more parties be identified as an "offender" and one or more parties as a "victim." In contrast, some incidents are merely designated as "involved parties" incidents thereby effectively negating statutory requirements for a presumptive or mandatory arrest. There are several reasons why this may occur, such as the lack of probable cause due to insufficient evidence or both parties denying that any assault or threat occurred.

In practice, police decisions are affected by the inherent ambiguity of the police-citizen encounter. As a result, officers need to rely on experiences and personal values to interpret ambiguous situations, determine legal requirements, and assess the potential consequences of their decisions. There is a vast body of research addressing the significance of incident, victim, offender, organizational, and community characteristics (for a summary of this research see Buzawa & Buzawa, 2003; Hirschel et. al., 2007).

Parents assaulted in their own homes by adolescent and young adult children have many attributes of what Christie (1986) refers to as "ideal" victims. They are often physically weaker than their attackers, engaged in what others define as proper activities (caring for home and children), are where they should be (in the household), and are assaulted by persons who are or were dependent upon them. However, research suggests such assumptions are inaccurate as many juvenile assault arrests have been reported to be in response to parental abuse (Buzawa, 2006; Chesney-Lind, 2004).

Adult partners, for whom domestic violence pro-arrest policies were primarily intended, may often be considered as "ideal" for the status of victim, but in some cases, police may deem this classification as inappropriate. Police may be less likely to identify a victim and provide assistance in cases where adult partners are suspected of using drugs or alcohol, where claims are made by both parties regarding the use of violence, and/or in cases where divorced or separated partners have a history of calling the police. Further, women who do not conform to behavioral expectations of "victim," and are angry, hostile, or aggressive, are often less likely to have their offenders arrested or receive assistance (Hanmer & Stanko, 1985; Saunders, 1995; Sheptycki, 1993).

THE IMPACT OF MINOR STATUS ON THE ARREST DECISION

There is a considerable body of research suggesting that minor status impacts the likelihood of arrest in domestic violence cases. Society's ambivalence toward parental use of force against children has always affected the probability that parents will be identified as aggressors in domestic violence incidents involving children. The legal right of parents to use "reasonable" corporal punishment is recognized in the majority of states (Healey, 1997). Therefore, even acts of severe violence resulting in injury often do not result in the arrest of the parent. The involvement of a minor often prompts referral to child protective services rather than criminal prosecution. Rather than impose legal sanctions, the governmental response to physical child abuse has been to uphold parental rights, to discourage removal of the victim from the household, and to "provide support to parents in their role at home through the provision of home-based services and psychological services, even after physical child abuse has been established" (Costin et al., 1996). Finkelhor, Wolak, & Berliner (2001) have found that many victims, parents, and police believe juvenile victimizations are simply not defined as crimes that should necessitate police intervention.

It has also been suggested that the police response is influenced by both the absolute and relative social positions of victims and offenders in the family unit (Black, 1971; 1976; 1980). Those holding the roles of "son" or "daughter," "brother," or "sister" have relatively little power compared to parents and other adults in the household. Since domestic violence most often occurs inside residences, this suggests that children will always have less power than their parents or other adult figures and that the police are more likely to act in the interests of the adult (Black, 1980: 123).

Based on observational data collected in 1966, Donald Black concluded: "In modern America . . . hardly anyone is lower than juveniles. . . . The police readily use their authority against a juvenile who is criticized by a parent, but when the situation is reversed—with a juvenile complaining against an adult—they show no sympathy at all, and usually treat the complaint itself as an offense" (Black, 1980: 155). Black characterized the police response to parental complaints against juveniles as more penal and moralistic than complaints made against adults. However, when juveniles complained about an adult, they were often criticized for questioning adult authority (Black, 1980).

Thirty-five years after Black's data collection, there are no empirical data suggesting that police attitudes toward juvenile offenders in domestic situations have changed. However, what *has* changed is the availability of greater police power to make misdemeanor arrests coupled with pro-arrest or mandatory arrest policies that appear to *require* police to intervene more aggressively in response to *all* victims and offenders in cases of domestic violence.

There are several reasons why police actually may use domestic violence statutes as a powerful tool to uphold and support parental authority. First, while the statutes now typically apply to all family members, these statutes often fail to *explicitly* discuss juveniles as primary aggressors (or victims) of domestic violence. Rather, the interest in children is usually limited to the impact of young children (under age 13) witnessing violence, especially against women. Recommended or required police action regarding children often consists of rules for filing reports to the appropriate agencies if the responding officers suspect a child has been harmed in an incident involving adult partners. As a consequence, we expect this to be reflected in police practices (Reiner, 1985).

Juveniles may not find a parent or caretaker arrested for several reasons. First, as described earlier, the legal right of parents to use corporal punishment to discipline children extends to juveniles, perhaps superseding pro-arrest domestic violence laws. Second, police are hesitant to question or undermine parental authority except in cases of extreme physical abuse or neglect. Third, since child protection laws allow some latitude in the use of force by parents, it is possible that the police do not define these types of incidents as criminal offenses.

Accompanying the reluctance to arrest parents, there has been a growing propensity to criminalize juvenile status offenses that were previously regarded as non-criminal (Chesney-Lind, 2002). Domestic violence cases involving children as offenders and parents as victims that were previously processed as cases involving "incorrigibles" or "persons in need of supervision" have been reclassified as assaults (Acoca, 1999; Belknap, Winter, & Cady, 2001; Chesney-Lind, 2002)

THE IMPACT OF GENDER ON THE ARREST DECISION

There is evidence that the gender of the involved parties also impacts police arrest decisions. The vast majority of domestic violence calls involve male offenders and female victims. The key issue, however, is not what gender constitutes the modal category of offender, but whether, given similar circumstances, the odds of arrest are similar for males and females.

There are various theories as to why each gender may have a greater likelihood of arrest. Females could be at greater risk for arrest compared to males due to their lack of social power (Chesney-Lind, 1997). Some researchers have argued that in male-against-female intimate violence, females are less likely to be accorded the status of victim due to their inferior social status relative to men (Dobash & Dobash, 1979; Ferraro, 1989; Hanmer, Radford, & Stanko, 1989). This orientation may come into play when police evaluate the behavior of the involved parties and determine whether a crime has been committed. Alternatively, they could be at increased risk for arrest as officers may perceive female offenders as more "out of character" and their behavior as more socially unacceptable (Chesney-Lind, 1997; Swan & Snow, 2006).

On the other hand, female offenders may be less likely to be arrested than male offenders. Male victims of domestic violence may be less likely than female victims to be accorded the status of victim. It has been well documented that males are less likely to report assaults by females (Langley & Levy, 1977; McLeod, 1984; Straus, Gelles, & Steinmetz, 1980). A contributing factor to their reluctance to report is the expectation of a limited police response. This is certainly plausible. The general population views assaults committed by females less seriously than assaults committed by males (Straus, 1993). Further, since police more often deal with female than male victims of domestic violence, they may have a difficult time viewing males as victims (Buzawa & Austin, 1993). Therefore, when a male victim meets the legal criteria of victim, he may have greater difficulty than a female victim in having an assault defined as a criminal offense, obtaining the help and assistance required, and/or having an arrest made.

There are scant empirical data examining this issue. While numerous studies have documented that arrest rates for women are growing more rapidly than for men, there is a lack of specificity as to the relative likelihood of arrest across domestic relationships controlling for incident characteristics. However, in an analysis of NIBRS 2000 data, Hirschel et al. (2007) reported that there were no significant gender differences in arrest rates in incidents involving intimate partner and acquaintances, but men were more likely to be arrested in cases of "other domestics" controlling for other incident characteristics. However, this difference lessened when a gun, knife, or object was used.

THE IMPACT OF BEING BOTH FEMALE AND A JUVENILE ON THE ARREST DECISION

There is a growing body of empirical evidence that finds girls, being both of minor status and female, are at an increased risk for arrest than either boys or adults (Chesney-Lind, 2002). In a recently released report by the Girls Study Group, it was reported that while the arrest rate for juvenile females between 1980 to 2003 increased much more than for male juveniles, juvenile males were still five times more likely to be arrested for aggravated assault. This is further exacerbated by the fact that the greatest increase in police arrests has been in the area of simple assaults, and, as in the case of adult women, a far higher proportion of simple assaults is committed by juvenile females than by males (Zahn et al., 2008).

What is particularly noteworthy is that if we consider that the Hirschel et al. (2007) study, using 2000 NIBRS data, reported similar overall arrest rates for females and males, the fact that the Girls Study Group found such an increased likelihood for arrest for juvenile females suggests that adult females may actually be less likely to be arrested.

The vast majority of research exploring the role of gender in domestic violence research has typically been limited to its role in police (or criminal justice) responses to intimate partner violence by adult males against adult females (Bachman & Saltzman, 1995; Edwards, 1989; Ferraro, 1989; Hanmer, Radford, & Stanko, 1989; Klinger, 1995; Stanko, 1989; Stark & Flitcraft, 1996; Tjaden & Thoennes, 2000). However, domestic violence statutes now typically encompass minor age victims and offenders in a wide range of domestic relationships. Further, research suggests that girls are more likely than boys to assault a family member (Franke, Huynh-Hohnbaum, & Chung, 2002). As a result, it has been suggested that the dramatic increase in domestic violence arrest rates has disproportionately increased arrest rates for females of minor age (Chesney-Lind, 2002).

In fact, this pattern has been seen as a backlash to the aggressive implementation of domestic violence arrest policies and/or statutes. While their initial intent was to protect women, "they are now being used as a means to 'control unruly children' by parents" (Chesney-Lind & Pasko 2004: 17), or as the result of a redefinition by police of a crime from what was previously identified as a family conflict or disturbance (Chesney-Lind & Pasko, 2004; Stahl, 2008).

Black (1980) argues that the increased likelihood of a juvenile female's arrest is the result of her decreased social status compared to male juveniles. As a result, an assault by a female juvenile against a parent or a sibling assault that reaches police attention is more likely to result in an arrest than a male juvenile assault (Black, 1980). In fact, it has been argued that juvenile females are "at the very bottom of the social scale" (Dougherty, 1998: 145) and are least likely to have their interests represented.

CURRENT STUDY

The preceding literature review suggests that the likelihood of arrest may be greater for juvenile females than for juvenile males or adult females or males. In this study we examine the comparative likelihood of arrest for juvenile females, juvenile males, adult females, and adult males in both domestic and non-domestic acquaintance cases. Four primary research questions are examined:

1. Controlling for seriousness of offense, are juvenile females more likely than juvenile males, and male and female adults, to be arrested in non-intimate partner domestic and acquaintance cases?
2. Do gender and age of the victim impact the likelihood of arrest?
3. Are the effects similar for non-intimate partner domestic violence and acquaintance cases?
4. Are differential impacts observed for specific subcategories of non-intimate partner domestic violence cases?

The initial sample comprised all assault and intimidation cases contained in the National Incident-Based Reporting System (NIBRS) calendar year 2000 data set. These cases came from 2,819 jurisdictions in 19 states. Very few intimate partner violence cases involved parties under the age of 18. Therefore, these cases were deleted from the data set. In addition, stranger cases were also deleted from the data set since the dynamics of stranger cases differ markedly from cases involving parties who know each other. All cases with offenders or victims under 13 were taken out of the sample since "juvenile" has been operationally defined for this study as a person who is at least13 and under 18 years of age. The final sample is thus composed of 208,280 domestic and acquaintance cases with involved parties aged 13 and over.

This chapter examines whether age and gender impact the police response to calls for assistance. Descriptive information on the background characteristics of the offenders, incidents, and the police response is presented in table 2.1. This information is organized according to whether the offender was (1) a juvenile female; (2) an adult female; (3) a juvenile male; or, (4) an adult male.

Nearly three-quarters (71.7%) of the cases involved acquaintances as opposed to people in domestic relationships (28.3%: see table 2.1). Juvenile female offenders (35.4%) were the most likely to be involved in a domestic incident. While the vast majority of female adult (87.2%) and male adult offenders (87.8%) committed their offenses against adult victims, female juvenile and male juvenile offenders were equally likely to have adult or juvenile victims.

A total of 65.2% of the offenders were white, 33.9% black, and 0.9% were of other races, with adult female offenders (37.6%) more likely than offenders in the other groups to be black. Only 12.2% of the offenders were suspected by the responding police officers to be under the influence of drugs or alcohol. Adult males (16.5%) were more likely than adult females (9.8%) to be under the influence, while few juvenile females (2.2%) or juvenile males (3.3%) were noted to be under the influence.

Most of the incidents were classified as simple assaults (63.5%), committed with personal weapons (59.6%), and producing either an apparent minor injury (47.8%) or no injury (46.2%). In terms of age and gender an interesting pattern emerges. Adult males (20.2%) were the most likely to have committed aggravated assault, followed by juvenile males (16.7%), adult females (14.6%), and juvenile females (12.1%). Though the percentages are smaller, this pattern is repeated both for the use of a weapon and the infliction of serious physical injury.

The majority (63.9%) of incidents took place in a home or residence, though this was more likely for adult females (67.8%) and adult males (66.1%) than for juvenile females (56.4%) or juvenile males (51.2%). About one-third (34.9%) of the incidents resulted in arrest with juvenile females (41.4%) and juvenile males (41.2%) more likely to be arrested than either adult females (30.5%) or adult males (34.2%).

The preceding analysis clearly shows that juveniles are more likely to be arrested than adults. However, these higher arrest rates might be explained by juveniles committing more serious offenses than adults. To examine this issue, we investigated the likelihood of arrest controlling for seriousness of offense. The results of this analysis are presented in table 2.2, page 44.

Table 2.1. Offender, Victim, and Incident Characteristics and Police Disposition by Offender Gender and Age

		Offender			
	Juvenile female	Adult female	Juvenile male	Adult male	Total
Offender characteristics					
Race					
Asian/Pacific Islander	60	198	160	578	996
	0.4%	0.4%	0.6%	0.5%	0.5%
Black	5062	17098	9170	38297	69627
	34.6%	37.6%	31.8%	32.9%	33.9%
American Indian/Alaskan Native	80	217	100	520	917
	0.5%	0.5%	0.3%	0.4%	0.4%
White	9410	27975	19386	77156	133927
	64.4%	61.5%	67.3%	66.2%	65.2%
Closest offender-victim relationship					
Domestic	5241	13018	8961	31771	58991
	35.4%	28.3%	30.7%	26.9%	28.3%
Acquaintance	9570	33062	20238	86242	149112
	64.6%	71.7%	69.3%	73.1%	71.7%
Offender suspected of having used drugs					
Yes	328	4532	963	19467	25290
	2.2%	9.8%	3.3%	16.5%	12.2%
Victim characteristics					
Race					
Asian/Pacific Islander	58	186	117	547	908
	0.4%	0.4%	0.4%	0.5%	0.4%
Black	4216	15494	7200	33108	60018
	28.9%	34.1%	25.1%	28.5%	29.3%
American Indian/Alaskan Native	30	166	55	413	664
	0.2%	0.4%	0.2%	0.4%	0.3%
White	10281	29570	21327	82221	143399
	70.5%	65.1%	74.3%	70.7%	70.0%

continued on next page

Table 2.1. (Continued)

			Juvenile female	Adult female	Juvenile male	Adult male	Total
Victim juvenile/adult		Juvenile	7262	5920	14735	14354	42271
			49.0%	12.8%	50.5%	12.2%	20.3%
		Adult	7549	40160	14464	103659	165832
			51.0%	87.2%	49.5%	87.8%	79.7%
Incident characteristics							
Most serious offense		Aggravated assault	1790	6729	4883	23885	37287
			12.1%	14.6%	16.7%	20.2%	17.9%
		Simple assault	11140	29489	20321	71158	132108
			75.2%	64.0%	69.6%	60.3%	63.5%
		Intimidation	1881	9862	3995	22970	38708
			12.7%	21.4%	13.7%	19.5%	18.6%
Most serious victim injury		Serious physical	339	1552	1182	7123	10196
			2.6%	4.3%	4.7%	7.5%	6.0%
		Apparent minor	6460	17702	11674	45125	80961
			50.0%	48.9%	46.3%	47.5%	47.8%
		No injury	6132	16964	12348	42805	78249
			47.4%	46.8%	49.0%	45.0%	46.2%
Weapon		Weapon	980	4324	2788	15353	23445
			7.1%	10.1%	10.4%	13.9%	12.1%
		Personal weapon	9605	25127	17573	63070	115375
			69.8%	58.9%	65.4%	57.3%	59.6%
		No weapon	3175	13195	6514	31716	54600
			23.1%	30.9%	24.2%	28.8%	28.2%

Location					
Home/residence	7558	29570	13367	74041	124536
	56.4%	67.8%	51.2%	66.1%	63.9%
Elsewhere	5839	14014	12725	37923	70501
	43.6%	32.2%	48.8%	33.9%	36.1%
Police disposition					
arrest					
Yes	6125	14073	12030	40399	72627
	41.4%	30.5%	41.2%	34.2%	34.9%

Table 2.2. Number and Percentage of Cases Resulting in Arrest by Offender
Gender and Age and Seriousness of Offense

		Incident was cleared by arrest		
		Most serious offense		
		Aggravated assault	Simple assault	Intimidation
Offender	Juvenile female	958	4798	369
		53.5%	43.1%	19.6%
	Adult female	2948	10136	989
		43.8%	34.4%	10%
	Juvenile male	2415	8627	988
		49.5%	42.5%	24.7%
	Adult male	11391	25828	3180
		47.7%	36.3%	13.8%

As can be seen from an examination of table 2.2, for all four gender-age categories seriousness of offense increases the likelihood of arrest. For both aggravated and simple assault, juvenile females have the highest arrest rates (53.5% and 43.1%), followed by juvenile males (49.5% and 42.5%), adult males (47.7% and 36.3%), and adult females (43.8% and 34.4%). For intimidation, the pattern varies slightly. Juvenile males have the highest arrest rate (24.7%), followed by juvenile females (19.6%), adult males (13.8%), and adult females (10%).

An issue of interest is whether the likelihood of arrest is affected by the gender and age of the victim. Are, for example, juveniles more likely to be arrested when they offend against adults as opposed to other juveniles? The results of this investigation are presented in table 2.3.

As can be observed in table 2.3, with one exception arrest rates do not vary much when the victim is a juvenile. Cases involving juvenile females assaulted by adult females are far less likely to result in arrest than any other combination of juvenile victim and adult or juvenile offender. When, however, the victim is an adult a very different pattern emerges. Both male and female juvenile offenders are far more likely to be arrested than male or female adult offenders. While juvenile females are arrested in 45.8% of the cases in which an adult female is the victim, and juvenile males are arrested in 47.4% of these cases, the comparative arrest rates for adult female and adult males are 29.0% and 32.9% respectively. When the victim is an adult male, the arrest rate for juvenile females is 48.9%, while for juvenile males it is 44.2%. For adult female offenders the arrest rate is 33.8%, and for adult male offenders it is 34.5%.

Thus far we have not examined whether the trends we have observed are similar for non-intimate partner domestic and acquaintance cases. Since we had already observed that likelihood of arrest is strongly associated with

Table 2.3. Number and Percentage of Cases Resulting in Arrest by Victim and Offender Gender and Age

		Incident was cleared by an arrest			
		Victim			
		Juvenile female	Adult female	Juvenile male	Adult male
Offender	Juvenile female	2340	2682	271	826
		36.2%	45.8%	34.0%	48.9%
	Adult female	1459	8883	510	3211
		20.3%	29.0%	36.1%	33.8%
	Juvenile male	1072	3483	4322	3138
		33.6%	47.4%	37.5%	44.2%
	Adult male	2315	14291	3039	20720
		36.5%	32.9%	38.0%	34.5%

seriousness of offense, and that most of the cases involved simple assault, we decided to limit this phase of the analysis to cases of simple assault. We conducted separate analyses of non-intimate partner domestic and acquaintance cases to observe whether there were any differences in the effect of victim and offender gender and age on the likelihood of arrest. The results are presented in tables 2.4 and 2.5 (page 48).

An examination of table 2.4 indicates that with regard to acquaintance cases both female and male juvenile offenders were far more likely than adult offenders to be arrested for an assault on an adult. This is similar to what was reported for the full sample. However, with regard to juvenile victims a different pattern emerges. Juvenile females were most likely to be arrested when the victim was a female, juvenile males when the victim was a male.

A similar analysis of the non-intimate partner domestic cases revealed that yet again when the victim was an adult both female and male juvenile offenders were more likely than adult offenders to be arrested. However, when the victim was a juvenile, adult females were much less likely to be arrested than any of the other categories of offender (table 2.5).

Since a number of different victim-offender relationships are included under non-intimate partner domestic violence cases, we decided to conduct additional analyses on these cases in the light of these relationships. Four relationship categories were constructed representing victims who were: (1) parents, step-parents, and grandparents; (2) siblings and step-siblings; (3) children, step-children, offspring of girlfriends or boyfriends, and grandchildren; and (4) in-laws and other family members. Of prime interest here is the effect that the victim offender relationship has on the likelihood of arrest for each of the four categories of offenders.

Table 2.4. Number and Percentage of Simple Assault Acquaintance Cases Resulting in Arrest by Victim and Offender Gender and Age

| | | Incident was cleared by an arrest | | | |
| | | Victim | | | |
		Juvenile female	Adult female	Juvenile male	Adult male
Offender	Juvenile female	1671	583	127	245
		37.3%	41.3%	28.1%	47.5%
	Adult female	496	4099	106	1282
		29.1%	30.1%	29.0%	33.2%
	Juvenile male	540	515	2934	1053
		32.7%	39.6%	36.9%	41.5%
	Adult male	563	5223	992	7978
		29.5%	30.5%	30.5%	31.2%

We believe that identifying the extent of juvenile involvement in these "other domestic" relationships is an area that has received little attention. As noted earlier, only a small percentage of juvenile domestic assault incidents involve intimate partners. Table 2.6 reveals that the vast majority of juveniles who come into contact with the police under domestic assault statutes are the result of incidents involving parents or grandparents. Juvenile incidents involving parents or grandparents are over three times more likely than incidents involving siblings and approximately 10 times more

Table 2.5. Number and Percentage of Non-Intimate Partner Domestic Cases Resulting in Arrest by Victim and Offender Gender and Age

| | | Incident was cleared by an arrest | | | |
| | | Victim | | | |
		Juvenile female	Adult female	Juvenile male	Adult male
Offender	Juvenile female	215	1552	48	352
		45.7%	51.2%	45.7%	52.9%
	Adult female	665	2446	272	764
		37.7%	42.0%	40.0%	45.8%
	Juvenile male	269	2039	310	957
		46.1%	53.4%	50.2%	52.2%
	Adult male	1241	4955	1248	3600
		43.3%	49.2%	47.7%	47.1%

Table 2.6. Number and Percentage of Simple Assault Domestic Non-Intimate Partner Cases Resulting in Arrest by Offender Gender, Age, and Victim-Offender Relationship

| | | Incident was cleared by an arrest | | | |
| | | Victim-offender relationship | | | |
		Parent/ grandparent	Sibling	Child/ grandchild	Other family
Offender	Juvenile female	1977	438	32	179
		53.2%	49.9%	41.6%	41.5%
	Adult female	1136	1154	1534	1235
		48.2%	43.1%	39.8%	34.2%
	Juvenile male	3268	952	57	331
		54.7%	48.6%	41.0%	44.3%
	Adult male	3826	3774	3740	3376
		52.9%	46.8%	47.5%	39.4%

likely than incidents involving other family members. In contrast, adults are fairly likely to be equally involved in domestic incidents involving parents or grandparents, children, siblings, and other family members. Obviously, juveniles are considerably less likely to have children. Clearly, their primary issues involve conflicts with parents and grandparents.

As also can be seen from an examination of table 2.6, arrest is most likely for all four categories of offenders when the victim is a parent or grandparent. With their overrepresentation in incidents where a parent or grandparent is the victim, juveniles are clearly disproportionately impacted by this finding. The pattern is somewhat more varied for the other categories of victim. Arrest is next most likely when the victim is a sibling for all offender categories except adult males. Adult females and juvenile males are least likely to be arrested when the victim is a child/grandchild. Juvenile females are least likely to be arrested when the victim is a child/grandchild or other family member. Adult males are least likely to be arrested when the victim is another family member.

DISCUSSION

These findings represent preliminary results that will hopefully lead to a more comprehensive analysis of the role played by age and gender in the decision to arrest. As noted in our review of the literature, prior research has almost exclusively focused on the increasing arrest rate for females without examining the *relative* likelihood of arrest for males in similar types of incidents. In addition, research examining gender has tended to aggregate all offenses and/or all domestic relationships. Finally, while prior research has addressed the disproportionate arrest of juvenile females compared to male juveniles, it has not similarly contrasted juvenile arrest rates with those of adults.

Our findings highlight the importance of these distinctions. We can summarize three key findings. First, we found that differences in assault rates were primarily attributable to gender, not age. Adult males were the most likely to have committed aggravated assault, followed by juvenile males, adult females, and juvenile females. Therefore, the findings discussed earlier reporting that men were overall more violent than females in non-intimate partner domestic assaults as well as with acquaintances are supported by these data. The distinction regarding the seriousness of the offense, including the use of a weapon or whether an injury was incurred, is more likely to be affected by gender, rather than age, with males committing the more serious offenses.

Second, we found that differences in arrest rates were primarily attributable to age, not gender. In all cases, the seriousness of offense increased the likelihood of arrest. For both aggravated and simple assault, juvenile females have the highest arrest rates followed by juvenile males, adult males, and adult females. For intimidation, the pattern varies slightly. Juvenile males have the highest arrest rate, followed by juvenile females, adult males, and adult females.

Third, we found that juveniles were far more likely to be arrested for assaulting adults, whereas adults were far less likely to be arrested for assaulting juveniles, with adult females having the lowest arrest rate, regardless of whether the adult assaulted was male or female. This was true for both non-intimate partner domestic assault and acquaintance relationships. These three general conclusions closely parallel Black's observations (1980) discussed earlier regarding the social power of juveniles as compared to adults.

Findings also parallel the Massachusetts study where it was reported that the odds for juvenile arrest were about 3.5 times that of adults (Hotaling & Buzawa, 2001). However, that study was limited to domestic assaults, including intimate partner incidents, and also included juveniles under the age of 13. We believe that the fact that the data for the current study involved a large-scale national data set and included acquaintance relationships as well as "other domestics" suggests this is an area worthy of further inquiry.

We believe there should be considerable concern regarding the extent to which we are criminalizing youth and failing to protect them when victimized. Police policies and training on other types of domestic relationships, and particularly incidents involving juveniles are not typical. Conversely, training on intimate partner violence is now routine in most police agencies. Further, a growing number of police agencies are focusing on the identification of a primary aggressor in cases of intimate partner violence. Absent any specific training, police can be expected to be more likely to listen to the adult's version of an incident, and also more inclined to assume parents have authority in incidents involving children.

In addition, the focus on comparing juvenile girls with boys discussed earlier may miss another critical bias by our criminal justice system that is against juveniles overall. We emphasize that we are not minimizing the significance of the bias against girls relative to boys. As noted, we did find a modest difference in overall arrest rates for juvenile females compared to juvenile males for aggravated assault (53.5% vs. 49.5%, see table 2.2), and that simple assault acquaintance incidents where juvenile females assaulted adult males were the most likely to result in an arrest (table 2.4). However, we did not find differences between female and male juveniles in overall simple assault arrest rates (table 2.2), and found a slightly decreased likelihood for arrest in cases of intimidation (19.6% vs. 24.7%, see table 2.2). Also, adult female offenders rather consistently had the lowest arrest rate in all relevant analyses (see tables 2.2, 2.3, 2.4).

Hopefully, our criminal justice system will begin to focus on the juvenile use of violence and how a decision is made when it is perpetrated against an adult. There is a growing body of research addressing women's use of violence, and indicating that a high proportion of these incidents involve self-defense or are in response to prior acts of abuse. In the case of juveniles, a history of victimization may be compounded by the fact that juveniles are not given the same credibility as adults by virtue of their age.

This research was intended to be descriptive in nature and provide preliminary findings that need to be considered in the light of other factors that have not been examined in this chapter. Foremost among these is race, which has been shown in previous studies to impact the likelihood of arrest (see, e.g., Bachman & Coker, 1995; Hirschel et al., 2007). Our data do, in fact, show higher arrest rates for some minorities and we plan to examine this finding in detail as we continue to analyze the relative roles played by a variety of incident, offender, and victim variables in order to better understand our findings.

NOTES

This project was supported by Grant No. 2001-WT-BX-0501 awarded by the National Institute of Justice, Office of Justice Programs, U.S. Department of Justice. Points of view in this document are those of the authors and do not necessarily represent the official position or policies of the U.S. Department of Justice.

1. The increase in cases known to police is not indicative of actual incidence rates. The NCVS reported that there was a 21% decrease in intimate partner violence between 1993 and 1998.

REFERENCES

Acoca, L. (1999). Investing in girls: A 21st century challenge. *Juvenile Justice* 6(1): 3–13.

Bachman, R., & Coker, A. L. (1995). Police involvement in domestic violence: The interactive effects of victim injury, offender's history of violence, and race. *Violence and Victims* 10: 91–106.

Bachman, R., & Saltzman, L. E. (1995). *Violence against women: Estimates from the redesigned survey* (BJS Publication No. 154–348). Washington, DC: Bureau of Justice Statistics, U.S. Department of Justice.

Belknap, J., Winter, E., and Cady, B. (2001). *Assessing the Needs of Delinquent and Preadjudicated Girls in Colorado: A Focus Group Study*. A report to the Colorado Division of Youth Corrections: Denver, Colorado.

Black, D. J. (1971). The social organization of arrest. *Stanford Law Review* 23: 1087–1111.

Black, D. J. (1976). *The behavior of law*. New York: Academic Press.

Black, D. J. (1980). *The manners and customs of the police*. New York: Academic Press.

Bourg, S., & Stock, H. V. (1994). A review of domestic violence statistics in a police department using a pro-arrest policy: Are pro-arrest policies enough? *Journal of Family Violence* 9: 177–189.

Buzawa, E., & Austin, T. (1993). Determining police response to domestic violence victims. *American Behavioral Scientist* 36: 610–623.

Buzawa, E., Austin, T., & Buzawa, C. (1995). Responding to crimes of violence against women: Gender differences vs. organizational imperatives. *Crime & Delinquency* 41: 443–466.

Buzawa, E., & Buzawa, C. (2003). *Domestic violence: The criminal justice response*. Third Edition. London: Sage.

Buzawa, E., & Hotaling, G. T. (2000). *The police response to domestic violence calls for assistance in three Massachusetts towns*. Washington, DC: Office of Community Policing, U.S. Department of Justice.

Chesney-Lind, M. (2002). Criminalizing victimization: The unintended consequences of pro-arrest policies for girls and women. *Criminology and Public Policy* 1(2): 81–90.

Chesney-Lind, M. & Pasko, L. J. (2004). *The female offender: Girls, women and crime, second edition*. Thousand Oaks, CA: Sage.

Comach, E., Chopyk, V., & Wood, L. (2000). *Mean streets? The social locations, gender dynamics and patterns of violent crime in Winnipeg*. Ottawa: Canadian Centre for Police Alternatives.

Costin, L. B., Howard, J. K., & Stoesz, D. (1996). *The politics of child abuse in America*. New York, NY: Oxford University Press.

Dobash, R. E., & Dobash, R. (1979). *Violence against wives: A case against the patriarchy*. New York: Free Press.

Dunrose, M. R., Harlow, C. W., Langan, P. A., Motivans, M., Rantala, R. R., & Smith, E. L. (2005). *Family violence statistics including statistics on strangers and acquaintances*. Washington, DC: Bureau of Justice Statistics, Department of Justice.

Edwards, S. M. (1989). *Policing domestic violence: Women, law and the state*. London: Sage.

Eigenberg, H. (ed.). (2001). *Women battering in the United States: Till death do us part*. Prospect Heights, IL: Waveland.

Elliott, D. S. (1989). Criminal justice procedures in family violence crimes. In M. Tonry & N. Morris (eds.), *Family Violence* (427–480). Chicago: University of Chicago Press.

Feder, L. (1998). Police handling of domestic violence calls: Is there a case for discrimination? *Crime & Delinquency* 44(2): 139–153.

Federal Bureau of Investigation. (1996). *The structure of family violence: An analysis of selected incidents*. Washington, DC: Federal Bureau of Investigation.

Federal Bureau of Investigation. (1999). *Incidents of family violence: An analysis of 1998 NIBRS data*. Washington, DC: U.S. Department of Justice.

Federal Bureau of Investigation (FBI). (2006). *Crime in the United States, 2005*.

Felson, R. B., & Ackerman, J. (2001). Arrests for domestic and other assaults. *Criminology* 39: 655–676.

Felson, R., & Paré, P. P. (2005). The reporting of domestic violence and sexual assault by nonstrangers to the public. *Journal of Marriage and Family*, August 67(3).

Ferraro, K. (1989). The legal response to women battering in the United States. In J. Hanmer, J. Radford, & E. Stanko (eds.), *Women, policing, and male violence* (155–184). London: Routledge & Kegan Paul.

Finkelhor, D., Wolak, J., & Berliner, L. (2001). Police reporting and professional help seeking for child crime victims: A review. *Child Maltreatment* 1(6): 17–30.

Franke, T. M., Huynh-Hohnbaum, A. L. T., & Chung, Y. (2002). Adolescent violence: With whom they fight and where. *Journal of Ethnic & Cultural Diversity in Social Work* 11(3-4): 133–158.

Fyfe, J. J., Klinger, D. A., & Flavin, J. M. (1997). Differential police treatment of male-on-female spousal violence. *Criminology* 35: 455–473.

Hanmer, J., Radford, J., & Stanko, E. (1989). Improving policing for women: The way forward. In J. Hanmer, J. Radford, & E. Stanko (eds.), *Women, policing and male violence: International perspectives* (185–201). London: Routledge & Kegan Paul.

Healey, K. M. (1997). *Polices, practices and statutes relating to child abuse and neglect. Background Paper #3*. Child Abuse Intervention Strategic Planning Meeting, Washington, DC: National Institute of Justice.

Hirschel, D., & Buzawa, E. (2002). Understanding the context of dual arrest with directions for future research. *Violence Against Women* 8(12): 1449–1473.

Hirschel, D., Buzawa, E., Pattavina, A., & Faggiani, D. (2007). Domestic violence preferred and mandatory arrest laws: To what extent do they influence police arrest decisions? *Journal of Criminal Law and Criminology* 98(1): 255–298.

Hotaling, G. T., & Buzawa, E. (2001). *The nature, scope and response to assault victimization in Athol and Orange, MA*. Washington, DC: Office of Community Policing, U.S. Department of Justice.

Jones, D., & Belknap, J. 1999. Police responses to battering in a progressive pro-arrest jurisdiction. *Justice Quarterly* 16: 249–273.

Klinger, D. (1995). Policing spousal assault. *Journal of Research in Crime and Delinquency* 32: 308–324.

Langley, R., & Levy, R. (1977). *Wife beating: The silent crisis*. New York: Dutton.

Massachusetts Supreme Judicial Court. (1996). *Annual Report of the Massachusetts Court System*. Fiscal Years 1981–1996. Boston: Supreme Judicial Court.

Mastrofski, S. D., Snipes, J. B., Parks, R. B., & Maxwell, C. D. (2000). The helping hand of the law: Police control of citizens on request. *Criminology* 38(2): 307–342.

McLeod, M. (1984). Women against men: An examination of domestic violence based on an analysis of official data and national victimization data. *Justice Quarterly* 1: 171–192.

Mignon S., & Holmes W. (1995). Police response to mandatory arrest laws. *Crime and Delinquency* 41(4): 430–442.

Municipality of Anchorage. (2000). *Analysis of police action and characteristics of reported domestic violence in anchorage, Alaska ten year study, 1989–1998*. Anchorage, AK: Author.

National Center on Child Abuse and Neglect. (1996). *The third national incidence study of child abuse and neglect (NIS-3)*. Washington, DC: U.S. Department of Health and Human Services.

Office of the Attorney General, State of California. (1999). *Report on arrest for domestic violence in California, 1998*. Sacramento, CA: Author.

Oppenlander, N. (1982). Coping or copping out: Police service delivery in domestic disputes. *Criminology* 20: 449–465.

Reiner, R. (1985). *The Politics of the Police*. Brighton: Wheatsheaf.

Robinson, A. L., & Chandek, M. S. (2000). The domestic violence arrest decision: Examining demographic, attitudinal, and situational variables. *Crime & Delinquency* 46(1): 18–37.

Saunders, D. G. (1995). The tendency to arrest victims of domestic violence. *Journal of Interpersonal Violence* 10: 147–158.

Sheptycki, J. W. E. (1993). *Innovations in policing domestic violence*. Newcastle upon Tyne: Athenaeum.

Smith, D. A. (1986). The neighborhood context of police behavior. In A. J. Reiss, Jr., & M. Tonry (eds.), *Communities and Crime*, Vol. 8 of *Crime and Justice: A Review of Research* (313–341). Chicago: University of Chicago Press.

Stanko, E. A. (1989). Missing the mark? Police battering. In J. Hanmer, J. Radford, & B. Stanko (eds.), *Women, policing and male violence* (46–49). London: Routledge & Kegan Paul.

Stark, E., & Flitcraft, A. (2006) *Women at risk: Domestic violence and women's health*. Thousand Oaks, CA: Sage.

Straus, M. (1993). Physical assaults by wives: A major social problem. In R. J. Gelles & D. R. Loseke (eds.), *Current Controversies on Family Violence*. Newbury Park, CA: Sage.

Straus, M. A., & Gelles, R. J. (1990). How violent are American families: Estimates from the National Family Violence Resurvey and other studies. In M. Straus & R. Gelles (eds.), *Physical violence in American families: Risk factors and adaptations to violence in 8,145 families* (95–112). New Brunswick, NJ: Transaction.

Straus, M. A., Gelles, R. J., & Steinmetz, S. K. (1980). *Behind closed doors: Violence in American families*. New York: Doubleday.

Swan, S. C., & Snow, D. L. (2006). The development of a theory of women's use of violence in intimate relationships. *Violence Against Women* 12: 1026–1045.

Tjaden, P., & Thoennes, N. (2000). *Extent, nature, and consequences of intimate partner violence: Findings from the National Violence Against Women Survey.* Washington, DC: U.S. Department of Justice.

Wanless, M. (1996). Mandatory arrest: A step towards eradicating domestic violence, but is it enough? *University of Illinois Law Review* 2: 533–587.

Zahn, M., Brumbaugh, S., Steffensmeier, D., Feld, B. C., Morash, M., Chesney-Lind, M., Miller, J., Payne, A. A., Gottfredson, D., and Kruttschnitt, C. (2008). *Violence by Teenage Girls: Trends and Contexts.* Washington, DC: Girls Study Group, Office of Juvenile Justice and Delinquency Prevention.

Zorza, J., & Woods, L. (1994). *Analysis and policy implications of the new police domestic violence studies.* New York: National Center on Women and Family Law.

THREE

JAILING "BAD" GIRLS

Girls' Violence and Trends in Female Incarceration

Meda Chesney-Lind

Mass incarceration has long characterized the landscape of adult criminal justice in the United States. Unlike other nations of the developed world that have sought to decrease their reliance on incarceration or at least kept incarceration rates level, our country has opted for penal sanctions for a wide array of offenses committed by adults (Mauer & Chesney-Lind, 2003). As a result, the United States has the dubious distinction of being the world's top incarcerator (Sentencing Project, 2007). We took this turn, as a country, during the late seventies, when politicians successfully convinced the American people that community-based and rehabilitative programs did not "work" for adult offenders, and that what was needed was a new "get tough" approach on crime. And get tough we did. Between 1970 and today, the U.S. prison population increased a staggering eightfold (Austin et al., 2007: 6). The Pew Center on the States noted in a recent report on the phenomenon that our country now incarcerates nearly 1 out of 100 of our adult citizens (Warren et al., 2008).

While mass incarceration has characterized the adult criminal justice system since the eighties (with the number of prisoners soaring past 1.5 million) (Harrison & Beck, 2006), the juvenile justice system has, until recently, pursued a more mixed course. Some would contend that the juvenile justice system has all but abandoned its focus on the "best interests of the child" in favor of a harsh, adult-focused emphasis on punishment with sharp increases in waiving youth to adult courts among other developments (see Feld, 1999). While there has clearly been an erosion of the focus on rehabilitation particularly in court processes, the juvenile justice system has not mimicked the adult system in one important arena: imprisonment.

The reasons for the juvenile justice system's hesitation with imprisonment are complex, but the pattern is largely a product of federal initiatives now decades old that focused on youth imprisonment. The Juvenile Justice and Delinquency Prevention Act of 1974 emphasized the "de-institutionalization" of status offenders (youth taken into custody for non-criminal offenses like running away or truancy) and it also raised questions about the "disproportionate" confinement of minority youth. Both of these "core requirements" of the act, until recently, functioned to keep youth incarceration somewhat in check (see Chesney-Lind & Irwin, 2008). That pattern, though, has begun to change, and ironically, it is the detention and incarceration of girls, not boys, that marks this shift most dramatically. Unlike the adult system (where drug offenses explain a large part of the increase),[1] this chapter will show, this shift in juvenile incarceration is largely if not exclusively a product of the arrest, referral, and incarceration of girls for "person" or "violent" offenses. The chapter will also document the racialized aspect of this new gendered incarceration, and finally it will focus on the increasing evidence of human rights violations in the facilities that hold young women and men.

GIRLS IN THE JUVENILE JUSTICE SYSTEM: KEY TRENDS

Girls now account for nearly a third (29.1%) of juvenile arrests (Federal Bureau of Investigation [FBI], 2007). This is a remarkable shift from decades earlier when girls accounted for only about one in five juvenile arrests (Chesney-Lind & Shelden, 2004). Moreover, girls are increasingly being arrested for crimes of violence. In 2006, girls' arrests for "other assaults" increased by 18.7% while boys' arrests for that offense decreased by 4.3%. That arrest category actually surpassed girls' arrests for "runaway," long seen as a prototypically female offense. Finally, it was also one of the few arrest categories to show an increase, since girls' arrests, globally, actually declined by 17.6% between 1997 and 2006 (FBI, 2007, table 33).

More to the point, girls are now staying in the system after being arrested for these new "violent" offenses. Between 1985 and 2002, the number of girls' delinquency cases referred to court increased by 92% compared to a 29% increase in boys' cases (Snyder & Sickmund, 2006). In exploring the source of this increase, the report's authors observed that "For females, the largest 1985–2002 increase was in person offense cases (202%)." As an example, referrals of girls for "simple assault" increased by 238% and female referrals for "other person offenses" increased by 322% (the comparable male increases were 152% and 111% (Snyder & Sickmund, 2006: 160). Astonishingly, girls actually have proportionately more "person offense" referrals than boys: these offenses account for 26% of girls referrals to court compared to only 23% of boys' referrals (Snyder & Sickmund, 2006: 160).

WHAT'S GOING ON? ARE GIRLS GETTING MORE VIOLENT?

Not surprisingly these sorts of dramatic changes in girls' arrest and court-referral patterns have ushered in a media firestorm about girls' violence. Consider the relatively recent case of the beating of a Florida cheerleader. The internet and cable news channels were filled with the video of this assault, which was apparently released by Sheriff Grady Judd. Sheriff Judd appeared to be on a one-man crusade to vilify the girls in the case. In addition to releasing the video, his office released mug shots of the youths involved in the case, and made comments to the effect that "some of the girls joked in the holding cell" and "showed no remorse" (WKMG, 2008). Ultimately, the girls, who range in age from 14 to 17 are being tried as adults, and they were charged with "battery," "false imprisonment," and "kidnapping," charges that early news reports suggested could result in the girls "spending the rest of their lives in prison" (Edwards, 2008). Media interest in the case was so intense that the judge issued a "gag order" just as one of the young women charged in the case was bailed out by the Dr. Phil Show so that she could appear on the program; Good Morning America was also interested in interviewing the girls (WFTV, 2008).

Media coverage of the sort seen in this case is not unique. In the seventies, the media demonized female "revolutionaries" and "terrorists" as "sisters in crime," and that set the pattern for the ensuing decades. The eighties showcased the media discovery that there were girls in gangs, the nineties found that girls as well as boys are involved in school violence, and the turn of the century showcased the "mean" girl (see Chesney-Lind & Irwin, 2008). The popular press has, quite literally, been obsessed with girls' violence and aggression. Often the media frame is one that positions this behavior against stereotypical images of girlhood utterly devoid of this sort of behavior. The *Newsweek* issue on youth violence, as an example, included an insert on girl's violence complete with a picture of an African American girl wearing a bandana over her face, peering at the camera over the barrel of a gun, with the headline, "Girls Will Be Girls" (Leslie et al., 1993: 44). In many ways, though, this gender juxtaposition makes sense in a country that grew up reading Longfellow's poem about his daughter: "when she was good, she was very, very good, but when she was bad she was horrid." (Longfellow, 1992: 513).

Of course, the reality of girls' lives has always been much more complex. It turns out that self-report delinquency data routinely show that girls act out violently and have been so since the earliest self-report data were published (Elliot & Voss, 1974). Second, there appears to be very little evidence that these patterns have changed in the last decades despite the media frenzy on the topic. The CDC has been monitoring youthful behavior in a national sample of school-aged youth in a number of domains (including violence) at regular intervals since 1991 in a biennial survey entitled the Youth Risk Behavior Survey. Consistent with the points raised in the earlier chapter in this volume by Males, a review of the data collected over the nineties and into this century reveals that while 34.4% of girls surveyed in 1991 said that they had been in a physical fight in the last year, in 2007, only 26.5% of girls reported being in a fight, down from two years earlier when 28.1% said they'd fought in the last year Another shift in the last decade must also be mentioned, however, since it has substantial consequences for both girls and the juvenile justice system. While girls long reported that they have engaged in fights, their arrests, particularly in the sixties and seventies, did not necessarily reflect that reality. Instead, girls' arrests tended to emphasize the status offenses; by the nineties, that had changed dramatically, as more girls were arrested, particularly for seemingly "masculine" offenses like simple assault. Between 1997 and 2006, despite an overall decrease in girls' arrests, girls arrests for simple assault continued to climb, increasing by 18.7% while boys' arrests for the same offense declined by 4.3% (FBI, 2007, table 33).

Research increasingly suggests that these shifts in girls' arrests are not products of a change in girls' behavior, with girls getting "more" violent. Not only do other measures of girls' criminality (notably self-report and victimization data) fail to show an increase in girls violence, there's ample evidence that girls are more heavily policed, particularly at home and in school (see Chesney-Lind & Irwin, 2008). Specifically, girls are being arrested for assault because of arguments with their parents (often their mothers) (see Buzawa & Hotaling, 2006; Buzawa and Hirschel, chapter 2 in this volume), or being arrested for "other assault" for fighting in school because of new "zero-tolerance" policies enacted after Columbine (see New York ACLU and ACLU, 2007). In decades past, this violence would have been ignored or labeled a status offense, like being "incorrigible" or a "person in need of supervision." Now, an arrest for assault is made. This pattern suggests that the social control of girls is once again on the criminal justice agenda, with a crucial change. In this century, the control is being justified by girls' "violence" whereas in the last century, it was their "sexuality" (see Odem, 1995).

GIRLS' DETENTION TRENDS

The relabeling and upcriming of girls' delinquency has also had a dramatic and negative effect on girls' detention trends, undoing decades of "deinstitutionalization" trends. Between 1991 and 2003, girls' detentions rose by 98% compared to a 29% increase seen in boys' detentions (see figure 3.1).

Despite the hype about violent girls, it was relatively minor offenses that actually kept girls in detention. Thirty-nine percent of all the girls in

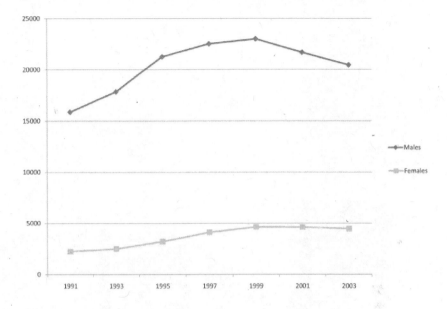

Figure 3.1. Detention Trends by Gender, 1991–2003

detention in the United States in 2003 were being held for either a status offense or a "technical violation" of the conditions of their probation, compared to only 25% of the boys (Snyder & Sickmund, 2006) (see figure 3.2, next page). Girls being detained for "violent" offenses were far more likely than boys to be held on "other person" offenses like simple assault (as opposed to more serious, part one violent offenses like aggravated assault, robbery, and murder). Over half (51.8%) of the girls but less than a third of the boys in detention (31.2%) were held for these minor forms of violence (Snyder & Sickmund, 2006: 210).

Research on detained youth in St. Louis suggested even more directly that girls were more likely than boys to be detained in non-serious cases. The researchers examined the detention decisions involved in serious (violent felonies) and non-serious cases (status offenses and misdemeanors) and found that even after controlling for factors like criminal history, girls were nearly twice as likely as their male counterparts to receive detention in non-serious cases (McGuire, 2002). A study of youth detained in Cook County added some other important information and perspective to these findings. Researchers found that while both boys and girls detention rates were about the same (41%), the reasons for the detention differed. Specifically, girls were being detained "as a result of their family situations" (often

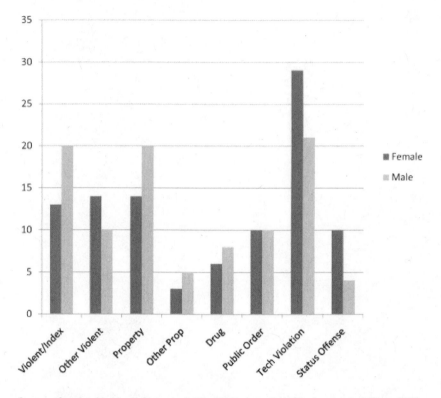

Source: Snyder, H. N., & Sickmund, M. 2006. Juvenile offenders and victims: 2006 national report. Washington, DC: U.S. Department of Justice, Office of Justice Programs, Office of Juvenile Justice and Delinquency Prevention, 210.

Figure 3.2. Offenses of Detained by Gender by Percentage, 2003

either "domestic violence" or "parents refusing to take the girl home") while boys were being detained because of the "seriousness of the offense" (Sherman, 2006: 34).

In addition to a distinctly gendered pattern in these increases, there also seemed to be clear race-based differences. For example, a study conducted by the American Bar Association and National Bar Association (2001) revealed that nearly half of girls in secure detention in the United States were African American. This is particularly interesting given that white girls made up a clear majority (65%) of the at-risk population (ABA & NBA, 2001: 20). More recent data analyzed by the National Council on Crime and Delinquency (see figure 3.3) showed that African American

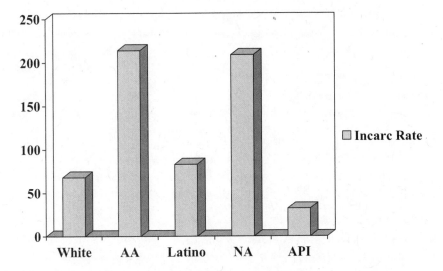

Source: Analysis of data reported by National Council on Crime and Delinquency 2006, 37.

Figure 3.3. U.S. Female Residential Custody Rates by Race, 2003

and Native American girls were held in custody at three times the rate of white girls. African American girls were incarcerated at a rate of 214 per 100K compared to 68 per 100K for white girls. For Native Americans, it was essentially the same at 209 per 100K Latino girls were also more likely to be incarcerated than their white counterparts (National Council on Crime and Delinquency, 2007: 37).

Another troubling gender and race-based pattern in the use of detention was the reliance on private facilities since the early 1980s. The use of private facilities has a particular importance for girls, as they tend to make up a larger proportion of the institutionalized population in private versus public facilities. Also interesting to note is the fact that 45% of the girls in private settings were detained for status offenses in 1997 (Snyder & Sickmund, 1999). This is compared to 11% of boys who were detained in private facilities for status offenses. Such a trend is likely a product of a racialized juvenile justice system, where the evidence suggests that white girls who come into the system as status offenders get labeled as child welfare cases while their African American and Latina counterparts are processed as criminals (Miller, 1994; Chesney-Lind & Irwin, 2007).

Girls are also more likely than boys to return to detention after their first detention. Essentially once girls were released on probation in the 1990s, they were more likely than boys to return to detention, usually for a technical violation of the conditions of their probation. A study by the ABA and NBA (2001: 20) not only found that girls were more likely than boys to be detained, but that they were more likely "to be sent back to detention after release. Although girls' rates of recidivism are lower than those of boys, the use of contempt proceedings and probation and parole violations make it more likely that, without committing a new crime, girls will return to detention." Data from four sites involved in an initiative to seek alternatives to detention indicate that there is a gender gap in detention return, with girls more likely than boys to be returned to detention (often numerous times). More to the point, a significant proportion of girls' detentions involved technical violations rather than new offenses. Across the Juvenile Detention Alternatives Initiative (JDAI) sites, 53% of the girls returned to detention were placed there for "warrant, probation or parole violation, or program failure" compared to only 41% of the boys. The pattern became even more marked on subsequent detentions when 66% of the girls returning a second time (but only 47% of the boys) were returned for these technical violations (Sherman, 2005: 33).

GIRLS' EXPERIENCES IN DETENTION

There is considerable evidence to suggest that, like their experiences outside of institutions, girls' confront vastly different environments and obstacles than boys face while being detained. This trend has continued despite the fact that over half of all states have committed themselves to improving conditions for girls in the juvenile justice system, assessing girls' unique needs, and designing better programs for them. One enduring trend is that there continues to be a lack of programs for girls. In 1998, for example, Ohio judges reported that there were few sentencing options for girls. Two-thirds of judges surveyed disagreed with the statement that "there are an adequate number of treatment programs for girls" while less than one-third of judges disagreed with this statement regarding services for boys (Holsinger, Belknap, & Sutherland, 1999). In a San Francisco study, Schaffner, Shorter, Shick, and Frappier (1996: 1) concluded that girls were "out of sight, out of mind" and that girls tended to linger in detention centers longer than boys. In fact, 60% of girls were detained for more than seven days, while only 6% of boys were detained that long.

Another concern noted by researchers examining the girls held in detention in Philadelphia was the "misdiagnosis of mental health issues" (Ambrose, Simpkins, & Levick, 2000: 1). As the Female Detention Project found, 81% of the girls studied had reported experiencing a trauma of some sort (sexual abuse, physical abuse, witnessing violence, and abandonment).

The girls were diagnosed with "Oppositional Defiant Disorder" instead of "Post-Traumatic Stress Disorder" despite the fact that, according to the researchers, "many of the girls reported symptoms that are characteristics of Post-Traumatic Stress Disorder, but not ODD." Significantly, while ODD is "characterized by a persistent pattern of negativistic, hostile, disobedient and defiant—but not violent—behavior," most of these girls were detained for assaults, many school related. As a consequence of misdiagnosis, the girls were not getting the specific kind of treatment that they needed, many had used alcohol and other drugs, been hospitalized for psychiatric reasons, and about half had attempted suicide (Ambrose, Simpkins, & Levick, 2000, p. 2).

The failure of detention facilities to provide girls with adequate mental health services was also the subject of a report on court-involved girls in New York City. The study ran focus groups with some of these girls and reported that there was an "overwhelming sense of fear for their own physical safety while in facility care" due in large part to the "perceived lack of supervision and treatment of girls with mental health needs" (Citizen's Committee for Children, 2006: 20). The girls also reported that there was a need for "high quality pre-natal care and health services for pregnant girls." The girls specifically suggested that a girl who had been in detention while pregnant had a "difficult time getting enough food and not being able to rest properly." Girls in detention also needed help to deal with the stress of pregnancy and the "frustration and depression" of being separated from their children (Citizen's Committee for Children, 2006: 20).

There is also some evidence that girls are more vulnerable than boys to experiencing sexual abuse while being detained. In their study of 200 girls in California juvenile justice halls, Acoca and Dedel (1998: 6), found several examples of abuse, including "consistent use by staff of foul and demeaning language, inappropriate touching, pushing and hitting, isolation, and deprivation of clean clothing." In addition, girls underwent strip searches while being supervised by male staff.

Lack of female staff seems to place girls in vulnerable positions while being detained. In addition to increasing the chances that female wards will be abused by male staff, the lack of female staff also limits the programs and activities available for girls. Staff shortages in the Miami-Dade County Juvenile Detention Center for girls, for example, resulted in decreased outdoor recreation for girls. Ledermen and Brown (2000) reported that girls sometimes went as long as two weeks without outdoor recreation and were sometimes "locked down" due to shortage of staff. On some days, staff shortages resulted in girls' inability to attend school.

Why do girls languish in detention? The answers are not too hard to find, unfortunately, once one begins to review the literature on probation officers' (and other court officials') attitudes toward female delinquents. Research has consistently revealed that despite their less serious offense profile, girls in the juvenile justice system are regarded as "more difficult" to work with (Baines & Alder, 1996; Belknap, Winter, & Cady, 1997). A recent study of probation files in Arizona revealed stark gender and cultural stereotypes that worked against girls. Specifically, the authors found that "common images found in girls' probation files included girls fabricating reports of abuse, acting promiscuously, whining too much, and attempting to manipulate the court system." Girls were universally seen as "harder to work with," "had too many issues," and were "too needy" (Gaarder, Zatz, & Rodriquez, 2004: 14). Even when girls were abused, they were somehow partially responsible for the abuse in the eyes of probation officers: "They feel like they're the victim. They try from, 'Mom kicked me out' to 'Mom's boyfriend molested me' or 'My brother was sexually assaulting me.' They'll find all kinds of excuses to justify their actions. Because they feel if I say I was victimized at home that justifies me being out on the streets..." (Gaarder, Zatz, & Rodriquez, 2004: 16).

GENDER AND TRAINING SCHOOLS — GIRLS' VICTIMIZATION CONTINUES

Girls' commitments to facilities increased by an alarming 88% between 1991 and 2003 while boys' commitments increased by only 23%. As a result, girls were 15% of youth "committed" to residential placements in 2003, up from 13% in 1991 (Snyder & Sickmund, 2006: 208). Moreover, while girls can be "committed" to a variety of what are called "residential placements," the largest share end up in "long-term secure" facilities or training schools (youth prisons, in actuality). Girls are also being committed to these facilities for different and less serious offenses than boys. In 2003, for example, well over a quarter (29%) were committed for either status offenses or technical violations, compared to only 14% of boys. About half (46.74%) of the girls committed for a "person" offense were committed for simple assault, while only 22.2% of boys doing time for violent offenses were committed for these less serious assaults (Snyder & Sickmund, 2006: 210).

A recent study of 444 incarcerated youth in Ohio provides clear evidence of this gender difference (Holsinger, Belknap, & Sutherland, 1999). Researchers found that girls were just as likely as boys to be incarcerated for "violent" offenses. Focus group data with incarcerated girls, however, indicated that girls were being incarcerated for minor infractions, and in some cases, for defending themselves (Belknap, Dunn, & Holsinger, 1997). Similarly, Acoca and Dedel in their case file reviews of girls in the juvenile justice system found "a shocking distortion of the number of 'violent' girl offenders. Frustration, anger and a lack of impulse control are often shared by the adult caretakers and the girls and, in some cases, the adults were the aggressors" (Acoca & Dedel, 1998: 97). Listing the types of events that caused arrest reveals a clear pattern: "She returned from a runaway, mom started questioning her, so she threw a batch of cookies at her"; "Father was hitting her, so she hit

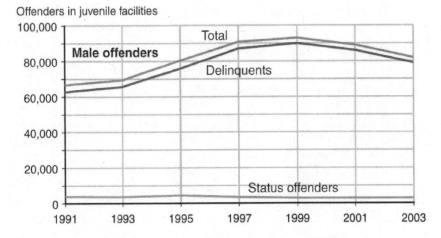

Figure 3.4. Trends in Male Incarceration, 1991–2003

him back and kicked him in the groin"; "My mom kept saying 'Hit me so I can call the police'"; and finally, "She was trying to sneak out of the house at night, but mom caught her and pushed her against the wall. She slapped mom" (Acoca & Dedel, 1998: 97). The authors concluded that a "majority" of the violence charges against girls were "non-serious mutual combat situations with parents" (Acoca & Dedel, 1998: 15). One can also see that in many instances these are either clearly child abuse cases or "status offense" cases that have been relabeled as "violent" offenses.

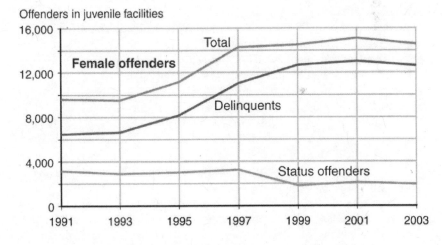

Figure 3.5 Trends in Female Incarceration, 1991–2003

Several recent scandals suggest that like their adult counterparts (women's prisons), juvenile prisons are often unsafe for girls in ways that are uniquely gendered. Take, for example, a recent investigation of conditions in the Hawaii Youth Correctional Facility in the summer of 2003 by the American Civil Liberties Union [ACLU]. According to the ACLU report, there were no female guards on duty at night on the girls' ward, one reported case of rape of a girl by a male guard, and several reports of girls exchanging sex for cigarettes. The report also noted that male guards made sexual comments to female wards, talked about their breasts, and discussed raping them. While wards noted that rape comments decreased after the rape incident, White (2003: 16) wrote, "wards expressed concern that the night shift is comprised entirely of male guards and they feel vulnerable after the rape because male guards could enter their cells at any time."

The ACLU report also discovered that wards reported being watched by male guards while they changed clothes and used the toilet. Male guards were also present when girls took showers. And, like their counterparts in detention, girls had not received outdoor recreation for a week due to lack of supervising staff and girls were told that the situation could last for up to a month (White, 2003). While critics of the ACLU report commented that the wards made up stories and severely exaggerated tales of abuse, in April of 2004, the guard implicated in the rape charge pleaded guilty to three counts of sexual assault and one count of "terroristic threatening of a female ward" (Dingeman, 2004). Although comprising a plea bargain, the legal rape case uncovered details indicating that the sexual abuse was more severe and alarming than wards originally reported to the ACLU.

More recently, the ACLU's Women's Rights Project and Human Rights Watch (HRW) conducted an investigation of the conditions of girls sent to two juvenile facilities in New York (Lansing and Tryon) (HRW & ACLU, 2006). They found many of the same problems identified in the Hawaii investigation, despite more limited access to wards and staff. Most notable among their findings was "use of inappropriate and excessive force by facilities staff against girls" (HRW & ACLU, 2006: 4).

Girls, who were former wards of the facility, complained specifically about excessive use of a "forcible face down 'restraint' procedure" that often resulted in the girls having "rug burns" and other abrasions as well as broken limbs as a result of this restraint process. Said one young girl: "You see kids walking around with rug burns on their faces from their temple all the way to the bottom of their chin, with crutches, one girl was in crutches and a case because they broke her arm and leg" (HRW & ACLU, 2006: 48). While such procedures are supposed to be reserved for extreme situations, the girls alleged that staff used the procedure in response to all sorts of minor infractions (such as not eating something they were allergic to, "improperly making their bed or not raising their hands before speaking") (HRW & ACLU, 2006: 5).

Girls also complained about sexual abuse at the hands of male staff as well as verbal abuse and degrading "strip searches," a severe lack of educational and vocational programming, and excessive idleness and security. As an example, "ill girls are bound in some combination of handcuffs, leg-shackles, and leather restraint belts any time they leave the facility" (HRW & ACLU, 2006: 5).

Again, as we have seen in other profiles, African American girls (who are only 18% of New York's youth population) comprised 54% of the girls sent to these facilities (HRW & ACLU, 2006:. 43). Many of these girls had histories of victimization and resultant mental heath issues. Roughly a third of all the girls were incarcerated for "property" crimes (mainly larceny); of the girls imprisoned for "crimes against person," over a third of these girls were there for "assaults," many of which involved family members (HWR & ACLU, 2006: 36).

An earlier Department of Justice investigation of Mississippi training schools provides even more horrific evidence of abuse (Boyd, 2003). In their letter to the governor of Mississippi, the investigators detail the conditions they found at Columbia Training School (where 75% of the girls were held for status offenses). They specifically detailed "unconstitutionally abusive practices such as hog-tying, pole-shackling, improper use and over use of restraints and isolation, staff assaulting youth, and OC spray abuse" (Boyd, 2003:. 5). Hog-tying was described in detail in the report:

> Approximately 10–15 boys and girls consistently described the practice, where youth are placed face down on the floor with their hands and feet shackled and drawn together. That is, youths' hands are handcuffed behind their backs. Their feet are shackled together and then belts or metal chains are wrapped around the two sets of restraints, pulling them together . . . several girls in Hammond Cottage told us that either they had been hog-tied or they had witnessed other girls being hog-tied. They reported that girls are typically tied for three-hour periods in the corners of the cottage and stated that girls are also hog-tied in the SIU [Special Intervention Unit]. Girls also reported being hog-tied in a SIU cell called the "dark room." (6)

The report also detailed examples of girls being "shackled to poles in public places" if they were "non-compliant" during military exercise (Mississippi uses a "military model for delinquent youth" stressing "vigorous" physical fitness) (Boyd, 2003: 2–5). Girls at Columbia reported being placed in the dark room for "acting out or being suicidal." The windowless isolation cell has lighting controlled by staff; it is also stripped of everything but a drain in the floor that serves as a toilet. When in use, the room is completely dark, and the girls are placed into the room naked. One girl reported being placed in the room for three days with "little access to water as her requests for water were largely ignored" (Boyd, 2003: 7). The report concluded "The conditions in the SIU are particularly inhumane. The cells are extremely hot with inadequate ventilation. Some girls are naked in a dark room where they must urinate and defecate in a hole that they cannot flush."

The report also found abuses that appear to grow out of the military style of the facility, which researchers have long suggested might not be appropriate for girls or women (Morash & Rucker, 1990). Specifically, the report notes that the program is "unsuitable for some of the troubled girls it serves." It goes on to state that the girls at Columbia "derive no benefits, physical or otherwise, from the program that is currently being administered." Harsh disciplinary practices are characterized as "training." Girls, for example, are "punished in the military field by being forced to run with automobile tires around their bodies or carrying logs. Girls reported being forced to eat their own vomit if they throw-up while exercising in the hot sun" (Boyd, 2003: 9). In another graphic example of abuse, the Columbia log book noted that one facility matron "punished a girl by requiring her to sleep one hour and walk one hour for two successive nights. This same girl also had to eat every meal standing for one week thereafter" (Boyd, 2003: 20). The problem of "unregulated punishments" included the hitting, choking, and slapping of girls. In one instance a 10-year-old girl was slapped by a male security guard (Boyd, 2003: 10).

The report further details major failures in the health area such that youth sent to the institution do not receive their prescribed medications. All the Mississippi facilities were failing to provide meaningful educational services, and were requiring youth, particularly girls, to "sit in silence for large blocks of time" because of chronic staff shortages (Boyd, 2003: 19–20). The letter contains a laundry list of deficiencies in the physical plant, including a dental clinic that had not been cleaned in "many months" with "spider webs, mouse droppings, and dead roaches everywhere" (Boyd, 2003: 34). Kitchen staff reported having to cover food to prevent cockroaches from dropping into the food from the hood above the stove, and the youth reported finding roaches in their food (Boyd, 2003: 35). Finally, and perhaps predictably, there is no meaningful grievance procedure at Columbia; youth reported that the mail was censored and was not mailed, if "anything negative about Columbia or the Columbia staff" was found (Boyd, 2003: 39).

While one might think that the excesses noted in these three states are unusual (or linked to one geographic region), that is sadly not the case. HRW earlier issued very critical reports on youth facilities in Georgia (HRW, 1996), Louisiana (HRW, 1995), and Colorado (HRW, 1997), and more recently, there have been scandals in Ohio and Texas as well. In Texas, where the Texas Youth Commission has had to fire more than 90 employees since 2000, a 16-year-old girl was granted early release after she attempted suicide as a result of being "molested repeatedly" by a male guard, who had earlier been accused of having raped four other girls (Fantz, 2008: 3).

HRW also notes that internal monitoring and oversight of the juvenile facilities in the United States are "dysfunctional" and independent, and out-side monitoring is "all but non-existent" (HRW & ACLU, 2006: 3–4). As a result, virtually all youth facilities in the United States, are "shrouded in secrecy and the girls who suffer abuse have little meaningful redress" (HWR & ACLU, 2006: 4). Sadly, scandals have long surfaced at girls' institutions (see Chesney-Lind & Shelden, 2004), and all of these incidents suggest that while authorities often use institutionalization as a means of "protect-ing" girls from the dangers of the streets and in their homes, many of the institutions that house girls not only perpetuate the gendered victimization that pervades girls' lives outside of these institutions, in some of the worst instances, the abuse that they suffer rivals that found in the most horrific of adult prisons.

INCARCERATION NATION: A DANGER TO GIRLS

The new millennium has signaled a dramatic reversal of previous decades of emphasis on the "deinstitutionalization" of girls. Today, girls are more likely to be arrested for violence and, once arrested, they were more likely to be detained or committed to residential facilities, often secure facilities with prison-like atmospheres and serious problems of abuse. Moreover, girls' deten-tions and commitments are longer now, and once serving their time, girls are more likely than before to return to detention and residential placement, thanks to recent legislative changes. One feature of girls and justice has not changed. Girls continue to experience rampant abuse and neglect at the hands of their justice system protectors, abuse that is in violation of international standards of human rights (HRW & ACLU, 2006). The persistence of neglect and abuse as well as the increase in girls arrests, court appearances, deten-tions, and commitments seems truly ironic given that since the seventies advocates, researchers, and legislators have pressed for increased services for and the decreased institutionalization, abuse, and neglect of girls.

Despite lip service to "deinstitutionalization," the juvenile justice system has always been ambivalent about releasing girls from formal supervision (see Chesney-Lind & Shelden, 2004). As a result, girls are now arguably the recipients of the worst of both worlds in the current juvenile justice system. That is to say girls in the new millennium are enduring the effects of a juvenile system that is becoming more punitive toward youth while also not shedding its more historic role of being deeply involved in the moral and social policing of girls (see Chesney-Lind & Irwin, 2007). This latter impulse is often bolstered by data showing the extensive victimization girls experience in home or on the streets (see Acoca & Dedel, 1998), which often backstops demands to place girls in detention and training schools "for their own protection."

An example of this trend can be seen is the 1995 Washington State "Becca's Bill" implemented in response to the murder of Rebecca Headman, a 13-year-old chronic runaway. After a series of runaway incidents and repeated calls to the police by her parents, Rebecca was murdered while on the streets. Under Becca's Bill, apprehended runways could be detained in a crisis residential center for up to seven days. Between 1994 and 1997, youth detention rates increased by 835% in Washington State and, by 1997, girls made up 60% of the detained population (Sherman, 2000). According to Sherman (2000), while there was Becca's Bill designed to save youths (mostly girls) from the streets in Washington by placing them in detention, there were no long-term community-based programs for runaway girls. In addition, as has been clearly shown, detention centers were certainly not universally safe havens for girls.

According to Corrado, Odgers, and Cohen (2000), the reliance on detention rather than treatment in the community was a trend in Canada as well. Looking at delinquency data and sentencing practices leading up to girls' detentions, Corrado, Odgers, and Cohen (2000: 193) found that "the sentencing recommendations made by youth justice personnel are primarily based on the desire to protect female youth from high-risk environments and street-entrenched lifestyles." Furthermore, they argue that reliance on detention came partly because of the ". . . inability of community-based programs to protect certain female youth, the difficulties these programs have in getting young female offenders to participate in rehabilitation programs, when they are not incarcerated, and the presence of some, albeit usually inadequate, treatment resources in custodial institutions" (Corrado, Odgers, & Cohen, 2000: 193).

Detention numbers are also affected by court personnel who confront a shortage of programs for girls and few safe, community-based alternatives (Sherman, 2005). At the same time that detention and arrest were being used to protect girls from the dangers of the streets, many jurisdictions, as was noted, were cracking down on youths' probation and court order violations. Through this mechanism, status offending girls are swept into detention, now relabeled as criminal offenders through contempt of court and probation violations. And, while those in the system may argue that they are forced to detain girls "for their own protection," a review of the conditions in these facilities as well as the services provided suggests that they are anything but protective.

GIRLS AND JUVENILE JUSTICE: WHAT DOES THE FUTURE HOLD?

Currently, Congress has had a series of hearings to reauthorize the Juvenile Delinquency Act, and one of the key issues that has surfaced is "conditions of confinement" (Fitzpatrick, 2008). The reauthorization of the act in 2002 supported the continued focus on girls. Specifically, the act required states, again, to create "a plan for providing needed gender-specific services for the prevention and treatment of juvenile delinquency" and denotes a category of funding for "programs that focus on the needs of young girls at risk of delinquency or status offenses" (Sharp & Simon, 2004). Perhaps this time, as more girls enter the various juvenile justice systems, the states will take more seriously the unique needs of girls.

Recent reports from a number of national organizations such as the American Bar Association, the National Bar Association (ABA & NBA, 2001), and the Child Welfare League (Sharp & Simon, 2004) have, once again, focused critical attention on the unmet needs of girls in the juvenile justice system. Beyond the continued claim that girls lack adequate gender-specific programming, there is also the undeniable fact that the girls in the juvenile justice system need considerable advocacy to protect them from the abuse of the system itself, which, like its adult counterpart, seems increasingly unable to protect those in custody from sexual and physical abuse (HRW, 1996a). Essentially, girl offenders have always been the recipients of what Ruth Wells described as "throwaway services for throwaway girls" (Wells, 1994). Now, sadly, we can add that the lack of girls' services promotes their placement in facilities that continue the sort of abuse they experienced in their families and on the streets (Acoca & Dedel, 1998).

Advocacy for community-based programming is critical, since it is clear that the girls in the juvenile justice system cannot wait another generation for things to change. As their numbers increase daily in the detention centers and training schools, and as the horrific conditions that characterize all too many of them are exposed, it is long past time to pay attention to girls. Imagine how different the juvenile justice system would look if we, as a nation, decided to take girls' sexual and physical victimization seriously and arrested the perpetrators rather than criminalizing girls' survival strategies and jailing them for daring to escape.

NOTE

1. Prisoners incarcerated on drug offenses make up more than half of all federal inmates and the number of drug offenders in state prisons has increased 13-fold since 1980 (Sentencing Project, 2008, http://www.sentencingproject.org/IssueAreaHome. aspx?IssueID=5, June 3, 2008).

REFERENCES

Acoca, L. (1999). Investing in girls: A 21st century challenge. *Juvenile Justice* 6(1): 3–13.

Acoca, L., & Dedel, K. (1998). *No place to hide: Understanding and meeting the needs of girls in the California juvenile justice system*. San Francisco: National Council on Crime and Delinquency.

Ambrose, A. M., Simpkins, S., & Levick, M. (2000). *Improving the conditions for girls in the juvenile justice system: The female detention project.* Washington, DC: American Bar Association.

American Bar Association and the National Bar Association. (2001). *Justice by gender: The lack of appropriate prevention, diversion and treatment alternatives for girls in the justice system.* Washington, DC: American Bar Association and the National Bar Association.

Austin, J., Clear, T., Duster, T., Greenberg, D., Irwin, J., McCoy, C., Mobley, A., Owen, B., & Page, J. (2007). *Unlocking America: Why and how to reduce America's prison population.* JFA Institute (Washington, DC). http://www.nicic.org/Library/022716 (accessed 14 July 2008).

Baines, M., & Alder, C. (1996). Are girls more difficult to work with? Youth workers' perspectives in juvenile justice and related areas. *Crime & Delinquency* 42(3): 467–485.

Belknap, J., Dunn, M., & Holsinger, K. (1997). *Moving toward juvenile justice and youth-serving systems that address the distinct experience of the adolescent female.* Gender Specific Work Group Report to the Governor. Office of Criminal Justice Services, Columbus, OH. February.

Belknap, J., Winter, E., & Cady, B. (2001). *Assessing the needs of committed delinquent and pre-adjudicated girls in Colorado: A focus group study.* A Report to the Colorado Division of Youth Corrections, Denver, CO.

Blumstein, A. (1995). Youth violence, guns, and the illicit-drug industry. *The Journal of Criminal Law & Criminology* 86: 10–34.

Blumstein, A., & Cork, D. (1996). Linking gun availability to gun violence. *Law and Contemporary Problems* 59: 5–24.

Blumstein, A., & Wallman, J. (2000). *The crime drop in America.* Cambridge: Cambridge University Press.

Boyd, R. (2003). *CRIPA investigation of Oakley and Columbia Training Schools in Raymond and Columbia, Mississippi.* http://i.cdn.turner.com/cnn/2008/images/04/01/oak.colu.miss.findinglet.pdf (accessed 15 July 2008)

Buzawa, E., & Hotaling, G. T. (2006). The impact of relationship status, gender, and minor status in the police response to domestic assaults. *Victims and Offenders* 1: 1–38.

Brener, N. D., Simon, T. R., Krug, E. G., & Lowry, R. (1999). Recent trends in violence-related behaviors among high school students in the United States. *Journal of the American Medical Association* 282(5): 330–446.

Bureau of Criminal Information and Analysis. (1999). *Report on arrests for domestic violence in California, 1998.* Sacramento: State of California, Criminal Justice Statistics Center.

Calahan, M. (1986). *Historical corrections statistics in the United States, 1850–1984.* Washington, DC: Bureau of Justice Statistics.

Cauffman, E., Feldman, S. S., Waterman, J., & Steiner, H. (1998). Posttraumatic stress disorder among female juvenile offenders. Journal of the American Academy of Child and Adolescent Psychiatry 31: 1209–1216.

Centers for Disease Control and Prevention. (1992–2002). *Youth risk behavior surveillance—United States, 1991–2001.* CDC Surveillance Summaries. U.S. Department of Health and Human Services. Atlanta: Centers for Disease Control.

Chesney-Lind, M. (1999). Media misogyny: Demonizing 'violent' girls and women. In J. Ferrel & N. Websdale (eds.), *Making trouble: Cultural representations of crime, deviance, and control* (115–141). New York: Aldine.

Chesney-Lind, M. (2000). What to do about girls? In M. McMahon (ed.), *Assessment to assistance: Programs for women in community corrections* (139–170). Lanham, MD: American Correctional Association.

Chesney-Lind, M., & Belknap, J. (2004). Trends in delinquent girls' aggression and violent behavior: A review of the evidence. In M. Putallaz & P. Bierman (eds.), *Aggression, antisocial behavior and violence among girls: A developmental perspective.* New York: Guilford Press.

Chesney-Lind, M., & Irwin, K. 2008. *Beyond bad girls: Gender, violence, and hype.* New York: Routledge.

Chesney-Lind, M., & Pasko, L. (2004) *The female offender: Girls, women and crime.* Second Edition. Thousand Oaks: Sage.

Chesney-Lind, M., & Shelden, R. (2004). *Girls, delinquency and juvenile justice.* Third Edition. Belmont, CA: Thompson-Wadsworth.

Children's Defense Fund and Girls Incorporated. (2002, August). *Overview of gender provisions in state juvenile justice plans.* Washington, DC: Children's Defense Fund and Girls Incorporated.

Citizen's Committee for Children of New York, Inc. (2006). Girls in the juvenile justice system: Understanding service needs and experiences. New York: Citizen's Committee for Children.

Cook, P. J., & Laub, J. H. (1998). The unprecedented epidemic in youth violence. In M. Tonry & M. H. Moore (eds.), *Youth violence. Crime and justice: A review of research* (27–64). Chicago: University of Chicago Press.

Corrado, R., Odgers, C., & Cohen, I. M. (2000). The incarceration of female young offenders: Protection for whom? *Canadian Journal of Criminology* 2: 189–207.

Currie, E. (1998). *Crime and punishment in America.* New York: Metropolitan Books.

Datesman, S., & Scarpitti, F. (1977). Unequal protection for males and females in the juvenile court. In T. N. Ferdinand (ed.), *Juvenile delinquency: Little brother grows up.* Newbury Park, CA: Sage.

Dembo, R., Sue, S. C., Borden, P., & Manning, D. (1995). Gender differences in service needs among youths entering a juvenile assessment center: A replication study. Paper presented at the Annual Meeting of the Society of Social Problems. Washington, DC.

Dembo, R., Williams, L., & Schmeidler, J. (1993). Gender differences in mental health service needs among youths entering a juvenile detention center. Journal of Prison and Jail Health 12: 73–101.

Dingeman, R. (2004). Ex-guard guilty in sex assault. *Honolulu Advertiser.* Posted 30 April 2004, on http://the.honoluluadvertiser.com/article/2004/apr/30/in/in14a.html.

Edwards, A. (2008). Teens in Lakeland cheerleader-beating case face adult court, restrictions. *Orlando Sentinel.* http://www.orlandosentinel.com/news/local/crime/orl-bk-cheerleader-beating1208apr12,0,3903732.story?track=rss (accessed 8 May 2008).

Elliott, D., & H. Voss. (1974). Delinquency and dropout. Lexington: D.C. Heath.

Fantz, A. (2008). "Sex abuse, violence alleged at teen jails across the U.S." CNN. com/crime. http://www.cnn.com/2008/CRIME/04/04/juvenile.jails/ (accessed 26 June 2008).

Federal Bureau of Investigation. (2007). *Crime in the U.S. 2006.* Washington, DC: U.S. Government Printing Office. http://www.fbi.gov/ucr/cius2006/ (accessed 14 July 2008).

Feld, B. (1999). *Bad kids: Race and the transformation of the juvenile court.* New York: Oxford University Press.

Female Offender Resource Center. (1977). *Little sisters and the law.* Washington, DC: American Bar Association.

Fitzpatrick, E. (2008). News briefs: Advocates seek to reform JJDP Act. *Youth Today.* March 1. http://www.youthtoday.org/publication/article.cfm?article_id=1485 (accessed 15 July 2008).

Gaarder, E., Zatz, M. S., & Rodriguez, N. (2004). Criers, liars and manipulators: Probation officers' views of girls. *Justice Quarterly* 21 (3, September): 547–578.

Gelsethorpe, L. (1989). *Sexism and the female offender.* Aldershot, England: Gower Publishing.

Girls Incorporated. (1996). *Prevention and parity: Girls in juvenile justice.* Indianapolis: Girls Incorporated National Resource Center.

Harms, P. (2002, January). Detention in delinquency cases, 1989–1998. *OJJDPAP Fact Sheet #1.* Washington, DC: U.S. Department of Justice.

Harrison, P. M., & Beck, A. J. (2006). *Prisoners in 2005.* Bureau of Justice Statistics Bulletin. Washington, DC: U.S. Department of Justice.

Harvard Civil Rights Project. (2000, June 15–16). *Opportunities suspended: The devastating consequences of zero tolerance and school discipline.* Report from a National Summit on Zero Tolerance. Washington, DC.

Holsinger, K., Belknap, J., & Sutherland, J. L. (1999). Assessing the gender specific program and service needs for adolescent females in the juvenile justice system. A Report to the Office of Criminal Justice Services, Columbus, OH.

Huizinga, D. (1997). Over-time changes in delinquency and drug use: The 1970s to the 1990s. Unpublished report. Washington, DC: Office of Juvenile Justice and Delinquency Prevention.

Human Rights Watch, Children's Rights Project. (1995). Children in Confinement in Louisiana. New York: Human Rights Watch.

Human Rights Watch, Children's Rights Project. (1996). Children in Confinement in the State of Georgia. New York: Human Rights Watch.

Human Rights Watch. (1996a). *All too familiar: Sexual abuse of women in U.S. state prisons.* New York: Human Rights Watch.

Human Rights Watch, Children's Rights Project. (1997). Children in Confinement in Colorado. New York: Human Rights Watch.

Human Rights Watch & American Civil Liberties Union. (2006). *Custody and Control: Conditions of Confinement in New York's Juvenile Prisons for Girls.* New York: Human Rights Watch and ACLU.

Joe Laidler, K. A., & Chesney-Lind, M. (1996). Official rhetoric and persistent realities in troublesome behavior: the case of running away. *Journal of Contemporary Criminal Justice* 12(2): 121–150.

Kempf-Leonard, K., & Sample, L. L. (2000). Disparity based on sex: Is gender-specific treatment warranted? *Justice Quarterly* 17: 89–128.

Kersten, J. (1989). The institutional control of girls and boys. In M. Cain (ed.), *Growing up good: Policing the behavior of girls in Europe* (129–144). London: Sage.

Lederman, C. S., & Brown, E. N. (2000). Entangled in the shadows: Girls in the juvenile justice system. Buffalo Law Review 48: 909–925.

Leslie, C., Biddle, N., Rosenberg, D., and Wayne, J. (1993). Girls will be girls. *Newsweek* (August 2): 44.

Longfellow, H. W. (1992). There was a little girl. In J. Bartlett & J. Kaplan (eds.), *Familiar Quotations*. 16th Edition. Boston: Little Brown and Co.

Madigan, E. (2004). Bullying by school kids gets lawmakers' attention. *Stateline.org* http://www.stateline.org/stateline/ (accessed 19 June 2004).

Mann, C. R. (1984). *Female crime and delinquency*. University of Alabama Press.

Mauer, M., & Chesney-Lind, M. (2003). *Invisible punishment: The collateral consequences of mass imprisonment*. New York: New Press.

McGuire, D. (2002). The interactive effects of race, sex and offense severity on detention processing decisions. *Journal for Juvenile Justice and Detention Services* 12: 259–277.

McCormack, A., Janus, M. D., & Burgess, A. W. (1986). Runaway youths and sexual victimization: Gender differences in an adolescent runaway population. Child Abuse and Neglect 10: 387–395.

Miller, J. (1994). Race, gender and juvenile justice: An examination of disposition decision-making for delinquent girls. In M. D. Schwartz & D. Milovanovic (eds.), *The intersection of race, gender and class in criminology*. New York: Garland Press.

Morash, M., & Rucker, L. (1990). A critical look at the idea of boot camp as a correctional reform. *Crime and Delinquency*: 204–222.

National Council on Crime and Delinquency. (2007). *And justice for some: Differential treatment of youth of color in the juvenile justice system*. Oakland, CA: National Council on Crime and Delinquency.

New York ACLU and Racial Justice Program, ACLU. (2007). *Criminalizing the classroom: The over-policing of New York City schools*. New York: NYCLU and ACLU.

Odem, M. (1995). *Delinquent daughters: Protecting and policing adolescent female sexuality in the United States, 1885–1920*. Chapel Hill: University of North Carolina Press.

Office of Juvenile Justice and Delinquency Prevention. (1998). *Guiding principles for promising female programming: An inventory of best practices*. Nashville, TN: Green Peters and Associates.

OJJDP. (2004). *Census of juveniles in residential placement databook: Offense Profile of detained residents*. Retrieved June 5, 2004 from www.ojjdp.ncjurs.org/ojstatbb/openpage.asp (accessed 5 June 2004).

Olweus, D., Limber, S., & Mihalic, S. (2002). *Blueprints for violence prevention: BULLYING prevention program*. Denver, CO: Center for the Study and Prevention of Violence, Institute of Behavioral Science, University of Colorado at Boulder.

Rafter, N. H. (1990). *Partial justice: Women, prisons and social control*. New Brunswick, NJ: Transaction Books.

Ray, D. (2002, March 20). Letter to Glenda MacMullin, American Bar Association. Re: National Girl's Institute.

Reitsma-Street, M., & Offord, D. R. (1991). Girl delinquents and their sisters: A challenge for practice. *Canadian Social Work Review* 8: 11–27.

Robinson, R. (1990). *Violations of girlhood: A qualitative study of female delinquents and children in need of services in Massachusetts.* Unpublished doctoral dissertation, Brandeis University.

Russ, H. (2004, February). The war on catfights. *City Limits* (magazine): 19–22.

Schaffner, L., Shorter, A. D., Shick, S., & Frappier, N. S. (1996). *Out of sight, out of mind: The plight of girls in the San Francisco juvenile justice system.* San Francisco: Center for Juvenile and Criminal Justice.

Sentencing Project. (2007). *Facts about prisons and prisoners.* Washington, DC: The Sentencing Project. http://www.sentencingproject.org/Admin/Documents/publications/inc_factsaboutprisons.pdf (accessed 14 July 2007).

Sharp, C., & Simon, J. (2004). *Girls and the juvenile justice system: The need for more gender responsive services.* Washington, DC: Child Welfare League.

Sherman, F. (2000). What's in a name? Runaway girls pose challenges for the justice system. *Women, Girls and Criminal Justice* 1(2): 19–20.

Sherman, F. (2005). *Detention reform and girls: Challenges and solutions.* Baltimore: Annie E. Casey Foundation.

Sickmund, M., Sladky, T. J., & Kang, W. (2004). *Census of juveniles in residential placement databook.* Washington, DC: U.S. Department of Justice. http://www.ojJJDPAp.ncjrs.org/ojstabb/cjrp/ (accessed 6 October 2008).

Siegal, N. (1995). Where the girls are? *San Francisco Bay Guardian* (4 October): 19–20.

Smart, C. (1976). *Women, crime and criminology: A feminist critique.* London: Routledge and Kegan Paul.

Snyder, H. N. (2001). *Law enforcement and juvenile crime. Juvenile offenders and victims national report.* Washington, DC: U.S. Department of Justice, Office of Justice Programs, Office of Juvenile Justice and Delinquency Prevention.

Snyder, H. N. (2002). *Juvenile arrests 2000.* Washington, DC: U.S. Department of Justice, Office of Justice Programs, Office of Juvenile Justice and Delinquency Prevention.

Snyder, H. N., & Sickmund, M. (1999). *Juvenile offenders and victims: 1999 national report* (NCJ 178257). Washington, DC: U.S. Department of Justice, Office of Justice Programs, Office of Juvenile Justice and Delinquency Prevention.

Snyder, H. N., & Sickmund, M. (2006). Juvenile offenders and victims: 2006 national report (NCJ 178257). Washington, DC: U.S. Department of Justice, Office of Justice Programs, Office of Juvenile Justice and Delinquency Prevention.

Stahl, A. (2003, September). Delinquency cases in juvenile courts. *OJJJDPAP Fact Sheet #31.* Washington, DC: U.S. Department of Justice.

Steffensmeier, D. J., & Steffensmeier, R. H. (1980). Trends in female delinquency: An examination of arrest, juvenile court, self-report, and field data. *Criminology* 18: 62–85.

Tyler, K. A., Hoyt, D. R., Whitbeck, L. B., & Cauce, A. M. (2001). The impact of childhood sexual abuse or later sexual victimization among runaway youth. Journal of Research on Adolescence 11: 151–176.

Viner, E. (2003, 21 October). Personal communication with the author (Chesney-Lind).

Warren, J., Gelb, A., Horowitz, J., Riordan, J. 2008. *One in 100: Behind Bars in America*. Washington, DC: Pew Center on the States. http://www.pewcenteron-thestates.org/uploadedFiles/8015PCTS_Prison08_FINAL_2-1-1_FORWEB.pdf (accessed 14 July 2008).

Wells, R. (1994). America's delinquent daughters have nowhere to turn for help. *Corrections Compendium* 19: 4–6.

WFTV. (2008). *Teen accused in taped beating asks judge to let her tell her story*. http://www.wftv.com/news/16479101/detail.html (accessed 8 July 2008).

White, B. (2003). American Civil Liberties Union report on the Hawaii Youth Correctional Facility. http://www.acluhawaii.org/pages/news/030826youthcorrection.html (accessed 3 June through 23 July 2008.

WKMG. (2008). *Girls in cheerleader beating joked in holding cell after arrests*. from http://local6.com/news/15830263/detail.html (accessed 8 May 2008).

PART II

GIRLS' VIOLENCE:
INSTITUTIONAL CONTEXTS AND CONCERNS

FOUR

THE GENDERING OF VIOLENCE
IN INTIMATE RELATIONSHIPS

How Violence Makes Sex Less Safe for Girls

Melissa E. Dichter
Julie A. Cederbaum
Anne M. Teitelman

INTRODUCTION

Adolescence, the developmental stage between childhood and adulthood, is a
time when youth begin to explore sexual and romantic intimacy with others
as part of their biological, psychological, and social maturation. Although
such intimate relationships can be, and ideally are, supportive, nurturing,
enjoyable, and healthy, in some cases the relationships are marked by violence, coercion, and abuse. It is often observed that both male and female
adolescents use aggression or violence in intimate relationships, however, a
range of social, psychological, and biological factors shape the context of this
violence, including motivation, meaning, and impact, in ways that put girls
at particular risk of negative consequences. Adolescent girls are particularly
susceptible to adverse consequences associated with (primarily heterosexual)
sexual activity, including unwanted pregnancy and sexually transmitted infections. Violence from an intimate or sexual partner can further exacerbate
these risks by interfering with methods of risk reduction on the part of
adolescent girls, such as abstinence from sex or use of protective elements,

such as condoms. Sexual risk prevention messages that ignore the impact of violence on adolescents' intimate relationships and discussions of partner violence that deny gender differences in experience or risk are misleading and fail to offer adequate support to adolescent girls who are negotiating violent intimate relationships.

In this chapter, we argue that when we consider adolescents in intimate relationships, we *must* consider violence, and when we consider violence in intimate relationships, we *must* consider gender. Furthermore, when thinking about young people, we must also recognize the significance of adolescent development more broadly. Adolescence is a stage during which identity development and role confusion prevail: adolescents typically struggle with the dual role of child and adult as they experience pubertal and sexual maturation, physical growth spurts, and the emergence of complex and abstract reasoning. During this time, individuals are learning to define who they are and who they want to be. This is a time of great change and vulnerability as individuals begin to break away from their parents and families, and elevate the importance of peers (Erikson, 1950, 1959; Micucci, 1998). Elkind (1998) describes the experience of physical and biological development that occurs during adolescence as the "perils of puberty" as adolescents learn to navigate their changing bodies and those of their peers.

It is often difficult for young people—boys and girls—who are in the process of coming to understand who they are to: (a) deviate from peer norms, (b) feel empowered and/or able to create limits with intimate partners, and (c) seek advice or assistance from adults prior to the onset of dating and intimacy. Adolescent girls face particular vulnerabilities associated with violence in intimate relationships. Adolescent girls involved in violent relationships may be unaware of ways to gauge the healthiness of relationships and may lack the self-efficacy needed to modify the parameters of the relationships. Threats of violence, shame, and violence-related trauma may further impose barriers to changing or removing oneself from an unhealthy relationship. This intersection of developmental and relational challenges puts adolescent girls at increased risk of suffering negative effects of partner violence. Adolescent girls' experience of partner violence is different from that of adolescent boys' as a result of biological, psychological, and social factors that lead to differences in types of violence experienced, severity of violence, motivations for violence, and, ultimately, the biological, psychological, and social impacts of such violence. Partner violence can have particularly damaging effects on an adolescent girl in a sexual relationship and can make sex more risky for adolescent girls.

In this chapter, we first review the role of gender in debates on gender symmetry in partner violence among adolescents. We use this review to illuminate what's missing in popular measurements of violence in the lives of adolescent girls in intimate relationships: sexual violence. We then describe the ways in which the experience of violence is different for adolescent girls and boys. We next discuss the gender-based experiences of sexual activity among adolescents, highlighting the risks of adverse consequences. The chapter ends with an analysis of the intersections of gender, violence, and sexual risk.

PARTNER VIOLENCE IN ADOLESCENCE: THE GENDER SYMMETRY/ASYMMETRY DEBATE

Over the last 30 years, scholars and advocates have been locked in a contentious debate about whether or not violence against intimate partners is gendered. Some argue that violence in intimate relationships is deeply gendered and is primarily a problem of violence against women and girls. Others claim that gender is not a factor in such violence, focusing instead on data showing that both males and females use violence against opposite-sex intimate partners and claiming that the violence is mutual or symmetrical across gender lines. These debates are illustrated in the most recent edition of the book *Current Controversies on Family Violence* (Loseke, Gelles, & Cavanaugh, 2005; see chapters by Dutton & Bodnarchuk, Loseke & Kurz, Yllö & Straus).

Claims of gender symmetry selectively rely on research conducted with adolescent or young adult populations (typically high school or college students) in dating (as opposed to marital or cohabiting) relationships. Such relationships help to support claims of gender symmetry because of higher rates of female-perpetrated violence in this population compared to older and married populations. Further, gender symmetry arguments tend to base their claims on narrow measures of violence—counting individual acts of violence ("hits"), exclusive of context around the violence, and limiting to physical violence acts or outcomes.[1] Through this narrow lens that focuses only on acts (outside of context) and emphasizes physical violence, partner violence, especially among adolescents, does appear gender-symmetric. Nationally representative studies of adolescents that count acts of violence also report that rates of psychological and physical victimization are essentially the same for males and females. This includes the most widely cited health and psychosocial data for the nation, the National Longitudinal Study of Adolescent Health (Add Health). The most recent reports on violence found that among adolescents age 12–21 years who had been in heterosexual relationships, 29% of females and 28% of males reported experiencing psychological violence from an opposite-sex partner. Twelve percent of both females and males reported experiencing physical violence from an opposite-sex partner (Halpern et al., 2001). Reported rates of *perpetration* of partner violence among adolescents tend to be either similar between boys and girls or to reveal girls perpetrating more violence than boys. For example, Roberts and Klein (2003) found that nationally, 21% of males and 22.1% of females reported perpetrating partner violence. Others (e.g., Foshee, 1996; O'Keefe, 1997) find similar results.

What these statistics fail to elucidate, however, is the *context* of violence. While these data support that differences in reported rates of perpetration and victimization are consistently statistically insignificant by sex, these data do not provide any insight into potential differences in *effects* of the violence among adolescent males and females. The data also conceal the prevalence and gender breakdown of other forms of violence, in particular, sexual violence, *which is not measured*. When including sexual violence and the context within which acts of physical, psychological, and sexual violence occur, gender *asymmetry* is clear. When looking more deeply into the context of violence in intimate relationships, we see that boys and girls are not equally impacted by violence in their intimate relationships. Although adolescent boys also experience adverse outcomes from violence perpetrated by their female partners, when looking within a gendered context we see that the experience and risk for girls is quite different. Without an understanding of the factors that influence the violence, the picture of violence in adolescents' intimate relationships is distorted.

THE MISSING PIECE: SEXUAL VIOLENCE

Sexual violence, including forced or coerced sex, attempted forced sex, or unwanted sexual touching, is often excluded from studies of partner violence, *especially among adolescents*. This form of violence, however, is neither uncommon nor insignificant and adolescence is a particularly high-risk time for sexual violence. From childhood to adulthood, the highest risk of sexual violence among females occurs during mid-adolescence, from the ages of 14 to 18 (Humphrey & White, 2000). Unlike physical and psychological violence, the gender breakdown regarding sexual violence is not symmetric. Females are far more likely than males to be victims of sexual violence and males are perpetrators more often than females. Available data comes from many studies that ask specifically about "forced sexual activity" or "rape." Sexual violence, however, includes *coerced and unwanted* sexual activity that is not considered, or stops short of, forced sex or rape. Although some coerced or unwanted sexual activity or pressure may fail to meet legal standards of completed rape, the meaning and impact of such violence may be no less significant for the victim. Limiting measurement to more narrow terms, therefore, is both arbitrary and misleading. Because of these limits, very little is known about the true rates of coercive or forced sexual activity. This lack of data leads to insufficient tools to effectively intervene with young women in relationships at risk for violence.

When using a broader and more inclusive framework of sexual violence, we find much higher victimization rates for adolescent girls. Smith, White, and Holland (2003) found that 29.5% of college students had experienced sexual violence from a dating partner while they were in high school. Among rural adolescents, Vicary, Klingaman, and Harkness (1995) found that 23%

of females reported unwanted sexual activity and 15% reported rape from male dating partners. Rosen (2004), found that among first-time adolescent mothers (ages 13–21years), 28.6% reported sexual coercion (including forced or coerced sex, or sex without a condom) from their intimate partners in the past 12 months and 31.4% reported sexual coercion from an intimate partner prior to the past year. What these studies highlight is the prevalence of unwanted sexual activity reported by young women. What we are not able to ascertain is the context of the violence. What are the circumstances that surround the events? This lack of information limits us from truly understanding the importance of looking at the issue of sexual violence and using a broader scope.

CONTEXT: INTENTION, MEANING, AND IMPACT

Thus far, we have seen evidence of outcomes from measuring multiple types of violence. In addition to including multiple types of violence in measurement, however, we must also take context into account in order to gain a more complete picture of the issue of partner violence. When we count individual acts of violence, we know only that the act has occurred but not the intention or meaning of the behavior for the perpetrator or the victim. The context often reveals that not all acts are equal. For example, depending on the context, a slap could be received as playful or humorous, or threatening and hurtful. In response to a slap, an individual could become excited or aroused or angry or fearful. The impact of the act on the recipient's behavior depends on the meaning of the act and the context in which it occurred. Therefore, it is imperative to take this more holistic approach to understanding partner violence among adolescents. For example, we see gender differences when considering intention, meaning, and impact of violent acts against adolescent intimate partners.

Even when the reported frequencies are similar, as they tend to be for physical and psychological violence, researchers have noted for at least a decade that the experience of violence for boys and girls is not the same (for a review, see Barter, 2009). Male-perpetrated violence is often more severe than female-perpetrated violence and females are more likely than males to suffer injuries from partner violence (Foshee, 1996; Molidor & Tolman, 1998; Muñoz-Rivas et al., 2007). Possibly due to this higher risk of injury, females are more likely than males to feel fearful as a result of partner violence (Molidor & Tolman, 1998; O'Keefe & Treister, 1998). Males are less likely to feel threatened by violence from females. This difference may be attributed, in part, to physical size differences between males and females. In Molidor and Tolman's (1998) study, boys were significantly more likely than girls (53.8% vs. 10.3%) to report that they responded to violence from their partner with laughter, or that they ignored it. When you do not think that the person hitting can hurt you, then the act becomes a joke or game. However, when you fear the outcome of the action, the effect manifests extremely differently. The effects of partner violence victimization, therefore, in the aggregate, are physically and psychologically more damaging for females than for males.

Adolescent boys, like adult males, tend to use violence against dating partners in an attempt to gain power in the relationship and to control their partners (Miller & White, 2003; O'Keefe, 1997). With violence causing fear in girls, males' use of violence may be successful in gaining dominance. Molidor and Tolman (1998) found that 12% of girls, compared with less than 2% of boys, reported that, in response to violence, they "obeyed" their partners. Adolescent girls, like adult females, frequently report that they have used violence in self-defense, to "fight back" or to express emotion rather than to dominate their partners (Barnett, Lee, & Thelen, 1997; O'Keefe, 1997). As such, they are hitting, but the motivation behind the hits varies dramatically from that of their male partners.

WHY GENDER MATTERS

In attempting to understand and explain these gender differences, we need to consider the social constructions and functions of gender. As Kristin Anderson (2005) reminds us, gender is a social construct, rather than an individual trait. She cautions against using an "individualistic approach to gender" that ignores the social context, including socioeconomic status and race in addition to gender, and encourages us to consider the ways in which violence interacts with gender within this social context. Particularly in heterosexual relationships, and particularly when sexual activity is involved, the gender context is critical in understanding the impact of violent behaviors. Contemporary U.S. society emphasizes the importance of males being "men" and men conforming to the norms of masculinity. "Real men," as Collins (2004) explains, are constructed as forceful and authoritative and, perhaps most critically, as *not* women. In a patriarchal society, men are assumed to be the dominant figures and masculinity is confirmed with power. Men hold the majority of power in societal institutions of business and government, and in highly regarded professions of medicine and law. When men do not have access to power in these public arenas, they may use violence to dominate in their private lives, often against women, also making sure that they are dominant over females and confirming their difference from females (Vandello et al., 2008). Although lack of power in public arenas may instigate violence in private lives, men who hold powerful public positions may also use violence against intimate partners.

Adolescence is the time for "boys" to transition into being "men" and to do this by distinguishing themselves from females and from adopting masculine traits. Lacking power in adult society due to their minority status, adolescents may be more likely to turn to violence to demonstrate dominance. Traditional gender role ideology endorses male dominance and use of violence or aggression in sexual relationships. Acceptance of aggressive, and even violent, verbal and physical sexual behavior is a pervasive and dominant norm of masculinity among adolescents (Tolman et al., 2003). Males who adhere to traditional gender role ideology are more likely than those who do not to promote acceptance of, and to perpetrate, partner violence (Santana et al., 2006). Members of racial minorities and other oppressed groups are, similarly, faced with reduced options for demonstrations of power. As Collins (2004) explains, "because so many African American men lack access to the forms of political and economic power that are available to elite white men, the use of their bodies, physicality, and a form of masculine aggressiveness become important" (109). Furthermore, being in a position subordinate to white people and adults, young black men may have an additional incentive to counteract subordination.

Power in society is stratified by age, gender, race, and social class (in addition to religion, education, employment, nationality, sexuality, ability, and more). These demographic factors interact and it may be difficult to distinguish the relevant factors. For example, studies have found higher rates of reported partner violence victimization among black adolescents than white adolescents (Eaton et al., 2006; Halpern et al., 2001; Rickert et al., 2004). There is little strong evidence, however, of a direct relationship between race and partner violence. Studies reporting differences in rates of partner violence by race have rarely controlled for other potentially mediating factors. Foshee and colleagues (2008) found that behavioral, attitudinal, and experimental variables mediated the relationship between race and perpetration of partner violence among adolescents.

Socioeconomic status, rarely measured among adolescents, may also account for disparities by race. A number of studies that examine differences by race (e.g., Howard & Wang, 2003; Foshee, 2006; Malik, Sorenson, & Aneshensel, 1997) have not controlled for socioeconomic status. Foshee and colleagues (2008) did assess aggregate-level socioeconomic status and found that adolescents living in more disadvantaged neighborhoods (measured as a composite of socioeconomic and demographic variables from the U.S. Census) were more likely than those from less disadvantaged neighborhoods to report perpetration of dating violence. There are also identified associations between neighborhood environments with high levels of community violence and poverty and partner violence (Glass et al., 2003; Malik, Sorenson, & Aneshensel, 1997). Other studies find higher rates of violence in urban areas, which are also more likely to have higher concentrations of minorities, compared with suburban or rural communities (Centers for Disease Control [CDC], 2006; National Institute of Justice [NIJ], 2005; Silverman, Raj, & Clements, 2004). Structural racism has created an environment in which African Americans are overrepresented in poor and underserved communities that provide little in the way of structural opportunities (White, 2002).

SEXUAL ACTIVITY AMONG ADOLESCENTS AND ITS CONSEQUENCES: GENDER-BASED EXPERIENCES

We have discussed thus far the gender-based experience of violence for adolescents in intimate relationships. The experience of sexual encounters in adolescence is also a gendered phenomenon. As described in this section, adolescent girls face particular risks related to sexual activity, particularly when they have relatively low power in a relationship. Following this section, we discuss ways in which violence interacts with sexual behavior and compounds risk.

Adolescence is a period of sexual maturation, when both boys and girls experience a surge in hormonal and physical body changes in preparation for sexual arousal and activity. This is the developmental period during which sexual debut—initiation of sexual intercourse, in particular—typically occurs. Similar to experiences of partner violence, *rates* of sexual activity tend to be similar between adolescent males and females; however, the *context* of initiation into sexual activity is often quite different. Sexual activity, like violence, is a gendered phenomenon in that the experience differs by gender. Sexual encounters do not occur within a vacuum but, rather, as Patricia Hill Collins (2004) explains, emerge around "sexual politics . . . a set of ideas and social practices shaped by gender, race, and sexuality that frame all men and women's treatment of one another, as well as how individual men and women are perceived and treated by others" (6). Almost half of all young people in high school in the United States report having had sexual intercourse; the rates do not significantly differ between males and females (CDC, 2008). However, girls are less likely than boys to be willing participants in their first experiences of sexual intercourse. Of their first experience of sexual intercourse, over 60% of males, and only 34% of females said that they "really wanted it to happen at the time." The majority of females (53%) had "mixed feelings" and 13% said that they "really didn't want it to happen" (Abma et al., 2004). Among young women, some findings report 10% of those who had sex before the age of 20 report that their first time was involuntary (Guttmacher Institute, 2006a). But "voluntariness" may be misleading: Abma, Driscoll, and Moore (1998) found that more than 25% of women who said that their first experience was "voluntary" also reported that it was not "wanted." In the most recent YRBS survey (CDC, 2008), 11.3% of girls reported having been physically forced to have sexual intercourse when they did not want to (compared with 4.5% of boys).

Whether forced, coerced, or wanted, sexual intercourse carries risk of resulting in unwanted pregnancy and contraction of sexually transmitted infections (STIs). Girls are more likely than boys to experience negative consequences from sexual activity and these undesirable outcomes have a potentially greater negative impact on female adolescents than they do on males.

Collateral Consequences: Adolescent Pregnancy

Rates of teenage pregnancy in the United States are the highest among countries in the developed world (Singh & Darroch, 2000; Terry-Human, Manlove, & Cottingham, 2006). While sexual behavior among U.S. adolescents is similar to those of other developed nations, U.S. adolescents are less likely to use contraception or do so consistently (Singh, Darroch, & Frost, 2001). This is particularly concerning as a sexually active young woman has a 90% chance of becoming pregnant within one year when she does not use contraceptives (Guttmacher Institute, 2006a) and more than 80% of adolescent pregnancies are unintended (Chandra et al., 2005). Almost a third (31%) of young women become pregnant at least once before they are 20 years old (Guttmacher Institute, 2006b). In 2006, the birth rate among 15- to 19-year-old females was 41.9 births per 1,000, an increase from the previous year and the first increase in fifteen years (Hamilton, Martin, & Ventura, 2007). As with disparities seen in risks for sexual violence, young ethnic minority women are particularly at risk for early pregnancy.

It is important to keep in mind that pregnancy in adolescence, while often unintended, is not always unwanted. Yet whether desired or not, despite norms in some communities where pregnancy at a young age is celebrated, in the larger U.S. society adolescents who become pregnant are often subject to multiple challenges, socially, economically, and medically. Pregnancy can become an adverse experience for both the teenager and for children of adolescent parents (Schwarz & O'Sullivan, 2007; Zeck et al., 2007).

Adolescent pregnancy affects girls' lives in profound ways—physically, socially, and psychologically. The fetus develops inside of the female body, affecting the female physiologically and may also cause her to face social stigma as her pregnancy becomes known (Wiemann et al., 2005). A male may be able to remain anonymous, or even unknowing, as the partner in pregnancy. The female partner is most likely to be held responsible for the outcome of the pregnancy and often becomes a single parent (Pearson, 2006). Females tend to bear the burden of child care, which may limit or thwart their educational and career options and aspirations. Although pregnancy may increase a teenager's sense of responsibility and educational aspirations, female adolescents typically find that parenting interferes with schooling and increases financial strain (Afable-Munsuz et al., 2006; SmithBattle, 2007). Adolescents who become pregnant are more likely than their adult counterparts to drop out of high school (Annie E. Casey Foundation, 1998) and are at increased risk of joblessness and poverty (Klein and the Committee on Adolescence, 2005).

Pregnancy can be a particularly high-risk time for partner violence, particularly for adolescents (CDC, 2006; Covington, Justason, & Wright, 2001; Pike & Wittstruck, 2000). Pregnant teens may experience increased violence because of jealousy from a partner who may resent the female's focus on her pregnancy instead of him or who may question whether he is the biological father. During pregnancy, girls may also increase their own use of violence in self-defense as a way to protect their unborn fetuses (Leiderman & Almo, 2001). Financial strain can also lead to dependence on partners for sustainability. The economic dependence may exacerbate power dynamics and increase the risk of violence.

Sexually Transmitted Infections (STIs)

The same behaviors that place young women at risk for pregnancy also place them at risk for STIs. The STIs for which adolescent girls and young adult women are at highest risk include chlamydia, herpes, gonorrhea, syphilis, human papillomavirus (HPV), and human immunodeficiency virus (HIV) (CDC, 2006). Although some are treatable, others (including herpes, HPV, hepatitis B and C, and HIV) lead to diseases that are typically chronic, often have no cure, have devastating social, mental, and medical health consequences, and may, ultimately, be fatal (as in the case of HPV leading to cervical cancer or HIV leading to AIDS). The high rates of STIs among adolescents are not unforeseen given that an earlier age of sexual intercourse has been linked to increased numbers of sexual partners during adolescence and inconsistent condom use (Hutchinson, 2002). However, reasons for inconsistent condom use, including threats of violence, are less known.

What we do know is that STIs are more likely to affect females than males (Aral et al., 2004; Kates & Leggoe, 2005). Physiologically and socially, females are more likely to contract infections from males through sexual activity than are males from females and adolescent females are more vulnerable than adults (Madkan et al., 2005). In addition to biological consequences, females experience social and psychological impacts. Among adolescent girls, STI diagnosis is associated with emotional distress, anxiety, and depression (Kahn et al., 2005; Salazar et al., 2006). Respondents to public opinion surveys indicate that women would be highly stigmatized, and more so than men, for having an STI (Lichtenstein, Hook, & Sharma, 2005; Smith, Mysak, & Michael, 2008). Thus, although STIs are of concern for both the female and make partner, young women with an STI are likely to experience both physiological and societal burdens as a result of the infection.

Prevention: Abstinence and Condom Use

Unwanted pregnancy and sexually transmitted infections, which carry great risks, particularly for adolescent girls, are preventable conditions. In order for an adolescent girl to keep herself safe from these adverse conditions, however, she needs some control in sexual relationships. The primary strategies for preventing unwanted pregnancy and STIs are abstinence from sexual intercourse or intercourse with male condom use. Less than two-thirds of sexually active high school students, however, report using a condom during their last experience of sexual intercourse (CDC, 2008). Perhaps because of the greater risks of negative outcomes associated with sexual intercourse, females are more likely than males to have positive attitudes about condom use and to desire safer sex practices (Mizuno et al., 2000; Tucker et al., 2007). Yet, given that the male condom is used on the male body, the male partner has more control over condom use and sex with male condom use requires the male partner's agreement and cooperation (Amaro, 1995; Rickert, Sanghvi, & Weimann, 2002). If her partner does not share her desire for safer sex practices, a young woman is faced with the sometimes unattainable challenge of safely saying "no" (Champion, Shain, & Piper, 2004; Tschann et al., 2002).

In conflict with prevention messages that emphasize the importance of negotiating with partners for safer sex, the dominant sexual scripts and traditional gender role ideologies suppress females' assertiveness. Girls are taught to "self-silence"—to withhold asserting their feelings or desires, especially around issues of sexuality or when their desires differ from their partners' and threaten the relationship (Bauman et al., 2007; Gavey, McPhillips, & Doherty, 2001). Girls are taught that the sexual domain is one in which the male partner leads, and where the female is submissive.

Boys are encouraged to express dominance in their intimate and sexual relationships. Finding that some sexually abusive boys were not psychologically abusive, Sears, Byers, and Price (2007) concluded that the boys were acting in accordance with a sexual script in which they are guided to "initiate and vigorously pursue sexual involvement" regardless of resistance from their partners. With peer reinforcement, such coercive behavior is viewed "as normative rather than as abusive" (501). Collins (2004) emphasizes the cultural significance of sex for young men in defining their manhood: "sexual intercourse with a woman initiates [boys] into manhood" (110)—having sex is a way for "boys" to become "men." In Code of the Street, Elijah Anderson (1999) also notes the importance of sex for urban African American male youth. Females are viewed as sexual opportunities and sexual conquests solidify a young man's prized masculine status. Anderson describes urban youth culture in which the "code of the street" dictates that, "To the young man, the woman becomes, in the most profound sense, a sexual object. Her body and mind are the object of a sexual game, to be won for his personal aggrandizement" (150).

Racial and economic oppression elevate the importance of sex for gaining power but also interfere with an adolescent's ability to responsibly handle the potential consequences of sex. As Anderson (1999) explains, "Casual sex with as many women as possible, impregnating one or more, and getting them to have his baby brings a boy the ultimate in esteem from his peers and makes him a man. Casual sex is therefore fraught with social significance for the boy who has little or no hope of achieving financial stability and hence cannot see himself taking care of a family" (177). There is, then, an inherent conflict between girls, who, because of social norms and adverse consequences, are motivated to avoid unprotected heterosexual sex and boys who feel social pressure to pursue heterosexual sex.

Social factors, including norms and sexual "scripts," additionally disadvantage females by ascribing power to males in sexual relationships, including as related to condom use (Amaro & Raj, 2000; Wingood & DiClemente, 2000; Zieler & Krieger, 1997). In adolescent relationships, for example, it is considered the boy's responsibility to carry condoms and initiate condom use, especially in casual or early stages of relationships, and girls who carry condoms are thought to be sexually intimate with multiple partners and are stigmatized as being promiscuous or "dirty." Girls are more often socialized to and expected to have a greater investment in maintaining a relationship and, thus, in more committed relationships, are less likely to suggest condom use as doing so can be perceived as a lack of trust in the partner and a threat to the continuance of the relationship (Bauman, Karasz, & Hamilton, 2007). Boys who subscribe to traditional gender norms are particularly likely to have negative views of condom use and are also likely to lack intention to use condoms during heterosexual intercourse (Noar & Morokoff, 2002; Santana et al., 2006).

Sexual messages from families often reinforce traditional sexual gender norms, which, in turn, disadvantage adolescent girls in negotiating safer sex. Fasula, Kim, Miller, and Wiener (2007) identified a sexual double standard in the ways mothers provided sexual risk reduction socialization. The sexual double standard is a social norm that affords the freedom and power to participate and direct heterosexual encounters to males. For example, daughters were discouraged from sexual risk preparedness, which mothers associated with promiscuity, while a proactive approach to condom preparation was provided to sons. Messages from families to wait to have sex can conflict with girls' experiences of pressure or coercion from peers or partners (Teitelman & Loveland-Cherry, 2004). However, evidence suggests that parent-adolescent communication about sexual pressure as well as girls' perceptions of their mothers having egalitarian gender norms are associated with more consistent condom use (Teitelman, Ratcliffe, & Cederbaum, 2008).

INTERSECTIONS OF GENDER, VIOLENCE, AND SEXUAL RISK

Partner violence further contributes to a female's vulnerability to adverse outcomes of sexual behavior. Adolescent females who experience partner violence victimization are also more likely than their non-victimized peers both to be pregnant and to be diagnosed with an STI (Coker et al., 2000; Decker, Silverman, & Raj, 2005; Kreiter et al., 1999; Miller et al., 2008; Roberts et al., 2005; Silverman et al., 2001; Silverman et al., 2004; Shrier et al., 1998; Upchurch & Kusunoki, 2004; Wingood et al., 2001). Partner violence intersects with sexual risk by increasing risk through mechanisms that decrease preventive behaviors. Numerous studies (e.g., Howard & Wang, 2003; Kreiter et al., 1999; Roberts, Auinger, & Klein, 2005; Silverman et al., 2004; Silverman et al., 2001; Wingood et al., 2001) have found that adolescent females who have experienced partner violence victimization are more likely than those who have not experienced partner violence victimization to have sexual intercourse without condom use (for a review, see Teitelman et al., 2007).

Prevention messages emphasize the need to negotiate for safer sex behaviors within a relationship. However, for a female in particular partner violence may interfere with her ability to safety and effectively pursue such negotiation. Partner violence can diminish a female's power in the relationship and, through both direct and indirect pathways, can erode a young woman's ability to have control over her own sexual risk behaviors.

When sex is forced, the victim, by definition, does not have control over the encounter. She is not able, in that case, to refuse sex or sex without male condom use. Even in the absence of forced sex, however, other abusive behaviors from male partners can lead to sexual relationship power imbalances that can lead to increased difficulty for females in navigating their sexual safety. When an adolescent female has experienced physical and/or psychological violence, and threats of violence, from a male partner, she may, reluctantly, acquiesce to her partner's wishes or demands in order to protect herself from further violent victimization stemming from non-compliance.

Males who use violence against their female partners are less likely than males who do not use violence to endorse safer sex practices and respect a partner's wishes to minimize risks. Non-use of condoms can facilitate a male's ability to maintain control in the relationship. In a particularly odious scenario, adolescent males who had been identified as possibly abusive noted that they might choose not to use a condom if sex was forced or coerced because the condom application process could give the female victim an opportunity to escape (Silverman et al., 2006). Outcomes of sexual risk behaviors—such as pregnancy—can increase a female's vulnerability and her partner's ability to establish control over her. In a qualitative study, female adolescents reported that their abusive partners had attempted to impregnate them even against their wishes. Male partners refused to participate in using birth control or would "sabotage" a female's birth control efforts by, for example, poking holes in condoms or disposing of her birth control pills (Miller et al., 2007).

Male partners can gain and sustain dominance in a sexual relationship through violence and threats of violence that instill fear in their female partners and thereby decrease the females' relative power in the relationship (Felson & Messner, 2000; O'Keefe, 1997). Adolescent females who have been victimized by partner violence are likely to fear violent responses from their partners (Champion et al., 2004; Wingood et al., 2001). This fear is correlated with lack of negotiation ability (Crosby et al., 2002; Morokoff et al., 1997). If a young woman perceives or knows her partner to use violence as coercion or punishment, she may comply with his wishes and prioritize her immediate safety from violence over her other needs or desires.

Girls who have experienced partner violence victimization perceive themselves as having low sexual relationship power (Champion et al., 2004; Teitelman et al., 2008; Wingood et al., 2001). In a relationship with uneven power, one partner has greater control over decision-making than the other and has the ability to carry out behaviors against the wishes of the other (Pulerwitz, Gortmaker, & DeJong, 2000). Violence and perceptions of low power in the relationship can decrease one's sense of self-efficacy—the belief that she has the power to enact the behavior (Morokoff et al., 1997; Rickert et al., 2002). Low relationship power and decreased self-efficacy are associated with condom non-use among adolescent females (Gutierrez, Oh, & Gillmore, 2000; Jorgensen, King, & Torrey, 1980; Teitelman et al., 2008; Sionean & Zimmerman, 1999; Wingood et al., 2001).

Partner violence can have more indirect influence on sexual risk behaviors by eroding the victimized partner's sense of self-esteem or self-worth, associated with depression, self-harm, and substance use, each of which decreases her enthusiasm for self-protection as well as attempts and abilities in engaging in self-protective behavior. Adolescent girls who are victimized by dating violence are more likely than non-victimized girls to experience low self-esteem, depression, suicidality, and drug and alcohol use (Ackard, Neumark-Sztainer, & Hannan, 2003; Coker et al., 2000; Kreiter et al., 1999; Olshen et al., 2007; Roberts & Klein, 2003; Silverman et al., 2001). Among adolescent girls, low self-esteem, depressive symptoms, and substance use are, in turn, associated with self-silencing, decrease in self-respect and assertiveness, and sexual risk behaviors (Crosby et al., 2002; Lehrer et al., 2006). These same associations are not true for boys, who may experience depressed mood as a result of dating violence but have not been found to have experiences of low self-esteem and substance use to the same degree (Lehrer et al., 2006; Roberts & Klein, 2003).

CONCLUSION

Girls' experience with violence and sexual risk are intertwined epidemics impacted by racism, sexism, and classism (Roberts, 1999). Due to the biological, psychological, and social factors that lead to differences in types of violence, severity of violence, motivations for violence, and the biological, psychological, and social impacts of such violence, in relationships among adolescents, male-to-female partner violence is not the same as female-to-male partner violence. The effects of partner violence serve to decrease girls' ability to effectively negotiate abstinence from sexual risk behavior, thereby increasing her risk of becoming pregnant or contracting an STI. The burden of these consequences of sexual behavior, in turn, is, in general, greater for girls than it is for boys. As this chapter has documented, the evidence is clear that partner violence and sexual risk both occur within a societal context of gender power dynamics that cause the girls' experiences to be different from that of boys in profound ways.

This culmination of biological factors and familial and societal norms place young women in a unique position; there are pressures related to the expectations, roles, and outcomes. Because this developmental time is associated with identity and exploration of self, dialogue and negotiation for safer sex are difficult. This pressure on girls to consistently make "good" decisions to protect themselves from unintended outcomes of sex may be an unrealistic directive. Changes on a greater scale, the societal rather than individual level, may ultimately translate to safer sexual encounters for young women.

Neither sexual risk behaviors nor partner violence are experienced by an individual in a vacuum. Community environments, cultural gender roles, social location, and poverty interact and contribute to shaping individual identities and experiences. As others have noted (Roberts, 1999; Way, 1995), we need to consider these factors, and the related forms of oppression, when attempting to reduce negative outcomes, particularly for young women of color. In both research and practice, we need to integrate theoretical approaches that address gender power dynamics, building on our knowledge of individual health behaviors. As DiClemente, Salazar, Crosby, and Rosenthal (2005) suggest, a socio-ecological framework that includes individual, familial, relational, community, and societal factors is important for understanding the numerous factors that can impact sexual risk among adolescents. A more inclusive approach may also help explain the gap between intention and practice in situations where intended behavior is not under one's volitional control.

The evidence compels us to incorporate an understanding and awareness of sex and gender differences when considering partner violence—its etiology, pathways, and, most importantly, its potential consequences. As we think about adolescents' sexual behavior and associated outcomes, we are similarly compelled to take into account relationship dynamics and the impact of violence and power differentials. In doing so, we need to be careful neither to ignore the gender context nor hold a victim solely responsible for the consequences of behavior in the relationship.

NOTES

1. The Conflict Tactics Scales (CTS; Straus, 1979), including various versions of the original instrument (e.g., the Revised Conflict Tactics Scales [CTS2]; Straus, Hamby, Boney-McCoy, & Sugarman, 1996), is the most widely used instrument

to measure partner violence. This quantitative, self-report instrument asks about frequency of specific violent acts by either partner (e.g., *I hit my partner* or *My partner hit me*). Studies using the CTS often find gender symmetry in reported frequency of acts of violence (i.e., that females use violence in equal frequency to males), or that there are more reports of female-perpetrated violence than male-perpetrated violence. However, interpreting the findings at face value may be misleading. The instrument measures violent acts framed in terms of conflicts in dyadic relationships and has been widely criticized for failing to account for motivations or meaning of the violence, historical patterns of violence, or the initiator of the violence or conflict (e.g., DeKeseredy & Schwartz, 1998; Kimmel, 2002; Melton & Belknap, 2003). Furthermore, although the CTS2 includes subscales for injury, psychological violence, and sexual violence, literature supporting an argument of gender symmetry using the CTS2 or like instruments often reports only on the physical violence subscale and excludes the more gender disparate forms of violence (e.g., Archer, 2000; Straus, 2009).

REFERENCES

Abma, J., Driscoll, A., & Moore, K. (1998). Young women's degree of control over first intercourse: An exploratory analysis. *Family Planning Perspectives* 30: 12–18.

Abma, J. C., Martinez, G. M., Mosher, W. D., & Dawson, B. S. (2004). Teenagers in the United States: Sexual activity, contraceptive use, and childbearing, 2002. National Center for Health Statistics, *Vital Health Stat* 23: 1–48.

Ackard, D. M., Neumark-Sztainer, D., & Hannan, P. (2003). Dating violence among a nationally representative sample of adolescent girls and boys: Associations with behavioral and mental health. *Journal of Gender Specific Medicine* 6: 39–48.

Afable-Munsuz, A., Speizer, I., Magnus, J. H., & Kendall, C. (2006). A positive orientation toward early motherhood is associated with unintended pregnancy among New Orleans youth. *Maternal and Child Health Journal* 10: 265–276.

Amaro, H. (1995). Love, sex, and power: Considering women's realities in HIV prevention. *American Psychologist* 50: 437–447.

Amaro, H., & Raj, A. (2000). On the margin: Power and women's HIV risk reduction strategies. *Sex Roles* 42: 723–749.

Anderson, E. (1999). *Code of the street: Decency, violence, and the moral life of the inner city.* New York: W.W. Norton.

Anderson, K. L. (2005). Theorizing gender in intimate partner violence research. *Sex Roles* 52: 853–865.

Annie E. Casey Foundation. (1998). When teens have sex: Issues and trends. Baltimore, MD: Annie E. Casey Foundation.

Aral, S. O., Hawkes, S., Biddlecom, A., & Padian, N. (2004). Disproportionate impact of sexually transmitted diseases on women. http://www.cdc.gov/ncidod/EID/vol10no11/04-0623_02.htm (accessed 14 October 2005).

Archer, J. (2000). Sex differences in aggression between heterosexual partners: A metaanalytic review. *Psychological Bulletin* 126: 651–680.

Barnett, O. W., Lee, C. Y., & Thelen, R. E. (1997). Gender differences in attributions of self-defense and control in interpersonal aggression. *Violence Against Women* 3: 462–481.

Barter, C. (2007). In the name of love: Partner abuse and violence in teenage relationships. *British Journal of Social Work* 39: 211–233.

Bauman, L. J., Karasz, A., & Hamilton, A. (2007). Understanding failure of condom use intention among adolescents completing an intensive prevention intervention. *Journal of Adolescent Research* 22: 248–274.

Beckman, L. J., Harvey, S. M., Thorburn, S., Maher, J. E., & Burns, K. L. (2006). Women's acceptance of the diaphragm: The role of relationship factors. *The Journal of Sex Research* 43: 297–306.

Blum, R. W., Beuhring, T., Shew, M. L., Bearinger, L. H., Sieving, R. E., & Resnick, M. D. (2000). The effects of race/ethnicity, income, and family structure on adolescent risk behaviors. *American Journal of Public Health* 90: 1879–1884.

Centers for Disease Control and Prevention (CDC). (2006). *Sexually Transmitted Disease Surveillance, 2005*. Atlanta, GA: U.S. Department of Health and Human Services.

Centers for Disease Control and Prevention (CDC). (2007a). *Adolescent reproductive health: Home*. http://www.cdc.gov/reproductivehealth/AdolescentReproHealth/index.htm (accessed 20 September 2007).

Centers for Disease Control and Prevention (CDC). (2007b). *Sexually transmitted disease surveillance, 2006*. Atlanta: U.S. Department of Health and Human Services.

Centers for Disease Control and Prevention National Prevention Information Network. (n.d.). STDs today. http://www.cdcnpin.org/scripts/std/std.asp (accessed 15 October 2005).

Centers for Disease Control and Prevention (CDC). (2008). Youth risk behavior surveillance—United States, 2007. *Morbidity and Mortality Weekly Report* 57, No.SS-4.

Champion, J. D., Shain, R. N., & Piper, J. (2004). Minority adolescent women with sexually transmitted diseases and a history of sexual or physical abuse. *Issues Mental Health Nursing* 25: 293–316.

Chandra, A., Martinez., G. M., Mosher, W. D., Abma, J. C., & Jones, J. (2005). Fertility, family planning, and reproductive health of U.S. women: Data from the 2002 National Survey of Family Growth. *Vital Health Statistics* 23.

Coker, A. L., McKeown, R. E., Sanderson, M., Davis, K. E., Valois, R. F., & Huebner, E. S. (2001). Severe dating violence and quality of life among South Carolina high school students. *American Journal of Preventative Medicine* 19: 220–227.

Collins, P. H. (2004). *Black sexual politics: African Americans, gender, and the new racism*. New York: Routledge.

Covington, D., Justason, B., & Wright, L. (2001). Severity, manifestations, and consequences of violence among pregnant adolescents. *Journal of Adolescent Health* 28: 55–61.

Crosby, R. A., DiClemente, R. J., Wingood, G. M., Cobb, B. K., Harrington, K., Davies, S. L., Hook, E. W., & Oh, M. K. (2002). Condom use and correlates of African American adolescent females' infrequent communication with sex partners about preventing sexually transmitted diseases and pregnancy. *Health Education and Behavior* 29: 219–231.

DeKeseredy, W., & Schwartz, M. (1998). Measuring the extent of woman abuse in intimate heterosexual relationships: A critique of the Conflict Tactics Scales. Harrisburg, PA: VAWnet. www.vawnet.org (accessed 4 January 2010).

Decker, M. R., Silverman, J. G., & Raj, A. (2005). Dating violence and sexually transmitted disease/HIV testing and diagnosis among adolescent females. *Pediatrics* 116: 272–276.

DiClemente, R. J., Salazar, L. F., Crosby, R. A., & Rosenthal, S. L. (2005). Prevention and control of sexually transmitted infections among adolescents: The importance of a socio-ecological perspective—a commentary. *Public Health* 119: 825–836.

Dutton, D. G., & Bodnarchuk, M. (2005). Through a psychological lens: Personality disorder and spouse assault. In D. R. Loseke, R. J. Gelles, & M. M. Cavanaugh (eds.), *Current controversies on family violence*. Second Edition. Newbury Park, CA: Sage.

Eaton, D. K., Kann, L., Kinchen, S., Ross, J., Hawkins, J., Harris, W. A., Lowry, R., McManus, T., Chyen, D., Shanklin, S., Lim, C., Grunbaum, J., & Wechsler, H. (2006). *Youth Risk Behavior Surveillance—United States, 2005*. Atlanta, GA: Centers for Disease Control and Prevention.

Elkind, D. (1998). *All grown up and no place to go: Teenagers in crisis*. Revised Edition. Reading, MA: Addison-Wesley.

Erikson, E. H. (1950). *Childhood and society*. New York: Norton.

Erikson, E. H. (1959). Identity and the life cycle. *Psychological Issues* 1: 1–71.

Fasula, A. M., Kim, S., Miller, K. S., & Wiener, J. (2007). The sexual double standard in African American adolescent women's sexual risk reduction socialization. *Women & Health* 46: 3–21.

Felson, R. B., & Messner, S. F. (2000). The control motive in intimate partner violence. *Social Psychology Quarterly* 63: 86–94.

Foshee, V. A. (1996). Gender differences in adolescent dating abuse prevalence, types and injuries. *Health Education Research* 11: 275–286.

Foshee, V. A., Karriker-Jaffe, K. J., Reyes, H. L. M., Ennett, S. T., Suchindran, C., Bauman, K. E., & Benefield, T. S. (2008). What accounts for demographic differences in trajectories of adolescent dating violence? An examination of intrapersonal and contextual mediators. *Journal of Adolescent Health* 42: 596–604.

Gavey, N., McPhillips, K., & Doherty, M. (2001). "If it's not on, it's not on"—or is it?: Discursive constraints on women's condom use. *Gender & Society* 15: 917–934.

Glass, N., Fredland, N., Campbell, J., Yonas, M., Sharps, P., & Kub, J. (2003). Adolescent dating violence: Prevalence, risk factors, health outcomes, and implications for clinical practice. *JOGNN* 32: 227–238.

Gutierrez, L., Oh, H. J., & Gillmore, M. R. (2000). Toward an understanding of (em)power(ment) for HIV/AIDS prevention with adolescent women. *Sex Roles* 42: 581–611.

The Guttmacher Institute. (1999). Pregnancy risk assessment monitoring system state specific survey of new mothers. *Family Planning Perspectives* 31: 106.

The Guttmacher Institute. (2006a). *Facts on American teens' sexual and reproductive health*. New York: The Guttmacher Institute.

The Guttmacher Institute. (2006b). *U.S teen pregnancy statistics national and state trends by race and ethnicity*. New York: The Guttmacher Institute.

Halpern, C. T., Oslak, S. G., Young, M. L., Martin, S. L., & Kupper, L. L. (2001). Partner violence among adolescents in opposite-sex romantic relationships: Findings from the National Longitudinal Study of Adolescent Health. *American Journal of Public Health* 91: 1679–1685.

Hamilton, B. E., Martin, J. A., & Ventura, S. J. (2007). Births: Preliminary data for 2006. *National Vital Statistics Reports* 56: 7.

Hickman, L. J., Jaycox, L. H., & Aronoff, J. (2004). Dating violence among adolescents: Prevalence, gender distribution, and prevention program effectiveness. *Trauma, Violence, & Abuse* 5: 123–142.

Howard, D. E., & Wang, M. W. (2003). Risk profiles of adolescent girls who were victims of dating violence. *Adolescence* 38: 1–14.

Humphrey, J. A., & White, J. W. (2000). Women's vulnerability to sexual assault from adolescence to young adulthood. *Journal of Adolescent Health* 27: 419–424.

Hutchinson, M. K. (2002). The influence of sexual risk communication between parents and daughters on sexual risk behaviors. *Family Relations* 51: 238–247.

Jorgensen, S. R., King, S. L., & Torrey, B. A. (1980). Dyadic and social network influences on adolescent exposure to pregnancy risk. *Journal of Marriage and the Family* 42: 141–155.

Kahn, J. A., Slap, G. B., Bernstein, D. I., Kollar, L. M., Tissot, A. M., Hillard, P. A., & Rosenthal, S. L. (2005). Psychological, behavioral, and interpersonal impact of Human Papillomavirus and Pap test results. *Journal of Women's Health* 14: 650–659.

Kates, J., & Leggoe, A. W. (2005). HIV/AIDS policy fact sheet: The HIV/AIDS epidemic in the United States. http://www.kff.org/hivaids/upload/Fact-Sheet-The-HIV-AIDS-Epidemic-in-the-United-States-2005-Update.pdf (accessed 25 September 2005).

Kimmel, M. S. (2002). "Gender symmetry" in domestic violence: A substantive and methodological research review. *Violence Against Women* 8: 1332–1363.

Klein, J. D., and the Committee on Adolescence. (2005). Adolescent pregnancy: Current trends and issues. *Pediatrics* 116: 281–286.

Kreiter, S. R., Krowchuk, D. P., Woods, C. R., Sinal, S. H., Lawless, M. R., & DuRant, R. H. (1999). Gender differences in risk behaviors among adolescents who experience date fighting. *Pediatrics* 104: 1286–1292.

Lehrer, J. A., Shrier, L. A., Gortmaker, S., & Buka, S. (2006). Depressive symptoms as a longitudinal predictor of sexual risk behaviors among U.S. middle and high school students. *Pediatrics* 118: 189–200.

Leiderman, S., & Almo, C. (2001). *Interpersonal violence and adolescent pregnancy: Prevalence and implications for practice and policy*. Washington, DC: Healthy Teen Network.

Lichtenstein, B., Hook, E. W., & Sharma, A. K. (2005). Public tolerance, private pain: Stigma and sexually transmitted infections in the American Deep South. *Culture, Health & Sexuality* 7: 43–57.

Loseke, D. R., Gelles, R. J., & Cavanaugh, M. M. (2005). *Current controversies on family violence*. Second Edition. Newbury Park, CA: Sage.

Loseke, D. R., & Kurz, D. (2005). Men's violence toward women is the serious social problem. In D. R. Loseke, R. J. Gelles, & M. M. Cavanaugh (eds.), *Current controversies on family violence*. Second Edition. Newbury Park, CA: Sage.

Madkan, V. K., Giancola, A. A., Sra, K. K., & Tyring, S. K. (2006). Sex differences in the transmission, prevention, and disease manifestations of sexually transmitted diseases. *Archives of Dermatology* 142: 365–370.

Malik, A., Sorenson, S. B., & Aneshensel, C. S. (1997). Community and dating violence among adolescents: Perpetration and victimization. *Journal of Adolescent Health*, 21(5): 291–302.

Mantell, J. E., Dworkin, S. L., Exner, T. M., Hoffman, S., Smit, J. A., & Susser, I. (2006). The promises and limitations of female-initiated methods of HIV/STI protection. *Social Science & Medicine* 63: 1998–2009.

Mantell, J. E., Myer, L., Carballo-Diéguez, A., Stein, Z., Ramjee, G., Morar, N. S., & Harrison, P. F. (2005). Microbicide acceptability research: Current approaches and future directions. *Social Science & Medicine* 60: 319–330.

Martin, J. A., Kung, H., Matthews, T. J., Hoyert, D. L., Strobino, D. M., Guyer, B., & Sutton, S. R. (2008). Annual summary of vital statistics: 2006. *Pediatrics* 121: 788–801.

Maternal Child Health Bureau [MCHB]. (2006). *Child Health USA 2004*. http://www.mchb.hrsa.gov/chusa_06/popchar/0205ma.htm (accessed 18 September 2007).

Melton, H. C., & Belknap, J. (2003). He hits, she hits: Assessing gender differences and similarities in officially reported intimate partner violence. *Criminal Justice and Behavior* 30: 328–348.

Micucci, J. A. (1998). *The adolescent in family therapy*. New York: The Guilford Press.

Miller, E., Decker, M. R., Reed, E., Raj, A., Hathaway, J. E., & Silverman, J. G. (2007). Male partner pregnancy-promoting behaviors and adolescent partner violence: Findings from a qualitative study with adolescent females. *Ambulatory Pediatrics* 7: 360–366.

Miller, E., Decker, M., Silverman, J., Reed, E. A., Marable, D., & Raj, A. (2008). Adolescent intimate partner violence and contraceptive nonuse among adolescent females utilizing teen clinics. *Journal of Adolescent Health* 42: 8.

Miller, J., & White, N. A. (2003). Gender and adolescent relationship violence: A contextual examination. *Criminology* 41: 1207–1248.

Mizuno, Y., Kennedy, M., Seals, B., & Myllyluoma, J. (2000). Predictors of teens' attitudes towards condoms: Gender differences in the effects of norms. *Journal of Applied Social Psychology* 30: 1381–1395.

Molidor, C., & Tolman, R. M. (1998). Gender and contextual factors in adolescent dating violence. *Violence Against Women* 4: 180–194.

Morokoff, P. J., Quina, K., Harlow, L. L., Whitmire, L., Grimley, D. M., Gibson, P. R., & Burkholder, G. J. (1997). Sexual Assertiveness Scale (SAS) for Women: Development and validation. *Journal of Personality and Social Psychology* 73: 790–804.

Muñoz-Rivas, M. J., Graña, J. L., O'Leary, K. D., & González, M. P. (2007). Aggression in adolescent dating relationships: Prevalence, justification, and health consequences. *Journal of Adolescent Health* 40: 298–304.

The National Campaign to Prevent Teen Pregnancy. (2002). *Not just another single issue: Teen pregnancy's link to other critical social issues.* http://www.teenpregnancy. org/resources/data/pdf/notjust.pdf (accessed 5 January 2008).

National Institute of Justice. (2004). When violence hits home: How economics and neighborhood play a role. http://www.ojp.usdoj.gov/nij/pubs-sum/205004. htm (accessed 10 July 2008).

Noar, S. M., & Morokoff, P. J. (2002). The relationship between masculinity ideology, condom attitudes, and condom use stage of change: A structural equation modeling approach. *International Journal of Men's Health* 1: 43–58.

Norris, J., Stoner, S. A. Hessler, D. M., Zawacki, T., Davis, K. C., George, W. H., Morrison, D. M., Parkhill, M. R., & Abdallah, D. A. (2009). Influences of sexual sensation seeking, alcohol consumption, and sexual arousal on women's behavioral intentions related to having unprotected sex. *Psychology of Addictive Behaviors* 23: 14–22.

O'Keefe, M. (1997). Predictors of dating violence among high school students. *Journal of Interpersonal Violence* 12: 546–568.

O'Keefe, M., & Treister, L. (1998). Victims of dating violence among high school students: Are the predictors different for males and females? *Violence Against Women* 4: 195–223.

Olshen, E., McVeigh, K. H., Wunsch-Hitzig, R. A., & Rickert, V. I. (2007). Dating violence, sexual assault, and suicide attempts among urban teenagers. *Archives of Pediatric and Adolescent Medicine* 161: 539–545.

Pearson, J. (2006). Personal control, self-efficacy in sexual negotiation, and contraceptive risk among adolescents: The role of gender. *Sex Roles* 54: 615–625.

Pike, L. B., & Wittstruck, G. (2000). Maltreatment and adolescent pregnancy and parenting program: A community awareness model. Center on Adolescent Sexuality, Pregnancy and Parenting.

Pulerwitz, J., Gortmaker, S. L., & DeJong, W. (2000). Measuring sexual relationship power in HIV/STD research. *Sex Roles* 42: 637–660.

Quinn, T. C., & Overbaugh, J. (2005). HIV/AIDS in women: An expanding epidemic. *Science* 10: 1582–1583.

Rickert, V. I., Sanghvi, R., & Wiemann, C. M. (2002). Is lack of sexual assertiveness among adolescent and young adult women a cause for concern? *Perspectives on Sexual and Reproductive Health* 34: 178–183.

Rickert, V. I., Wiemann, C. M., Vaughn, R. D., & White, J. W. (2004). Rates and risk factors for sexual violence among an ethnically diverse sample of adolescents. *Archives of Pediatric Adolescent Medicine* 158: 1132–1139.

Roberts, L. (1999). Creating a new framework for promoting the health of African-American female adolescents: Beyond risk taking. *Journal of the American Medical Women's Association* 54: 126–128.

Roberts, T. A., Auinger, P., & Klein, J. D. (2005). Intimate partner abuse and the reproductive health of sexually active female adolescents. *Journal of Adolescent Health* 36: 380–385.

Roberts, T. A., & Klein, J. (2003). Intimate partner abuse and high-risk behaviors in adolescents. *Archives of Pediatric Adolescent Medicine* 157: 375–380.

Rosen, D. (2004). "I just let him have his way": Partner violence in the lives of low-income, teenage mothers. *Violence Against Women* 10: 6–28.

Rosenthal, S. L., Cohen, S. S., & Stanberry, L. R. (1998). Topical microbicides: Current status and research considerations for adolescent girls. *Sexually Transmitted Diseases* 27: 368–377.

Roth, J., Hendrickson, J., Schilling, M., & Stowell, D. W. (1998). The risk of teen mothers having low birth weight babies: Implications of recent medical research for school health personnel. *Journal of School Health* 68: 271–275.

Salazar, L. F., DiClemente, R. J., Wingood, G. M., Crosby, R. A., Lang, D. L., & Harrington, K. (2006). Biologically confirmed sexually transmitted infection and depressive symptomatology among African-American female adolescents. *Sexually Transmitted Infections* 82: 55–60.

Santana, M. C., Raj, A., Decker, M. R., La Marche, A., & Silverman, J. G. (2006). Masculine gender roles associated with increased sexual risk and intimate partner violence perpetration among young adult men. *Journal of Urban Health* 83: 575–585.

Schwarz, D. F., & O'Sullivan, A. L. (2007). State of the art reviews: Intervening to improve outcomes for adolescent mothers and their children. *American Journal of Lifestyle Medicine* 1: 482–489.

Sears, H. A., Byers, E. S., & Price, E. L. (2007). The co-occurrence of adolescent boys' and girls' use of psychologically, physically, and sexually abusive behaviours in their dating relationships. *Journal of Adolescence* 30: 487–504.

Short, M. B., Mills, L., Majkowski, J. M., Stanberry, L. R., & Rosenthal, S. L. (2003). Topical microbicide use by adolescent girls: Concerns about timing, efficacy, and safety. *Sexually Transmitted Diseases* 30: 854–858.

Shrier, L. A., Pierce, J. D., Emans, S. J., & DuRant, R. H. (1998). Gender differences in risk behaviors associated with forced or pressured sex. *Archives of Pediatric and Adolescent Medicine* 152: 57–63.

Silverman, J. G., Decker, M. R., Reed, E., Rothman, E. F., Hathaway, J. E., Raj, A., & Miller, E. (2006). Social norms and beliefs regarding sexual risk and pregnancy involvement among adolescent males treated for dating violence perpetration. *Journal of Urban Health* 83: 723–735.

Silverman, J. G., Raj, A., & Clements, K. (2004). Dating violence and associated sexual risk and pregnancy among adolescent girls in the United States. *Pediatrics* 114: e220–e225.

Silverman, J. G., Raj, A., Mucci, L. A., & Hathway, J. E. (2001). Dating violence among adolescent girls and associated substance use, unhealthy weight control, sexual risk behavior, pregnancy, and suicidality. *Journal of the American Medical Association* 286: 572–579.

Silverman, J. G., Raj, A., & Clements, K. (2004). Dating violence and associated sexual risk and pregnancy among adolescent girls in the United States. *Pediatrics* 114: 220–225.

Singh, S., & Darroch, J. E. (2000). Adolescent pregnancy and childbearing: Levels and trends in developed countries. *Family Planning Perspectives* 32: 14–23.

Singh, S., Darroch, J. E., & Frost, J. J. (2001). Socioeconomic disadvantage and adolescent women's sexual and reproductive behavior: The case of five developed countries. *Family Planning Perspectives* 33: 251–289.

Sionean, C., & Zimmerman, R. S. (1999). Moderating and mediating effects of socioeconomic status, perceived peer condom use, and condom negotiation on sexual risk behavior among African American and white adolescents. *Annals of the New York Academy of Sciences* 896: 474–476.

Smith, G., Mysak, K., & Michael, S. (2008). Sexual double standards and sexually transmitted illnesses: Social rejection and stigmatization of women. *Sex Roles* 58: 391–401.

Smith, P. H., White, J. W., & Holland, L. J. (2003). A longitudinal perspective on dating violence among adolescent and college-age women. *American Journal of Public Health* 93: 1104–1109.

SmithBattle, L. (2007). "I wanna have a good future": Teen mothers' rise in educational aspirations, competing demands, and limited school support. *Youth & Society* 38: 348–371.

Straus, M. A. (2005). Women's violence toward men is a serious social problem. In D. R. Loseke, R. J. Gelles, & M. M. Cavanaugh (eds.), *Current controversies on family violence.* Second Edition. Newbury Park, CA: Sage.

Straus, M. A. (2009). Why the overwhelming evidence on partner physical violence by women has not been perceived and is often denied. *Journal of Aggression, Maltreatment, and Trauma* 18: 552–571.

Straus, M. A., Hamby, S. L., Boney-McCoy, S. & Sugarman, D. B. (1996). The Revised Conflict Tactics Scales (CTS2). *Journal of Family Issues* 17: 283–316.

Teitelman, A. M., Dichter, M. E., Cederbaum, J. A., & Campbell, J. (2008). Intimate partner violence, condom use, and HIV risk for adolescent girls: Gaps in the literature and future directions for research and intervention. *Journal of HIV/AIDS Prevention in Children and Youth* 8: 65–93.

Teitelman, A. M., & Loveland-Cherry, C. (2004). Girls' perspectives on family scripts about sex, sexuality and relationships: Implications for promoting sexual health, reducing sexual risk. *Journal of HIV/AIDS Prevention for Children and Youth* 6: 59–90.

Teitelman, A. M., Ratcliffe, S., & Cederbaum, J. A. (2008). Parent-adolescent communication about sexual pressure, maternal gender norms about relationship power and HIV protective behaviors of minority urban girls. *Journal of the American Psychiatric Nurses Association* 14: 50–60.

Teitelman, A. M., Ratcliffe, S., Morales, M., & Sullivan, C. (2008). Sexual relationship power, intimate partner violence and condom use among minority urban girls. *Journal of Interpersonal Violence* 23: 1694–1712.

Terry-Human, E., Manlove, J., & Cottingham, S. (2006). Trends and recent estimates: Sexual activity among U.S. teens. http://www.childtrends.org/files/SexualActivityRB.pdf (accessed 18 July 2008).

Tolman, D. L., Spencer, R., Rosen-Reynoso, M., & Porche, M. V. (2003). Sowing the seeds of violence in heterosexual relationships: Early adolescents narrate compulsory heterosexuality. *Journal of Social Issues* 59: 159–178.

Tschann, J. M., Adler, N. E., Millstein, S. G., Gurvey, J. E., & Ellen, J. M. (2002). Relative power between sexual partners and condom use among adolescents. *Journal of Adolescent Health* 3: 17–25.

Tucker, J. S., Fitzmaurice, A. E., Imamura, M., Penfold, S., Penney, G. C., van Teijlingen, E., Shucksmith, J., & Philip, K. L. (2007). The effect of the national demonstration project *Health Respect* on teenage sexual health behaviour. *European Journal of Public Health* 17: 33–41.

Upchurch, D. M., & Kusunoki, Y. (2004). Associations between forced sex, sexual and protective practices, and sexually transmitted diseases among a national sample of adolescent girls. *Women's Health Issues* 14: 75–84.

Vandello, J. A., Bosson, J. K., Cohen, D., Burnaford, R. M., & Weaver, J. R. (2008). Precarious manhood. *Journal of Personality and Social Psychology* 95: 1325–1339.

Ventura, S. J., Curtin, S. C., & Mathews, T. J. (2001). Variations in teenage birth rates, 1991–98: National and state trends. *National Vital Statistics Reports* 48(6): 1–11.

Ventura, S. J., Mathews, T. J., & Hamilton, B. E. (2001). Births to teenagers in the United States, 1940–2000. *National Vital Statistics Reports* 49: 10.

Vicary, J. R., Klingaman, L. R., & Harkness, W. L. (1995). Risk factors associated with date rape and sexual assault of adolescent girls. *Journal of Adolescence* 18: 289–306.

Way, N. (1995). "Can't you see the courage, the strength that I have?" Listening to urban adolescent girls speak about their relationships. *Psychology of Women Quarterly* 19: 107–128.

Weinstock, H., Berman, S., & Cates, W. (2004). Sexually transmitted diseases among American youth: Incidence and prevalence estimates, 2000. *Perspectives on Sexual and Reproductive Health* 36: 6–10.

White, R. T. (2002). Reconceptualizing HIV infection among poor black adolescent females: An urban poverty paradigm. *Health Promotion Practice* 3: 302–312.

Wiemann, C., Rickert, V., Berenson, A., & Volk, R. (2005). Are pregnant adolescents stigmatized by pregnancy? *Journal of Adolescent Health* 36: 352.e1–352.e7.

Wingood, G. M., & DiClemente, R. J. (2000). Application of the theory of gender and power to examine HIV-related exposures, risk factors, and effective interventions for women. *Health Education and Behavior* 27: 539–565.

Wingood, G. M., DiClemente, R. J., McCree, D. H., et al. (2001). Dating violence and the sexual health of black adolescent females. *Pediatrics* 107: E72.

Ylló, K. A. (2005). Through a feminist lens: Gender, diversity and violence: Extending the feminist framework. In D. R. Loseke, R. J. Gelles, & M. M. Cavanaugh (eds.), *Current controversies on family violence*. Second Edition. Newbury Park, CA: Sage.

Zeck, W., Bjelic-Radisic, V., Haas, J., & Greimel, E. (2007). Impact of adolescent pregnancy on the future life of young mothers in terms of social, familial, and educational changes. *Journal of Adolescent Health* 41: 380–388.

Zieler, S., & Krieger, N. (1997). Reframing women's risk: Social inequities and HIV infection. *Annual Review of Public Health* 18: 410–436.

FIVE

POLICING GIRLHOOD?

Relational Aggression and Violence Prevention

Meda Chesney-Lind
Merry Morash
Katherine Irwin

The turn of the century has been characterized by an increased attention to girls' violence and aggression. Much of the intense media interest in girls' violence is the product of dramatic increases in girls' arrests for non-traditional, violent offenses. Between 1980 and 2000, for example, girls' arrests for aggravated assault, simple assault, and weapons law violations increased by 121%, 257%, and 134% (respectively). Boys' arrests also increased in these categories, but by far less (28%, 109%, and 20%). And the trend continues; as an example, between 1995 and 2004, girls' arrests for simple assault increased by 31.4%, while boys' arrests decreased by 1.4%. Arrests of girls for aggravated assault did drop (by 2.9%), but compare that to the 27.6% drop in boys' arrests for this offense (FBI, 2005: 285).

It is important, though, to keep these figures in perspective. Despite the increases seen in girls' arrest, girls still accounted for relatively small proportions of violent crime arrests of juveniles: 10% of murders or negligent manslaughter arrests, 3% of forcible rapes, 9% of robberies, and 24% of aggravated assaults (Snyder, 2004: 3). Data from the Federal Bureau of Investigation's National Incident-Based Reporting System further confirm the low level of girls' violence compared to boys'; relatively few (26%) victims who reported violent crimes by juveniles said that the offender was a female (McCurley & Snyder, 2004: 6). Girls were responsible for just 8% of victimizations for sexual assault, 6% of robberies, 22% of aggravated assaults, and 30% of simple assaults committed by a juvenile. In no category did they account for close to half of the victimizations.[1]

There are reasons to be somewhat skeptical of police and court statistics showing that girls are increasing their use of violence. Self-report data sources failed to corroborate this "surge" in girls' arrests for violence. In fact, self-report studies often found that girls were becoming less violent during the period that saw their arrests increase dramatically. The Centers for Disease Control and Prevention's biennial Youth Risk Behavior Survey found that between 1991 and 2005, there was a decrease in the percentage of girls who reported being in a fight, from 34.2% to 28.1% of girls. Boys' self-reported violence during the same time also decreased, from 50.2% to 43.4%, but in each year, it was still higher than the girls' rate (Centers for Disease Control and Prevention, 1992–2006; see also Steffensmeier et al., 2005).

Why the difference between official statistics and self-reports? Many suspect that zero tolerance policies in public schools and mandatory arrests for domestic violence may have led to more arrests of girls for acts that previously would have been considered either family matters, school matters, or for some other reason outside of the purview of the police and the courts (Bartollas, 1993; Russ, 2004; Chesney-Lind & Irwin, 2006). There also is some evidence that police and courts treat girls more harshly than boys (Horowitz & Pottieger, 1991), and that this practice inflates the official statistics for girls.

Although there is debate about whether girls are increasing or maintaining their use of violence, it is recognized that some girls have problems, sometimes serious problems, with violence, and that they hurt others. Given the importance of gender in our society, the etiology of girls' violence is likely to be influenced by gender, in combination with race, class, and ethnicity, and thus interventions must be carefully targeted to any gender-related and culturally specific causes. The need to understand the etiology of girls' violence is not in dispute here. Indeed, the authors of this article as well as other researchers have explored the context of girls' violence and the need for those seeking to intervene in this behavior to foreground these gender-related issues (see Artz & Reicken, 1997; Chesney-Lind & Belknap, 2004; Morash & Chesney-Lind, 2009).

While we very much support gender-responsive prevention and intervention efforts aimed at reducing girls' violence, we are troubled by another trend: focusing violence prevention and intervention efforts on the policing of girls' (and occasionally boys') non-violent, "covert," or "relational" aggression. In this chapter, we will discuss our reasons for raising questions about this approach, which some contend is a gender-balanced approach to violence prevention and "bullying."

In fact, we contend that public concern about "youth violence" and the many programs created to prevent and intervene in the "problem" offers an instructive and cautionary case study of the new gender-balanced approach in youth programming. Instead of just implementing programs for boys or taking programs developed for boys and then superficially adapting them for girls, policymakers and program designers in the post-Columbine years drew from the studies about girls and specifically responded to the idea that girls and boys experience and express violence and aggression differently, and they have made a specific effort to include these "indirect" or covert aggressions in violence prevention programs and policies. In this chapter, we will explore how this gender balanced strategy can go awry—in ways that we feel seriously disadvantage girls.

COVERT AGGRESSION AND GIRLS

The manipulative and damaging characteristics of girls' social worlds have been the subject of high-profile bestselling books like *Odd Girl Out* and *Queen Bees and Wannabes*, publications that prompted innumerable newspaper articles as well as hit movies, like *Mean Girls*, on the topic of girls' aggression. These works all rely on recent psychological research on aggression, particularly what is called "relational," "covert," or "indirect" aggressions (Underwood, Galen, & Paquette, 2001: 248). A critical assessment of this literature is vital, not only because of the media hype surrounding the topic, but more importantly, as we will document, because this line of research clearly informs current violence prevention and anti-bullying programs.

To critically assess this approach to girls' aggression, it first is important to understand the psychological concept of "aggression," and how this academic definition relates to commonsense understandings of aggression (which typically include fighting and other forms of violence). Psychologists define aggression as "behaviors that are intended to hurt or harm others" (Crick et al., 1999). This means that a wide variety of behaviors fall under the category ranging from rolling one's eyes and deliberately ignoring people to assault, rape, and murder. Owens et al. (2000) used focus groups to identify the following indirect forms of girls' aggression: talking about other girls; spreading rumors; breaking confidences; criticizing others' clothing, appearance, or personality; exclusionary behaviors; making prank phone calls; writing about other girls on desks; and sarcasm. As we shall see, this area of research has created an interesting set of conversations about the harms of "indirect" or "covert" aggression. Yet, we also need to keep in mind that there may be some problems with a concept of "aggression" that is so inclusive that such disparate behaviors are covered by the same concept. While an understanding of all forms of aggression is important, the degree of harm involved in such behavior is important to keep in mind as well.

Finally, we need to recall that this concept clearly includes both illegal and, however unpleasant, legal behaviors.

More to the point, there is increasing evidence that recognition of this "new" aggression can prompt more formal monitoring and intervention directed at behaviors assumed to be typical for school girls. For example, with support from the National Institute of Mental Health, Stephen Leff, a clinical psychologist at The Children's Hospital of Philadelphia, designed a school-based intervention, Friend to Friend, for urban, African American elementary school girls considered to be "at risk."[2] The "at risk" group included not just physically aggressive girls who often pushed, hit, or threatened others, but also relationally aggressive girls, who gossiped, left others out on purpose, and threatened to withdraw friendships. Certainly it is laudable to assist all children, including boys, in developing positive relationships with each other; however, is it useful to prohibit students—especially girls who are allegedly most prone to the relationally aggressive behaviors—from gossiping, leaving others out, and threatening to withdraw friendship for the purpose of reducing bullying and physical aggression? And is it accurate to consider the behaviors of relational aggression to be serious bullying?

Some examples suggest an affirmative answer to these questions. Finessa Ferrell-Smith, a research analyst for the National Conference of State Legislatures, equated bullying with relational aggression in the statement,

> Although relational aggression can be as psychologically or emotionally destructive as the more direct and physical bullying behavior of boys, many school harassment policies focus on physical or direct violence and do not address relational aggression. In addition, female bullying is less likely to come to the attention of school personnel, even though students report that it is common. (Ferrell-Smith, 2003: 1)

A resource made available for the Office of Community Oriented Policing Services (COPS) within the National Institute of Justice advocates that bullying be addressed with a "multifaceted, comprehensive approach" that includes "establishing a schoolwide policy that addresses indirect bullying (e.g., rumor spreading, isolation, social exclusion), which is more hidden, as well as direct bullying (e.g., physical aggression)" (Sampson, 2002:. 19). Notice that relational aggression is again folded into the mix of behaviors that constitute bullying. Also, *Monitor on Psychology*, a publication of the American Psychological Association, included an article in a special issue on *Psychology and the Prison System*. In the article, "Girls Use a Different Kind of Weapon," Tori DeAngelis (2003) notes that relational aggression "may lead girls into trouble" (51), and that "[w]hile no one has shown a tie between high levels of relational aggression and girls' propensity to break the law, psychologists in the juvenile justice system say they see the behavior all the time" (51). DeAngelis goes on to describe an innovative program that trains foster care parents to recognize and address girls' relational aggression. Similarly, the emerging research on girls' aggression is closely linked with and serves as a partial basis for the concept of "indirect bullying," as it appears in Olweus' anti-bullying program. A problem with the conceptual mixing of the notion of relational aggression with bullying is that it can open the door, or widen the net, for greater social control and scrutiny of particularly girls' behaviors, without attention to whether these behaviors actually constitute harmful bullying. For this reason, it is important to examine the literature on indirect or covert aggression as well as gender differences in these domains closely and carefully, and to fully consider what behaviors constitute bullying.

At this point, it is useful to distinguish bullying from aggression. Olweus (1993: 8–10) defines bullying as either physical or relational aggression, repeated over time, that involves a perpetrator or perpetrators who have more power (e.g., strength) than the victim. Aggression is a more general concept, and aggression as it is relevant to youth development varies along three dimensions (Dishion, French, & Patterson, 1995). Aggression can be physical or non-physical, overt, or covert. It can be a one-time event or continue over time. And it can escalate, decrease, or stay at the same level. Unfortunately, none of the recommendations for increased attention to (especially girls, and at least in one case, African American urban girls) relational regression include cautions about the difference between relational aggression and bullying, and the variations in severity of aggression. In fact, some of the program models and recommendations conflate girls' relationship aggression with bullying and other illegal activities.

A CRITICAL LOOK AT RESEARCH ON GIRLS' AGGRESSION

Early research has concluded that, as a group, boys exhibit significantly higher levels of aggression than girls (see Crick & Grotpeter, 1995, for review). This is consistent with arrest statistics illustrating higher rates of violent crime (i.e., murder, forcible rape, robbery, and aggravated assault) for male versus female youth (FBI, 2005). The perception that males are more aggressive, however, might be more of a factor of *how* aggression is defined, which historically tended to reflect more overt manifestations. Increasingly, in both the empirical and popular literature, the concept of "relational aggression" has been discussed and associated with girls.

As noted earlier, the concept of relational or covert aggression relates to a repertoire of passive and/or indirect behaviors (e.g., rolling eyes, spreading rumors, ostracizing, and ignoring), used with the "intent to hurt or harm others" (Crick & Grotpeter, 1995; Crick et al., 1999), and thus the concept expands the range of behaviors that are considered aggressive in nature. On one end of the spectrum are covert, non-physical forms of aggressive behaviors identified in social science research, while on the other end are overt, physical forms of aggressive behaviors that are typically described as violence in common discourse.

By identifying a "relational," "covert," or "indirect" aggression, rather than physical types of aggression, researchers argued that they shattered the myth of the non-aggressive girl (see Bjorkqvist & Niemela, 1992). These researchers note that girls are as aggressive as boys when these indirect aggressions are considered. In fact, they claimed that they were not only shattering myths, but that they were unraveling years of gender bias in which male researchers tended to only look at male problems. Bjorkqvist and Niemela (1992:. 5) argued that researchers, ". . . the majority being males, . . . may, for personal reasons, find male aggression easier to understand and a more appealing object of study." Consequently, the "discovery" of female aggression was seen as taking on old "stereotypes." It also seemed to end a long history of male-biased research and to provide a more gender-balanced approach to explaining adolescent development.

While this characterization of the "discovery" has been widely accepted, there are reasons to be a bit more skeptical that this concept benefits girls. First, does this aggression really challenge stereotypes and myths about girls? Recall that the behaviors included in relational or indirect aggression include retaliating against or manipulating another person by spreading rumors about them, giving them the silent treatment, or threatening to end a relationship. In essence, this research is arguing that girls and women are manipulative, sneaky, mean spirited, and backstabbing. These ideas are hardly new, which may, in fact, be one reason that the public and the media embraced them so quickly.

What this area of research is really doing is systematically measuring a set of attributes that have always been associated with girls and women (i.e., their devious and venomous natures), and then intellectually equating these "aggressions" to boys' violence. Consider researchers' contention that the "discovery" of girls' meanness is part of a gender-balanced project and a systematic assessment of problems that are "relevant to both sexes" (Crick et al., 1999). Looking back at two decades of work, scholars Smith and Brain (2000) concluded that "indirect aggression is more evident in females, and this applies also to bullying," and because indirect aggression is so hard to pin down and discourage, there are important issues related to "tackling it." In the name of gender balance and equity, we are actually providing new ways to devalue and demonize girls and suggesting the need to police their behavior even more assiduously.

Implicit in this "discovery" is also the contention that there is a significant gender difference in this behavior, and that "girls are more likely than boys to engage in relational, as opposed to overt, aggression" (Crick, 1996: 2317). As we note, while this notion is intuitively appealing, since it tracks gender stereotypes, research addressing this question, though, has been decidedly mixed. Consistent with the view that girls and boys are similarly aggressive, Crick and Grotpeter (1995), for example, found that girls in their sample of third- through sixth-grade students were significantly more relationally aggressive than were boys. Similarly, Bjorkqvist and Niemela (1992) found that when types of verbal aggression (e.g., gossiping, spreading rumors, etc.) were included in their overall measurement of aggression, only 5% of the variance in the composite measure of aggression was explained by gender. This suggests that, by using a broader definition of aggression, both boys' and girls' unique forms of aggression were accounted for in their study, and gender differences were largely erased.

However, there are a number of studies finding no differences between boys' and girls' perpetration of relational aggression (Prinstein, Boergers, & Vernberg, 2001; Hart et al., 1998; Putallaz et al., 1999; Crick & Grotpeter, 1995; Rys & Bear, 1997; McMaster et al., 2002). There are a few studies concluding that boys are actually more relationally aggressive than girls are (Craig, 1998; Hennington et al., 1998; Little et al., 2003; Wolke et al., 2000). When we shift to the problem of bullying, according to Olweus' research, boys perpetrate the majority of indirect bullying experienced by girls (see also Whitney & Smith, 1993). Note that if Olweus' findings are correct, girls are indirectly victimized more often by boys than by girls; yet this phenomenon rarely makes it into any of the popular books on the topic, which instead showcase girl-on-girl aggression almost exclusively (Chesney-Lind, 2002).

Looking at the research, there are a few possible reasons for these divergent findings. These reasons include the way that aggression is defined as well as how it is measured. For example, Olweus was examining *bullying*, which includes direct or indirect victimization carried out repeatedly over time. In contrast, *relational aggression* can include, but is not limited to, single hurtful acts. Boys might be more likely than girls to practice indirect aggression repeatedly. These differing findings might also be due to sample size and representativeness. Olweus' research studied large samples ranging from 900 to 130,000 students, and, in contrast, the relational aggression research tended to draw from smaller samples with 500 or fewer students (sometimes as few as 105, see Storch, Werner, & Storch, 2003). The small-sample studies may reflect atypical school environments or populations of youth.

In addition, Olweus relied on students' self-reports of victimization to identify bullying problems, and Little et al. (2003) used self-report methods to measure aggression. In contrast, many relational aggression researchers identify aggressors through peer nominations (see De Los Reyes and Prinstein, 2004, for a review of self vs. peer reports of victimization). In general, classmates tend to nominate boys as more physically aggressive and girls as relationally aggressive; though self-reports confirm the boys' greater involvement in physical aggression, they show boys and girls to be similar in relational aggression (Odgers and Moretti, 2002: 106).

.Another reason for the conflicting findings regarding the difference between girls' and boys' relational aggression might be that the use of indirect aggression depends on a combination of gender and developmental stage. Girls may be more aggressive than boys in early childhood, but by late adolescence, girls and boys might be equal in their perpetration of relational aggression (Bjorkqvist, 1994, Chessler, 2001; Roecker-Phelps, 2001; Paquette & Underwood, 1999; Prinstein, Boergers, & Vernberg, 2001; Rys & Bear, 1997; Storch et al., 2003; Little et al., 2003).

To date it is not clear whether girls are really more relationally aggressive than boys are. What we do know, however, is that the existing literature suggests that the early conclusions drawn by Crick and colleagues were overstated (see also Underwood, Galen, & Paquette, 2001). The truth is that we need studies with larger samples and multiple measurement techniques in order to definitively state, once and for all, that girls are equally or even more relationally aggressive than boys are. Also, it is probably necessary to distinguish between single relationally aggressive acts and relational aggression that is repeated over time, and to make a very clear distinction between relational aggression and actual bullying.

IS RELATIONAL AGGRESSION A SERIOUS PROBLEM?

One of the core claims in the emerging literature has been that relational aggression is a major problem that had been ignored. These aggressions, we have been told, exist underneath the radar of most parents and virtually all teachers, since teachers and parents have their hands full dealing with the much more obvious physical aggression and violence of boys. As a result, "the day-to-day aggression that persists among girls, a dark underside of their social universe, remains uncharted and unexplored. We have no language for it" (Simmons, 2002: 69). Simmons, in fact, opens *Odd Girl Out* with her own story. In her case, when she was eight, a "popular" friend of hers began to whisper to Rachel's best friend that they should run away from Rachel. One day they did on the way to dance class at a local community theater, and she spent much of that year trying to make sense of their desertion. As she puts it, "the sorrow is overwhelming" (2) so "now is the time to end the silence" (3). Paying attention to this aggression as both academics and journalists who highlight the problem would have us do, means that Simmons' experience is not unique. Not only do the behaviors "intend" to harm, they in fact *do* measurable harm arguably to both the victim and the perpetrator. Let's review the evidence to see if this is, in fact, the case.

First, it appears that relational aggression is one of the most common forms of aggression among children (see Crick, Bigbee, & Howes, 1996). Here researchers have argued that the commonplace nature of it implies that it should be taken seriously. Specific arguments for the damage caused by relational aggression are that girls report relational aggression to be very hurtful and distressing (Crick, 1995; Galen & Underwood, 1997), and that victims of relational aggression experience difficulties with peer rejection, depression, isolation, and loneliness (Crick & Bigbee, 1998; Crick & Grotpeter, 1995, 1996: Nansel et al., 2001; Prinstein, Boergers, &Vernberg, 2001; Storch et al., 2003; Werner & Crick, 1999). Similar to the findings that girls are more aggressive than boys are, the connection between victimization by relational aggression and negative outcomes is inconsistent and questionable. In some studies, relational aggression does not lead to isolation (Storch et al., 2003) or depression (Werner & Crick, 1999; Storch, Werner, & Storch, 2003). Moreover, support from peers may mediate the relationship between relational aggression and loneliness (Storch et al., 2003).

To date, the vast majority of studies in this area have been cross-sectional rather than longitudinal, meaning that researchers cannot establish the temporal order between the onset of relational aggression and other problems among youth. Of the few longitudinal studies conducted, the time period examined was very short. For example, one study (Crick, 1996) looked at third- through sixth-grade students for six months and established that relationally aggressive girls persist in their behaviors through most of a school year. This finding hardly establishes a temporal order among all the factors under investigation. In fact, the researchers have tended to imply causation when in fact they have only established correlations (and inconsistent correlations at that) of victimization through relational aggression, victimization with isolation, depression, and peer rejection. This is a significant shortcoming of the current literature.

More importantly, there is some evidence to suggest that some "indirect" or "relational" aggression is actually prosocial, rather than antisocial, for youth (Underwood et al., 2001; Xie et al., 2002). Specifically, from a narrative study of aggression among 475 seventh-grade youth, Xie and colleagues found that "social aggression" (which they defined as "concealed social attack") was associated with "higher network centrality" among adolescents (Xie et al., 2002:. 205). Expanding on the meaning of this, they speculate that "the majority of socially aggressive children and adolescents may be neither socially incompetent nor suffering from deficits in social cognition" (219); instead, they argue that youth who use indirect aggression might actually have "higher social intelligence" than their counterparts who do not know that "socially aggressive behaviors serve important functions for the individual and social groups" (219).

In contrast to the failure of scientists to identify any long-term negative consequences of relational aggression, the bullying research has identified several negative outcomes of direct bulling. For example, Olweus (1993) stated that bullying is part of a repertoire of antisocial and conduct-disordered behavior that starts in adolescence and becomes progressively worse as time goes on. This statement stems from the finding that 60% of bullies in grades 6–9 were convicted of a crime by age 24 (Olweus, 1993).

It is important to note that this likelihood of arrest was only true for the perpetrators of direct bullying, and it was not true for youth who engaged only in indirect bullying.

In short, although popular books like Simmons' claimed that there were many harms associated with indirect aggression, the truth is that, to date, aggression researchers have failed to identify any long-term negative consequences of indirect aggression in contrast to clear evidence of harm associated with physical aggression.

DOES RELATIONAL AGGRESSION LEAD TO PHYSICAL AGGRESSION?

Turning now to the idea that relational and physical aggression comprise two types of the same underlying behavior, perhaps with one leading to the other, there is reason to question this version of "equality." Researchers have generally supported the idea that relational and physical aggression are different types of the same underlying behavior, because relational and physical aggression are moderately correlated (see Crick & Grotpeter, 1995). As Crick and Grotpeter (1995: 715) argued, "the moderate magnitude of this correlation [r = .54, p < .01] is what one would expect for two constructs that are hypothesized to be *different* forms of the *same* general behavior." If they lacked any correlation, then these behaviors would be seen as completely different, and if they were highly correlated they would be viewed as the same behavior. We, however, argue that establishing a moderate correlation is not sufficient enough to state that physical and relational aggression are two parts of a whole. Finding a considerably larger correlation between relational and physical aggression, Little et al. (2003: 83) agreed with our conclusion, based on the additional finding that the two types of aggression were differently related to other variables.

Finally, and most importantly, is relational aggression a step in the development of a pattern of violence? Recall that it is violence prevention that started the whole anti-bullying initiative and supplies the justification for intervention into the lives of young people. There is certainly reason to continue to be concerned about youth violence in the United States. While youth violence has been dropping in the last decade, the United States still has the highest rate of firearm-related deaths among youths in the industrialized world (U.S. Department of Health and Human Services, 2001) and, as of 2003, violence was still the second leading cause of death for 15- to 24-year-olds (CDC, 2006). Death statistics are just the most serious outcomes of violence, and do not include the physical injuries that youth sustain and survive on a daily basis as the outcome of physical violence. Even if we accept the findings of studies showing high correlations between relational and physical violence, it is as plausible, if not more plausible, that a common cause accounts for this correlation, rather than a tendency for relational aggression to lead to physical aggression.

Indeed, other more careful research has failed to confirm a clear progression from covert or relational aggression to violence. Data from a longitudinal study of 475 youth followed from grade 7 into adulthood showed that while physical aggression "significantly increased a person's risk for school dropout and criminal arrest," and verbal aggression "significantly increased teen parenthood," social/relational aggressions "were not predictive of developmental maladjustment." The authors wrote, in fact, that these results "suggest that subtle aggressive behaviors may be normative in development" (Xie et al., 2002: 219).

GENDER RESPONSIVE OR GENDER BLAMING: THE EMERGENCE OF THE GIRL BULLY

> Linda, aged 12, was allegedly victimized by her classmates because she was "too posh." It appears that Linda had made friends with another girl in the class and they went around together. The alleged ringleader of the small bully group tried to destroy this friendship and eventually succeeded, leaving Linda fairly isolated. Later on, another girl in the bully group persuaded Linda to give a party at her home, then made sure no one came. Linda's self-confidence was completely destroyed. (Olweus, 1993: 8)

Linda's story was one of those chosen by Dan Olweus to open his book *Bullying at School: What We Know and What We Can Do*. When the book first appeared in 1993, bullying was considered a normal aspect of adolescent life both in the United States and Norway. Olweus, a psychology professor at the University of Bergen, in Norway, had been up to that point best known in the academic community for his research on aggression among adolescent boys (Olweus, 1977, 1978, 1979). His interest remained largely scientific and academic until 1982, when the suicides of three adolescent boys who had been severely bullied shocked Norway. In Olweus' (1993: 2) own words, the triple suicide "triggered a chain of reactions, the end result of which was a nationwide campaign against bully/victim problems in Norwegian primary and secondary/junior schools." Having spent a decade researching peers and aggression, Olweus found himself taking a leadership position in the northern European anti-bullying movement, lending a scientific and research-based perspective to the design and implementation of national "anti-bullying" strategies. Ultimately he would create his own intervention curricula.

Bullying at School, a book that Olweus intended for teachers, parents, school administrators, and legislators, would become central to framing the problem as well as offering potential "solutions." In fact, Linda's "story" was gleaned from newspaper accounts and was "slightly adapted" for inclusion in Olweus' book. But including "Linda's story" before launching into the research and facts about bullying implied that the problem of bullying had both a female and a male face.

That Linda's friends were certainly cruel, at least in this constructed account, is undeniable. However, the narrative item immediately following Linda's in Olweus' book details a far more serious situation.

> Schoolboy Philip C. was driven to his death by playground bullying. He hanged himself after being constantly threatened, pushed around and humiliated by three of his classmates. Finally, when the shy 16-year-old's examination notes were stolen days before he was due to sit an important exam, he could take no more. Frightened to tell his parents, Philip chose to die. When he came home from school, he hanged himself by a rope from his bedroom door. (Olweus, 1993: 8).

Note that girls' gossip and relational aggression is clearly equated and conflated with boys' violence in the positioning of these two accounts of "bullying." However, none of this would have necessarily been any concern in the United States, had not a critical event occurred in the late nineties that would propel bullying to the top of every school administrator's "to do list."

The horrific Columbine shootings of 1999 had a dramatic policy fallout that initially focused on gun violence, but gradually shifted to a national concern about "bullying." This shift was largely a product of the determined and effective opposition of the National Rifle Association to any form of gun control legislation (CBS, 2000), but it was also the product of an influential report by the Secret Service and the U.S. Department of Education that examined common traits among numerous school shooting incidents (or targeted events) in the United States. The finding that "almost three-quarters of the attackers [n = 29] felt persecuted, bullied, threatened, attacked or injured by others prior to the incident" (Vossekuil et al., 2002: 21) became one of the most noteworthy and oft-cited points made in the report.

Perhaps not surprisingly, Colorado set a national precedent by being one of the first states to link bullying and school violence and to pass anti-bullying legislation in 2001. While previous legislation addressing school violence had focused on zero tolerance policies, the Colorado anti-bullying legislation mandated that each school district adopt a bullying prevention and education policy and strongly encouraged schools to adopt anti-bullying programs (see the National Conference of State Legislatures, www.ncsl.gov). By May 2003, 32 states had introduced anti-bullying bills, and, according to the National Conference of State Legislatures, by September of 2006, 28 states had passed some sort of anti-bullying legislation.

While Colorado's approach encouraged the adoption of prevention programs, other states, such as Arizona, mandated that school personnel report suspected bullying incidents to appropriate officials. Once bullying became a behavior that could result in formal reporting, investigations, and mandatory punishments, states and schools needed to define what constituted bullying. In some states, like Georgia, bullying was limited to actions that caused or threatened bodily harm. Other states, including New Jersey, adopted broader definitions that also included actions or words meant to insult or demean students or to interfere with the orderly operation of the school. In fact, many states like Idaho and Mississippi have combined anti-bullying with anti-harassment policies. Maine specifically included sexual harassment in its anti-bullying legislation.

The merging of bullying and harassment problems is extremely problematic for girls. Girls are not only more likely than boys to be the victims of sexual harassment, especially in its most severe forms, they also have clear legal rights when they experience this form of sex discrimination. Those gains could well be lost when sexual harassment is relabeled as a form of "bullying"—a behavior that, remember, included indirect and relational aggression (Brown, Chesney-Lind, & Stein, 2005). More to the point, here, "violence" prevention initiatives that conflate covert and relational aggressions with direct aggression and violence seem to suggest that girls' non-violent "aggressions" are roughly equivalent to boy's violence—enter the "girl bully" and programs to control her, such as Olweus' Bullying Prevention Program.

GIRLS AND BULLYING PREVENTION

On the surface, the focus on bullying in the Olweus Bullying Prevention Program seems to offer schools an egalitarian approach to youth violence and an alternative to many of the more punitive, zero tolerance approaches also being implemented at the time. Instead of removing bullies from the school, the Olweus program was designed to intervene in bullying and change behaviors at early stages, working with bullies or potential bullies before they became more serious delinquents. The fact that self-reported rates of delinquency decreased when bullying prevention programs were implemented in research trials (Melton et al., 1998) seemed to suggest that schools do not need to suspend, transfer, or expel students to solve behavior problems.

So what about gender? For years, researchers had critiqued the fact that delinquency prevention and intervention programs were too often developed using data from studies of boys, then applied in practice to boys and girls (Kersten, 1989; Mann, 1984). In shaping his anti-bullying program, Olweus sought to avoid this problem. Although his primary research focus was boys' aggression, he was aware of emerging research about aggressive girls (Bjorkqvist & Niemela, 1992) and made sure to consider these research findings as he created his program. He also tested the program with girls as well as boys, and his guides to implementers thoroughly discussed the ways in which both genders experienced bullying (Olweus, 1993).

Olweus' attempts to address girls' aggression with his program emerged at the same time that collection of research findings about girls' developmental outcomes chronicled additional reasons to be concerned about the state of girlhood. Since Gilligan's path-breaking work in the eighties, a growing literature on girls' development documented that adolescence is a difficult time for girls, but later girl-focused books would increasingly locate the source of the problem not with sexism, ageism, or racism in the settings that girls find themselves in, but rather in girlhood itself (Chesney-Lind & Irwin, 2006). Certainly, the "mean girl" books of the nineties (particularly *Odd Girl Out*) identified the source of what might be described as a toxic girl culture as other girls.

Olweus' efforts to incorporate research regarding girls' aggression into bullying prevention seemed, on the surface, to offer an approach to violence prevention that includes the unique challenges that girls confront on the pathway to adulthood—being the "victim" of other girl's relational aggression. We are fundamentally concerned, though, that this "equity" is misleading, and that it has encouraged both negative attention to and inappropriate interventions with girls.

The programs' primary flaw was that it included an overly broad spectrum of behaviors into its definition of bullying. As noted earlier, Olweus (1993:. 9) contends "a student is being bullied or victimized when he or she is exposed, repeatedly and over time, to negative actions on the part of one or more other students." Furthermore, "such negative actions include intentionally inflicting, or attempting to inflict, injury or discomfort upon another" (Elliott et al., 2002: 7–8). Bullying was categorized as direct—physical or verbal attacks—or indirect—"making faces or obscene gestures, or intentional exclusion from a group" (Elliott et al., 2002:. 8).

According to the logic of the bullying prevention program, rolling one's eyes at another person is a less extreme form of bullying than hitting or punching them, but they are, at their core, both bullying. We argue that this construction of "aggression" is problematic, for a number of reasons. Notably, there is evidence to suggest that non-physical, but emotionally hurtful behaviors such as rolling eyes at, spreading rumors about, or excluding individuals from a group belong in a different category of behaviors than physical attacks, in terms of the dynamics involved, the consequences of the behavior, and the long-term implications of the behavior. Beyond the logical imprecision of conflating indirect or relational aggression with direct bullying (i.e., violence), there are important practical reasons to separate the two behaviors. As we have seen, bullying has been increasingly connected to school violence, particularly lethal school violence, in popular opinion and legislative action. For this reason, we argue that this conflation has encouraged public condemnation of and increasingly harsh punishments against girls absent any data to indicate that these interventions are either warranted or necessary.

In their attempts to educate the public about the consequences of bullying, proponents of the Olweus program contended that bullying is a serious problem and should not be treated as a normal part of growing up for either boys or girls. The data used to advance these claims were usually alarming. For example, in his bullying prevention literature, Olweus argues that long-term studies of bullying victims demonstrated that they were more prone to depression and low self-esteem than non-bullied individuals (Olweus, 1993). In addition, it was argued that "in some cases, the victims' devaluation of themselves becomes so overwhelming that they see suicide as the only possible solution" (Elliott et al., 2002: 12). The bullying prevention program encourages schools to make parents aware of the seriousness of bullying by circulating informational fliers and fact sheets about bullying. Included in one sample brochure is the statement that "60% of children who are identified as bullies in middle school go on to have arrest records. We need to address the behavior problems of these children at an early age, before it becomes [sic] even more serious" (Elliott et al., 2002: 69). Apparently, schools also suffer at the hands of bullies. In "schools with high levels of bullying problems, students tend to feel less safe and are less satisfied with school life" (Elliott et al., 2002: 13). The message is that bullies are making schools unsafe places to be. Moreover, if bullying is not stopped, society will have a worse time containing the bullies when they become even bigger menaces.

These arguments about the severity of the bullying problem come from research on the long-term effect of *boys'* direct bullying, not girls' or boys' indirect bullying, and the conclusion that direct bullies went on to have arrest records comes from research on boy bullies. Because the program defines bullying as direct and indirect behaviors, however, the public assumes that it is both types of bullying that lead bullies to become criminal, victims to develop depression and low self-esteem, and students, in general, to feel less safe and satisfied at school. And because the public perceives girls to be the major culprits of indirect bullying (although, as we have shown, this is actually not consistently found in the research literature), it is consequently assumed that it is *both* girls and boys who are responsible for these negative outcomes.

GENDER RESPONSIVE OR GENDER BLAMING?

As this chapter has noted, there are a number of reasons why trying to prevent girls' violence by curbing their "meanness" is a questionable strategy. First, relational aggression does not predict developmental maladjustment; there is evidence that it is normative and desirable for youth (Underwood, Galen, & Paquette, 2001; Xie et al., 2002). Aggression has the positive effects of making separation from others, individualization, competition, achievement, and the initiation of new relationships possible (Hadley 2003:391). Second, as already noted, it is debatable that girls are particularly inclined to use and/or approve of relational aggression, and if there are gender differences in these forms of aggression, they seem to end by late adolescence. Finally, relational aggression is not illegal, and any focus on it would expand the juvenile justice intervention net to a group of people that are not even likely to be involved in the physical violence that *is* illegal. Even if intervention into relational aggression for both boys and girls improves youths' social skills in school, peer group, or family settings—an outcome that is debatable, it cannot be viewed as a useful violence prevention strategy.

Even for girls who both act violently and who direct relational aggression toward other girls, how relational aggression is handled must be carefully thought through. Many girls are socialized to be conciliatory and to avoid conflict, so that they are included in relationships and liked by other people (Brown and Gilligan, 1992; Zahn-Waxler, 2000; Underwood, 2003). Indirect acts are sometimes the only way that girls have to express their anger or even their preferences for friends. Alternatives to physical and direct aggressions are, fundamentally, weapons of the weak, and as such, they are as reflective of girl's powerlessness as they are of girl's "meanness." Girls, women, and others in relatively powerless groups have not, historically, been permitted direct aggression (without terrible consequences). As a result, in certain contexts, and against certain individuals, relational aggressions were ways the powerless punished the bad behavior of the powerful. This was, after all, how slaves and indentured servants—female and male—got back at abusive masters, how women before legal divorce dealt with violent husbands, and how working women today get back at abusive bosses. As one psychologist put it, "There is reason to question any approach that potentially serves to discourage females from expressing anger and aggression and reminds them of their subordinate positions in society" (Zahn-Waxler, 1993: 81). Given the many negative contexts and experiences that contribute to girls' violence, a focus on their own meanness misses the mark in addressing the causes of that violence.

WHAT IS REALLY GOING ON HERE?

The indirect aggression, school violence, and bullying literatures suggest the need for interventions that will stop girls from being mean to each other, and perhaps to boys as well. Research on girls' lives, however, suggests the need for interventions that give girls a fuller picture of where their criticisms of other girls might come from. For example, numerous examples from Owens et al.'s (2000) focus groups suggest that gender relations and statuses are important in aggression in school settings, but not as an ordering mechanism that leads girls to mostly use indirect aggression and boys to use physical aggression. When girls (and boys) call girls sluts or make jokes by asking about pregnancy test results in prank phone calls, they are reflecting the common double standard that prohibits sexuality in teenage girls, but encourages it for boys. Moreover, Owen's focus group participants said they engaged in bitching and talking for "something to do," and she observed the male-dominated use of the playground and the small areas where girls indeed had little else to do but to "bitch." Again, gender arrangements are central to understanding girls and boys behavior. However, the decontextualization of research subjects from these gender arrangements can lead to recommendations for policing rather than empowerment.

NOTES

1. There are some situations and contexts where girls come closer to boys in their levels of violence, but none where they surpass boys. Particularly in large cities, significant numbers of girls are beaten by their peers, in most cases other girls (Singer et al., 1995). Also, probably due to their involvement in child care, among children younger than two who were victimized by a juvenile, 34% were victimized by a girl. In U.S. schools, national surveys in the United States reveal that boys are three times more likely to carry weapons than are girls (Odgers & Moretti, 2002: 104), but in selected inner-city schools there is no gender difference (Webster et al., 1993).

2. Similar programs targeting girls' relational aggression include the Empower Program designed by Rosalind Wiseman, author of Queen Bees and Wannabees, and the Girls' Leadership Institute founded by Rachel Simmons, author of Odd Girl Out.

REFERENCES

Artz, S., & Riecken, T. 1997. What, so what, then what? The gender gap in school-based violence and its implications for child and youth care practice. Child and Youth Care Forum 26: 291–303.

Bartollas, C. (1993). Little girls grown up: The perils of institutionalization. In C. Culliver (ed.), Female criminality: The state of the art (469–482). New York: Garland Press.

Bjorkqvist, K. (1994). "Sex differences in physical, verbal, and indirect aggression: A review of recent research." Sex Roles 30: 177–188.

Bjorkqvist, K., & Niemela, P. (1992). New trends in the study of female aggression. In K. Bjorkqvist & P. Niemela (eds.), Of mice and women: Aspects of female aggression (3–16). San Diego: Academic Press.

Bjorkqvist, K., & Niemela, P. (1992). Of mice and women: Aspects of female aggression. San Diego: Academic Press.

Brown, L., Chesney-Lind, M., & Stein, N. (2007). "Patriarchy matters: Toward a gendered theory of teen violence and victimization." Violence Against Women 13(12): 1249–1273.

Brown, L. M., Gilligan, C. (1992). Meeting at the Crossroads: Women's Psychology and Girls' Development. Cambridge: Harvard University Press.

CBS. (2000). "Colorado kills gun laws: Measures were inspired by Columbine." *CBS Evening News*. Denver, Colorado. 17 November, http://www.cbsnews.com/stories/2000/02/16/columbine/main161459.shtml

Centers for Disease Control and Prevention. (1992–2003). *Youth risk behavior surveillance—United States, 1991–2001. CDC surveillance summaries.* U.S. Department of Health and Human Services. Atlanta: Centers for Disease Control.

Centers for Disease Control and Prevention, National Center for Injury Prevention and Control. (2006). Web-based Injury Statistics Query and Reporting System (WISQARS) [online]. www.cdc.gov/ncipc/wisqars (accessed 18 July 2006).

Chesney-Lind, M. (2002). The meaning of mean. Review of *Odd girl out: The hidden culture of aggression in girls* by Rachel Simmons, *The secret lives of girls* by Sharon Lamb, and *Queen bees and wannabes* by Rosalind Wiseman. *Women's Review of Books* (November): 20–22.

Chesney-Lind, M., & Belknap, J. (2004). Trends in delinquent girls' aggression and violent behavior: A review of the evidence. In M. Putallaz & P. Bierman (eds.), *Aggression, antisocial behavior and violence among girls: A developmental perspective.* New York: Guilford Press.

Chesney-Lind, M, &. Irwin, K. (2006). *Beyond bad girls: Gender violence and hype.* New York: Routledge.

Chessler, P. (2001). *Women's inhumanity to women.* New York: Nation Books.

Craig, W. M. (1998). The relationship among bullying, victimization, depression, anxiety, and aggression in elementary school children. *Personality and Individual Differences*, 123–140.

Crick, N. R. (1996) The role of overt aggression, relational aggression, and prosocial behavior in the prediction of children's future social adjustment." *Childhood Development*, 67: 2317–2327.

Crick, N. R., Warner, N., Cass, J., O'Brien, K., Nelson, D., & Grotpeter, J. (1999). Childhood aggression and gender: A new look at an old problem." In Dan Bernstein (ed.), *Gender and Motivation*, (75–141). Lincoln: University of Nebraska Press.

Crick, N. R., & Bigbee, M. A. (1998). Relational and overt forms of peer victimization: A multi-informant approach. *Journal of Consulting and Clinical Psychology* 66: 337–347.

Crick, N. R., Bigbee, M. A., & Howes, C. (1996). Gender differences in children's normative beliefs about aggression: How do I hurt thee? Let me count the ways. *Child Development*, 67: 1003–1014.

Crick, N. R., & Grotpeter, J. K. (1995). Relational aggression, gender and social-psychological adjustment. *Child Development* 67: 710–722.

Crick, N. R., & Grotpeter, J. K. (1996) Children's treatment by peers: Victims of relational and overt aggression. *Development and Psychopathology* 8: 367–380.

DeAngelis, T. (2003). Girls use a different kind of weapon. *Monitor on Psychology*. 34: 51. Washington, DC: American Psychological Association.

De Los Reyes, A., & Prinstein, M. J. (2004) Applying depression-distortion hypotheses to the assessment of peer victimization in adolescents. *Journal of Clinical Child and Adolescent Psychology* 33: 325–335.

Dishion, T. J., French, D. C., & Patterson, G. R. (1995). The development and ecology of antisocial behavior. In D. Cicchetti & D. Cohen (eds.), *Develop-*

mental Psychopathology, Volume 2: Risk, Disorder, and Adaptation (421–471). New York: A Wiley-Interscience Publication.

Elliott, D., Olweus, D., Limber, S., & Mihalic, S. (1998). Book nine: Bullying prevention program. Boulder: Center for the Study and Prevention of Violence, Institute for Behavioral Sciences, University of Colorado, Boulder.

Federal Bureau of Investigation. (2005). Crime in the United States 2004. Washington, DC: Government Printing Office.

Ferrell-Smith, F. (2003). Tackling the schoolyard bully: Combining policy making with prevention. National Conference of State Legislatures. Washington, DC. http://www.ncsl.org/programs/cyf/schoolyard.htm

Galen, B. R., & Underwood, M. K. (1997). A developmental investigation of social aggression among children. Developmental Psychology 33: 589–600.

Gilligan, C., & Brown, L. M. (1992). Meeting at the Crossroads: Women's Psychology Girls' Development. Cambridge, MA: Harvard University Press.

Hadley, M. (2003). Relational, indirect, adaptive, or just mean: Recent work on aggression in adolescent girls: Part I. Studies in Gender and Sexuality 4: 367–394.

Hart, C. H., Nelson, D., Robinson, C. C., Olsen, S. F., & McNeilly-Choque, M. K. (1998). Overt and relational aggression in Russian nursery-school-age children: Parenting style and marital linkages. Developmental Psychology 34: 687–697.

Hennington, C., Hughes, J. N., Cavell, T. A., & Thompson, B. (1998).The role of relational aggression in identifying aggressive boys and girls." Journal of School Psychology 36: 457–477.

Horowitz, R., & Pottieger, A. E. (1991). Gender bias in juvenile justice handling of seriously crime-involved youths. Journal of Research in Crime and Delinquency 28: 75–100.

Kersten, J. (1989). The institutional control of girls and boys. In Maureen Cain (ed.), Growing up good: Policing the behavior of girls in Europe (129–144). London: Sage.

Little, T. D., Henrich, C. C., Jones, S. M., & Hawley, P. H. (2003). Disentangling the "whys" from the "whats" of aggressive behavior. International Journal of Behavioral Development 27: 122–133.

McMaster, L. E., Connolly, J., Pepler, D. J., & Craig, W. M. (2002). Peer to peer sexual harassment in early adolescence: A developmental perspective. Development and Psychopathology 14(1): 91–105.

Mann, C. (1984). Female crime and delinquency. Tuscaloosa: University of Alabama Press.

Melton, G. B., Limber, S. P., Cunningham, P., Osgood, D. W., Chambers, J., Flerx, V., Henggeler, S., & Nation, M. (1998). Violence among rural youth. Final report to the Office of Juvenile Justice and Delinquency Prevention. Washington, DC: United States Department of Justice, Office of Justice Programs, Office of Juvenile Justice and Delinquency Prevention.

Morash, M., & Chesney-Lind, M. (2009). Girls' violence in context. In M. Zahn (ed.), The delinquent girl (182–206). Philadelphia: Temple University Press.

McCurley, C., & Snyder, H. N. (2004). Victims of violent juvenile crime. Washington, D C: Juvenile Justice Bulletin. Office of Juvenile Justice and Delinquency Prevention, National Institute of Justice.

Nansel, T. R., Overpeck, M., Pilla, R. S., Ruan, W. J., Simons-Morton, B., & Scheidt, P. (2001). Bullying behaviors among U.S. youth. *Journal of the American Medical Association* 285(16): 2094–2100.

National Conference of State Legislatures, from education bill tracking database, http://www.ncsl.org/programs/educ/educ_leg_srch.cfm (accessed 1 November 2006).

Odgers, C. L., & Moretti, M. M. (2002). Aggressive and antisocial girls: Research update and challenges. *International Journal of Forensic Mental Health* 1(2): 103–119.

Olweus, D. (1977). Aggression and peer acceptance in adolescent boys: Two short-term longitudinal studies of ratings. *Child Development* 48: 1301–1313.

Olweus, D. (1978). *Aggression in the schools: Bullies and whipping boys.* Washington: Hemisphere.

Olweus, D. (1979). Stability of aggressive reaction patterns in males: A review. *Psychological Bulletin* 86(4): 852–875.

Olweus, D. (1993). *Bullying at school: What we know and what we can do.* Cambridge: Blackwell.

Owens, L., Shute, R., & Slee, P. (2000). "Guess what I just heard!": Indirect aggression among teenage girls in Australia. *Aggressive Behavior* 26(1): 67–83.

Paquette, J. A., & Underwood, M. K. (1999). Gender differences in young adolescents' experiences of peer victimization: Social and physical aggression. *Merrill-Palmer Quarterly* 45: 242–266.

Prinstein, M. J., Boergers, J., & Vernberg, E. M. (2001). Overt and relational aggression in adolescents: Social-psychological adjustment of aggressors and victims. *Journal of Clinical Child Psychology* 30(4): 479–491.

Putallaz, M., Kupersmidt, J. B., Grimes, C. L., & DeNero, K. (1999). Overt and relational aggression: Aggressors, victims, and gender. In J. B. Kupersmidt (Chair), *Social relationships and two forms of aggression: Gender considerations.* Symposium presented at the biennial meeting of the Society for Research in Child Development, Albuquerque, New Mexico.

Roecker, P. C. (2001). Children's responses to overt and relational aggression. *Journal of Clinical Child Psychology* 30(2): 240–252.

Russ, H. (2004, February 19–22). The war on catfights. *City Limits.* http://www.citylimits.org/content/articles/viewarticle.cfm?article_id=3024 (accessed).

Rys, G. S., & Bear, G. G. (1997). Relational aggression and peer relations: Gender and developmental issues. *Merrill-Palmer Quarterly* 43: 87–106.

Sampson, R. (2002). *Bullying in schools: Problem-oriented guides for police series* (Report No.12). Washington, DC: United States Department of Justice, Office of Community Oriented Policing Services.

Simmons, R. (2002). *Odd girl out: The hidden culture of aggression in girls.* New York: Harcourt.

Singer, M., Anglin, T., Song, L., & Lunghofer, L. (1995). Adolescents' exposure to violence and associated symptoms of psychological trauma. *Journal of the American Medical Association* 273(6): 477–482.

Smith, P. K., & Brain, P. (2000). Bullying in schools: Lessons from two decades of research. *Aggressive Behavior* 26(1): 1–9.

Snyder, H. N. (2004). *Juvenile arrests 2002.* Washington, DC: Juvenile Justice Bulletin. Office of Juvenile Justice and Delinquency Prevention, United States Department of Justice.

Steffensmeier, D., Schwartz, J., Zhong, H., & Ackerman, J. (2005). An assessment of recent trends in girls' violence using diverse longitudinal sources: Is the gender gap closing? *Criminology* 43(2): 355–406.

Storch, E. A., Nock, M. K., Masia-Warner, C., & Barlas, M. E. (2003). Peer victimization and social-psychological adjustment in Hispanic and African-American children. *Journal of Child & Family Studies* 12(4): 439–452.

Storch, E. A., Werner, N., & Storch, J. B. (2003). Relational aggression and psychosocial adjustment in intercollegiate athletes. *Journal of Sport Behavior* 26(2): 155–167.

Underwood, M. K. (2003). The comity of modest manipulation: The importance of distinguishing among bad behaviors. *Merrill-Palmer Quarterly* 49(3): 373–389.

Underwood, M. K., Galen, B. R., & Paquette, J. A. (2001). Top ten challenges for understanding gender and aggression in children: Why can't we all just get along? *Social Development* 10(2): 248–266.

U.S. Department of Health and Human Services. (2001). *Youth violence: A report of the surgeon general*. Rockville, MD: Department of Health and Human Services, Centers for Disease Control and Prevention, National Center for Injury Prevention and Control, Substance Abuse and Mental Health Services Administration, Center for Mental Health Services, and National Institute of Mental Health.

Vossekuil, B., Robert, A. F., Reddy, M., Borum, R., & Modzeleski, W. (2002). *The final report and findings of the Safe School Initiative: Implications for the prevention of school attacks in the United States*. Washington, DC: United States Secret Service and United States Department of Education.

Webster, D. W., Gainer, P. S., & Champion, H. R. (1993). Weapon carrying among inner-city junior high school students: Defensive behavior versus aggressive delinquency. *American Journal of Public Health* 83 (11): 1604–1608.

Werner, N. E., & Crick, N. R. (1999). Relational aggression and social-psychological adjustment in a college sample. *Journal of Abnormal Psychology* 108(4): 615–623.

Whitney, I., & Smith, P. K. (1993). A survey of the nature and extent of bullying in junior/middle and secondary schools. *Educational Research* 35(1): 3–25.

Wiseman, R. (2002). *Queen bees and wannabees: Helping your daughter survive cliques, gossip, boyfriends and other realities of adolescence*. New York: Crown Publishers.

Wolke, D., Woods, S., Bloomfield, L., & Karstadt, L. (2000). The association between direct and relational bullying and behavioral problems among primary school children. *Journal of Child Psychology and Psychiatry* 41(8): 989–1002.

Xie, H., Swift, D., Cairns, B. D., & Cairns, R. B. (2002). Aggressive behaviors in social interaction and developmental adaptation: A narrative analysis of interpersonal conflicts during early adolescence. *Social Development* 11(2): 205–224.

Zahn-Waxler, C. (2000). The development of empathy, guilt, and internalization of distress: Implications for gender differences and externalizing problems. In R. J. Davidson (ed.), *Anxiety, depression, and emotion: Wisconsin symposium on emotion, volume II* (222–265). New York: Oxford University Press.

SIX

"I DON'T KNOW IF YOU CONSIDER

THAT AS VIOLENCE ..."

Using Attachment Theory to Understand
Girls' Perspectives on Violence

Judith A. Ryder

INTRODUCTION

Public discourse often presumes a common understanding of girls' violence—as if we all know it when we see it. Our perceptions, however, are shaped by powerful media images drawing attention to the latest sensationalized case, be it a "baby-faced butcher" (Lovett, 2004), inner-city "gangstas" (Begum, 2006; Maher & Curtis, 1995), or "mean" suburban brawlers (Simmons, 2003; Burns, 2007; Scelfo, 2005). Such images garner authority from almost instantaneous video feeds and constant repetition, but are devoid of social or personal context. While some scholars reject *girls' violence* as a meaningless phrase dependent upon a universal or "generic construction of girlhood" (Batacharya, 2004: 62), others continue to debate what counts as violence, and by extension, whether it is going up or down (for discussion see Pollock & Davis, 2005; Steffensmeier et al., 2005). Terminology in these latter discussions is typically legalistic, relying on codified definitions of specific offenses enacted by individual girls. Such a narrow focus ignores the context of enacted violence as well as its antecedents, and in particular, fails to take into account the perspective of girls themselves. Moreover, by their nature such legalistic accounts lack a theoretical framework for understanding the violence.

It is the intent of this chapter to portray a fuller picture of violence in the lives of girls by analyzing interviews with young women incarcerated for a violent offense. Rather than take as a given the official label of the criminal offense for which the girls were adjudicated delinquent (robbery and assault), I review and compare the situational context and characteristics of those events. The girls' narratives identify similar patterns and motives for both criminal acts. The data also suggest that distinctions made by mainstream adult society about what is considered violent do not always correspond with those made by adolescents. For example, within the particular and personal context of conflicting peer relationships, assault may be redefined as an act of self-defense. Asked if she did violent things with her friends, 13-year-old Jackie[1] said no, explaining: "No, not if, if we had, um,—if we don't like nobody, if we don't like nobody and that person try to jump one of us, we gonna jump them—I don't know if you consider that as violence, but I don't think it is."

From the girls' standpoint, "violence" is a flexible and often ambiguous term that extends beyond their own illegal acts (Hartsock, 1996; Collins, 1990). To gain a more comprehensive understanding of the meaning of *girls' violence*, the discussion moves beyond the specifics of robberies and assaults to include participants' histories of victimization and loss. This widens the focus from girls' behaviors to girls' subjective experiences; the unit of analysis expands from individual girls to girls in the context of dynamic relational processes (Daiute & Fine, 2003). Girls' violence in this broad construction includes an extensive range of intertwined experiences: violence enacted by girls, witnessed by girls, and experienced by girls. The data indicate that much of the violence in the girls' lives occurred within the context of relationships, particularly relationships with adults responsible for their care and development. Using Bowlby's (1988) attachment theory to frame girls' perspectives and use of violence, I suggest that weakened bonds with primary caregivers left the young women susceptible to the stress of traumatic events. Lacking the intervention of other loving adults, and given the human need for attachment, girls used violence as a means of connecting with others—however maladaptive and misplaced that connection might have been.

SUBJECTIVITIES OF VIOLENCE

An essential dimension of feminist analysis is seeking to understand social life from the standpoints of women (Harding, 1987), and over the last 30 years researchers have begun to develop rich qualitative analyses of violence committed by *adult* women. Studies that specifically address robberies and assault include Maher's (1997) ethnographic study of crack cocaine users and sex workers in a Brooklyn drug market. Many of these women assumed a violent street persona as part of "a necessary survival strategy," resorting to assaultive behavior primarily in response to threats of harm. Robbing dates in this setting is also more about surviving on the margins than gaining economic independence. In her interviews with robbers, Miller (1998) found that while motivations were similar among men and women, the enactment of violence differed. Females used stereotypical perceptions of women as part of a gendered economic strategy wherein they appeared sexually available to men before robbing them, or were accomplices in male robberies of other men. Baskin and Sommers (1998) compared the situational context of robberies and assaults committed by women, and report that robberies were more likely to be planned, impersonal, and instrumental. Differences, however, "seemed to be more a matter of degree rather than categorical distinction" (124); all offenders shared a perspective centering on obtaining money, purchasing drugs, and using drugs. Although these and other studies provide thick and detailed descriptions of the use of violence, particularly assaults and robberies, Kruttschnitt and Carbone-Lopez (2006) contend, "we are only beginning to uncover the subjectivities of women offenders" (328). Certainly, there has been even less attention paid to violent female offenders still in their teenage years.

Despite significant social and legal consequences for female offenders, neither the diversity nor the specificity of girls' lives has been widely researched. Even as increasing numbers of young women are being arrested, detained, and committed to the juvenile justice system (Snyder & Sickmund, 2006), and numerous statistical studies are issued *on* and *about* girls' violence, our understanding of the context of such acts remains limited. Few reports consider how girls themselves define and understand the violence in their lives or how experiences of violence have affected them. By these omissions, such studies not only miss the "reality that girls experience various forms of violence in their everyday lives" (Hussain et al., 2006: 59), but they fail to see the interconnected and relational quality of such violence.

Exceptions include Phillips' (2003) study in which young college women (16 to 22 years old) discuss how physical aggression and violence is considered normal, even enviable, gendered behavior within the educational setting's group hierarchies. The young women explained they maintained their positions in the school's "pecking order" by verbally and physically bullying others, using intimidation, and picking fights. Brown (2003) also focused on the social context of schools, interviewing over 400 girls from diverse backgrounds enrolled in elementary through high school classes. Although physical violence was not pervasive, girls did engage in "fist fighting"—sometimes as a way of separating themselves from "white feminine ideals and behaviors they see as 'wussy' or weak," but also for revenge, self-respect, protection, and keeping the peace (112–114).

The ethnographic work of Jones (2004) examines how violence is enacted (or not) by girls located within one community's "bounded spheres of interaction" (Sullivan, 1989: 9). Her in-depth case studies reveal the ways young women must negotiate pervasive conflict and violence in distressed neighborhoods, sometimes finding the ability to fight and the reputation as a fighter to be "the most reliable social resources available to them" (61). Ness (2004) also conducted ethnographic fieldwork with girls who engage in fights in the community, and states that in some neighborhoods violence among girls is both normative and instrumental, providing security and a sense of mastery, status, and self-esteem. These and a growing number of studies present a detailed look at girls' use of violence and a description of the social and cultural context within which girls maneuver.

Researchers also have begun to focus on the need for a close examination of girls' own words to better comprehend the meanings of violence (Hussain et al., 2006; Flores, 2006; Schaffner, 2004). Findings from two related studies in Scotland indicate that girls' definitions of violence overlap with mainstream norms—but not completely. When asked about what counted as violence, groups of girls in various communities first spoke in general terms about physical behaviors such as hitting, kicking, or fighting. When girls talked about their *own* experiences, however, they described a much broader range of physical acts and incidents of victimization (e.g., sexual assault, self-harm, locked in a cupboard, pushed in a river), as well as verbal confrontations (e.g., name-calling, threats, and racial harassment), vandalism, and cruelty toward animals (Batchelor, Burman, & Brown, 2001: 3). A small subset described fighting as part of their sense of self and expressed pride in their "hard" reputation and the rewards it could bring. These self-identified "violent girls" also reported higher levels of self-harm than did others in the study, higher levels of verbal abuse, and significantly higher levels of physically violent victimization. This subset was similar to girls in the second study, all of whom had been sentenced to imprisonment for violent offending (Batchelor, 2005). Among the imprisoned girls, anger and aggression were frequently related to experiences of family violence and abuse, and the development of a negative worldview in which other people were perceived as being "out to get you." Despite its multiple forms and prevalence, girls found it difficult to talk about violence in their lives, vacillating between blaming individuals and explaining actions in their social context. Ultimately, the framework within which they made sense of violence was "intertwined with talk about interpersonal relationships and social context" (Burman, 2004: 100).

These projects correspond with those that suggest a link between victimization and violent offending (Chesney-Lind, 1989; Arnold, 1995; Gaarder & Belknap, 2002; Siegel & Williams, 2003), and also hint at the need to consider underlying mechanisms that may contribute to girls' violence. While girls' relationships to violence are best appreciated within the context of specific social, material, and gendered circumstances, we also need to examine the individual variation that exists, even among girls subject to similar circumstances (Robinson, 2007). Why, for example, is fighting taken up by some but not all girls, or is taken up in different ways? What meanings do girls bring to violence, and how might those be shaped by internal processes? Linking structural context with the "meaning that individuals differentially ascribe to events" (Ness, 2004: 46) has been instrumental in investigating boys' offending (Shaw, 1930/1966; 1936); such linkages can also enhance understanding of girls' actions.

One way to look at and think about this process is through the lens of attachment theory. Since Bowlby's theoretical groundwork (1969–1980; 1988) in association with Ainsworth's empirical studies (1972, 1979), attachment research has come to be recognized as key to explaining the normative processes of human development. As with developmental criminology and life course theories, attachment theory asserts the primacy of early childhood as a determinate of later life behavior. Attachment here, however, is conceptualized as the natural bonds of affection between infants and significant others, rather than an acquired state derived from sanctioning destructive impulses (Hirschi, 1969). The emphasis is on nurturing and supporting a child's innate need to maintain emotional bonds with others. Bowlby and other attachment theorists contend that this need is essential to survival, crucial in determining the course of child development, and influential throughout the lifespan (Lopez & Gover, 1993).

Children internalize interactions with caregivers and develop expectations about their own roles and those of others in relationships (Shapiro & Levendorsky, 1999). Whether children "develop in a socially cooperative way" depends in great measure on how they are treated (Bowlby, 1988: 9). Thus, if a child is neglected, abandoned, or abused, she will feel that the caregiver (the attachment figure) believes her to be bad and that indeed she is bad, essentially unloved and unwanted by anyone (Bowlby, 1973: 238). Such a profound disruption of the primary bond leaves the child alone to attend to her attachment needs and to master the effects of the trauma. Her working model of the world is impaired. Eventually, if others are not available to provide instrumental and expressive support (Margolin & John, 1997), a state of social "detachment" may result (Hayslett-McCall & Bernard, 2002). Perceiving a lack of meaning, control, or connection in her life, the child may assume there is no place where she is safe (Herman, 1997). Shengold (1989) underscores the effects of such psychological trauma on a child's attachment by explaining that because the terror of abandonment exceeds the child's terror of the abuser, she may not be able to "forgo attachment to the individual(s) who has caused the trauma" (Robinson, 2007: 38). Thus, a girl's own violence against others later in life becomes a reenactment of a much earlier developmental stage. She may seek connection with and be comforted by an abusive attachment rather than let it go, because it is familiar and similar to the original love object (Robinson & Ryder, 2007).

To expand on this perspective, in the following section I present results from a secondary analysis of interviews with female offenders, first examining the conditions under which specific violent offenses were enacted. Despite distinct legal charges, the girls' actions and the contexts of those actions demonstrate much similarity. I also use narrative data from a subset of the girls to locate the violence within histories of extensive victimization, loss, and detachment from primary caregivers. Attachment theory provides a framework for considering how detachment and the absence of nurturing others contribute to the processes that draw some girls into violence.

GIRLS' PERSPECTIVES ON VIOLENT OFFENDING

Semi-structured interviews were conducted with 51 female adolescents remanded to residential custody in New York State's Office of Children and Family services for a robbery (27%) or assault (73%).[2] Three-fourths of the girls self-identified as black or Hispanic.[3] The median age was 15, and the median level of education was eighth grade.[4] Four respondents were mothers.

When asked to talk about any violence they had participated in, the girls typically responded with a mix of deviant and delinquent behaviors. While there may be some common ground with normative (i.e., legal and adult) conceptualizations of violence, most girls in this study did not distinguish clearly between what was expedient, what was illegal, and what was violent: "We hopped cabs. We used to stole from malls, we jumped girls, robbed people's houses. We sold drugs." Seeking greater specificity, we asked each girl to focus on the most recent offense for which she was adjudicated and remanded to custody—the Instant Offense (IO).[5] In response, the girls talked about what happened, including their motivation and what, if any, planning went into committing the crime. They described the offense location and weapons, accomplices, and victims.

The Instant Offense: Robbery and Assault

Nearly two-thirds (65%) of the Instant Offenses were not planned. Robberies, more so than assaults, were likely to have had an element of precalculation (69% vs. 22%), but even these entailed minimal organization and were open to changes. Similarly, the unplanned crimes were not totally spontaneous, "out of the blue," or irrational, but often stemmed from a simmering conflict that burst into violence. One girl explained:

> We had this thing going. First they try to jump me, but they didn't succeed. The third day I only see two of them . . . She wasn't the one I wanted, but it wasn't nobody else there so I figured, they

didn't care who I was, because they had a problem with somebody I knew. They were trying to jump me, because of somebody else.

The young women offered multiple motives for using violence in the commission of the Instant Offense; five primary categories were inductively derived from interview data.

Demanding respect. Overall, 39% of the IOs were motivated by the demand for respect. Individually, nearly half of those adjudicated for an assault (47%) indicated that their need to be respected motivated their acts, in contrast with only 16% of robbery offenders. Racist and sexist insults were often the triggers, even more so when they were directed toward the girls' parents and other caregivers. Fifteen-year-old Joanne describes how the dynamics of a drug transaction quickly shifted to violence when the buyer disrespected her mother:

> This girl, she owed me money and I didn't mean to, I really didn't mean to hit her but she was talking about my mother and I was not trying to hear it. So I mauled her. I just beat her down ... She was like 'your mother did this, this, and this with this, this, and this person. The ho [whore] did this, this, and this ... She got into my personal issues and if it becomes personal—she's not getting up.

Retaliation/Revenge. While retaliation or revenge was the motivation for less than a third of all IOs combined (29%), it was the primary motivation for robberies (38%). One such robbery took place in a group home where Alona had previously lived.

> I was living in a group home in Queens and they kicked me out ... I got upset and told them I was going to get them back 'cuz I didn't want to move so me and [a peer] we robbed the group home. I told them I ain't wanna go to Brooklyn. I told them and they didn't wanna listen to me.

Similarly, in an assault case Lisa was enraged at being abandoned by a mother whose children she was babysitting. She took revenge on the children one day when the mother went out:

> ... and she didn't come back for a whole weekend, so, me and my sister got mad. So we got, um ... turned on the hot water, we put her kids hands under the hot water ... We had burnt their hands. 'Cause I was mad that she didn't, she didn't even, she didn't even come in, she didn't even call.

Self-defense. Just under one-fourth of the assault offenders (22%) explained their acts were motivated by self-defense or the defense of others. Countering a common image of girl-on-girl violence, the majority of these assaults were against authority figures (including teachers, police, and group home staff) who touched or hit the respondent first (see Schaffner, 2005). One girl described a situation in her classroom:

> I got up to the board without my teacher's permission and erased it [assignment] and when she turned around she grabbed me by my neck and threw me on the board. So I had a pen in my hand . . . I didn't mean to cut her neck but when I went to punch her, it got her from the neck and down . . . I don't like nobody touching me.

In another case, Maria felt she was defending herself from a "sneak" move by officials. When Maria called her social worker, the woman asked if Maria was okay and then asked her to come into the office. Upon arrival, Maria was presented with a warrant for her arrest for running away and told she was to be sent to a secure facility upstate. A fight ensued when two male officers sought to restrain her. In both cases, the girls' responses suggest a wariness and distrust of "caring" institutions and their representatives.

Financial gain. Interestingly, less than one-third of the robberies (31%) were motivated by financial gain, but in these cases girls were clear that the robbery was a quick solution to a lack of money. Kathy, who was involved in a carjacking ring, said "it was just the way we grew up—we couldn't make money on our own." Another explained that "we really did it because we didn't have any money to get smoke . . . to get weed." Only two assault offenders were motivated by financial gain. One girl said she "got greedy" for money to buy her boyfriend a Christmas present, and the other explained that her role was "to walk up to the girl and ask her for the time, then beat the shit out of her. Beat her up, distracting her, and my friend was supposed to snatch her chain and take her money."

Bored/seeking excitement. The final grouping included only two robberies, each with a similar explanation: "It wasn't really like a feeling that 'well I wanna rob somebody, I wanna hurt somebody.' It was just a feeling that I don't have anything to do. You know, a boring feeling."

Other Characteristics of the Instant Offenses

Location and weapons. Overall, most offending occurred outside (59%), but this was more often the case for robberies than assaults (85% vs. 50%). Generally, the location was a public area such as on the street or in a park; offenses seldom occurred in the subject's own neighborhood. Indoor locations included group homes; the residence of the victim or offender; classrooms; probation or social worker offices; and a social club.

In a third of all offenses, girls used *only* their own body as a weapon—specifically their fists, feet, and teeth. When comparing the two offenses and looking at all other weapons used, girls' bodies continued to be primary. Almost three-fourths of the assault offenders (72%) used either their own body only, or a box cutter/knife; nearly the same percentage of robbery offenders (69%) used either their own body only or used the threat of a weapon (displaying a box cutter/knife, a gun, or projecting their voice). One robbery offender used a gun to pistol whip the victim.

Accomplices and victims. Delinquent activity often involves others, and just over half (53%) of the young women were joined by at least one other person. Here there is a significant difference between offense types: 61% of the assault offenders acted on their own, while only 8% of the robbery offenders did so. Contradicting the stereotype of female offenders acting as accomplices to males, when young women did act with others, those others were typically female. Also, almost three-fourths of all victims were female (73%). Assault offenders were nearly as likely to have assaulted an adult as a juvenile, whereas over two-thirds (69%) of robbery offenders reported that their victims were over age 18. Robbery victims were more likely to be strangers, although overall, victims were evenly split between friends and strangers (47% each); 6% of assault victims were family members.

Each of the girls in this study was remanded to custody for either a robbery or an assault. These official labels are legal categories that serve classification and sentencing purposes. An examination of the criminal events from the girls' perspectives, however, indicates that despite some variation within each offense type the acts are generally more alike than different. For example, two categories (respect and revenge) reflect the motives of 68% of all offense events, and although robberies were more likely than assaults to be prearranged, include an accomplice, occur out of doors, and victimize a stranger, the planning and accomplishment of offenses were very similar. Legal offense labels serve administrative purposes but they do not reveal the details of a criminal event, nor do they contextualize or provide insight into the motivations behind the acts they are meant to represent. Furthermore, even as they recognized the personal risks of their behaviors ("What I got to show for this? I been stabbed, sliced, shot, and stitched up. I don't need this no more") the young women received significant benefits (i.e., respect, revenge, protection, money, excitement). Mainstream norms that shun fighting did not fit within the reality of the girls' world. Official labels also did not distinguish between "type" of offender and held little meaning for the girls: most of the young women were involved in a variety of illegal activities and at the time of the interview were uncertain as to which act of delinquency was their officially designated Instant Offense.

VIOLENCE IN THE CONTEXT OF GIRLS' LIVES

For girls living in chaotic and impoverished family situations and communities, violence and violent offending is often an unremarkable backdrop to daily life: "we used to get together and go to the movies sometimes but mainly it was selling drugs and robberies." Girls described their neighborhoods as "typical" and "normal," although "a lot of people are killed there" and distinct acts of violence often blurred together. For many, *violence* and the official labels of *robbery* and *assault* were elastic, their meanings dependent upon particular contexts and individuals' experiences. Elana, for example, recalled coming home from the grocery store and, walking into her building elevator, witnessing a woman stabbing a man. The woman was "stabbing him all in his chest. I was standing right there. Blood was all over my shirt." But, she added, "I don't see no violence with drug using." Many of the young women in this study "don't see no violence" even as they describe physical assaults all around them. This is the broad background against which we must consider girls' violent offenses. Representative of the dissonance between mainstream norms and the girls' perspectives, such ordinary violence and trauma are insidious in girls' lives.

To gain a more comprehensive understanding than can be achieved by comparing official offense labels, the following section assumes a broader definition of *girls' violence*. Shifting away from girls' behaviors in the enactment of robbery and assault, the discussion considers girls' experiences, particularly in the context of relationships. This perspective is important for, as emerging research has shown, maltreatment, victimization and trauma, and family fragmentation and insecure attachment are significant risk factors for girls' violent behaviors (Moretti, Catchpole, & Odgers, 2005).

In prior work I examined the role of attachment and childhood trauma in the development of violent behavior among young female offenders (Ryder, 2007). Narratives from open-ended questions, combined with results from a 23-item Trauma Inventory checklist, were analyzed to develop a comprehensive picture of trauma in the girls' lives (Ryder, Langley, & Brownstein, 2008). The quantitative data indicate the range and prevalence of experiences while the qualitative interview data portray the details of those experiences, including the disruption of attachment bonds.

The prevalence of the traumatic event items are shown in table 6.1, grouped into three domains: Domestic, Community, and Other. The domains are then subdivided by Loss, Experienced Violence, and Witnessed Violence. Columns indicate the percentage of girls who reported that an event had ever occurred and the median earliest age of occurrence and lifetime frequency of occurrence. The total number of traumatic lifetime events experienced by the 51 girls ranged from two to 18, with an average of nine.[6]

A subset of the narrative data provides greater depth, detailing extensive histories of violent victimization and traumatic events, as well as four

Table 6.1. Traumatic Events Inventory (N = 51)*

			Ever occurred* %	Earliest age (Median)	Frequency (Median # of times experienced)
Domestic Inside home; involving family	Loss	Death of a loved one	82	10	2
		Serious injury/illness of a loved one	77	12	2
		Parents separated or divorced	63	3	1
		Lost home	22	7	1
	Experienced violence	Kicked, bitten, or hit	69	8	6
		Awakened by gunfire	61	11	7
		Sexually bothered/forced sex	26	7	4
		Burned or scalded	18	5	1
	Witnessed violence	Witnessed kicking, biting, or hitting	47	8	6
		Witnessed burning or scalding	20	11	1
		Witnessed shooting or stabbing	18	12.5	1
		Witnessed someone sexually bothered/ forced sex	16	6	3

continued on next page

Table 6.1. (Continued)

		Ever occurred* %	Earliest age (Median)	Frequency (Median # of times experienced)
Community				
Outside home; involving acquaintance or stranger	Experienced violence			
Kicked, bitten, or hit		65	10	7
Sexually bothered/forced sex#		26	13	2
Shot or stabbed#		24	13.5	2
Mugged, burned or scalded		18	14	13
		13	1	1
	Witnessed violence			
Witnessed shooting or stabbing		61	13	3
Witnessed a killing#		51	12.5	3
Other				
Accident; hospital treatment		41	12	1
Fire or explosion		31	8	2
Any other upsetting event##		28	13	1
Serious physical illness		20	7.5	2
Kidnapped		2	15	—

* Actual numbers range from 44–51 because of missing data.

Question did not specify if event was domestic or community related.

Other events included being locked up, death of a pet, loss of best friend.

types of loss (Death of a Loved One, Loss of Home, Physical Absence, and Psychological Unavailability).[7] The young women had been scalded, kicked, bit, beaten, and stabbed by parents and relatives; sexually assaulted in their homes; and witnesses to similar assaults on siblings, cousins, and mothers. The few who reported their sexual victimization to adults were ignored, punished, or accused of lying. Over a fifth of the girls indicated they had lost their home and told of being evicted by landlords or forced to move because their buildings were unlivable. Nearly all of the girls had spent time in out-of-home placements and the disorienting process of moving among facilities or alternating between several residences and institutions was traumatic. Other losses included the death of loved ones, often under violent conditions. Girls were confronted with the physical absence of parents because of hospitalizations, divorce, incarcerations, and immigration. They experienced the loss of parents or primary caregivers who, although physically present, were emotionally unavailable because of addiction, illness or disability, or the distractions of attending to other children, work, or personal problems. In general, adults were incapable or unwilling to emotionally nurture the girls. As developmental criminology suggests, these events represent life transitions but, more significantly, they indicate the disruption and loss of primary emotional attachments.

The girls' perspectives and their Instant Offenses can be best understood when placed within the specific, gendered, and complex circumstances of their lives. The girls in this study describe growing up in families nearly devoid of supportive relationships. When asked whom they turned to when something was bothering them, and with whom they felt the safest and most secure, over two-thirds said there was no one. Most had been placed out of home at some point; of the offenses that occurred indoors, most were within a group home, suggesting that there was already a broken connection between offenders and their families. As a result, the bonds to primary caregivers weakened and became a source of pain, rather than serving as indirect control mechanisms as many criminological theories propose. Without other adults to help integrate traumatic events into their lives, the girls were vulnerable and left to survive on their own. Ever vigilant for cues that may signal a threat reminiscent of earlier danger or loss, the girls remained in a state of preparedness. When faced with a teacher's attack, a social worker's duplicity, or insults against a mother with whom bonds were tenuous, memories of prior experiences triggered a violent response.

In a very basic way, many of these girls also sought to achieve a connection with others through violence, using their own body. Jackie, the young woman who described jumping specific peers as self-defense (not as a form of violence) talked a great deal about how her mother had abandoned her as an infant, and specifically related many of her actions to her anger at that loss. Responsibility for her upbringing rotated among her father, an aunt, and city and state institutions, and, she emphasized, she "just didn't trust nobody" and "don't feel safe." Explaining why she cut a girlfriend, Jackie reveals her vulnerability to yet another loss and betrayal: "she was like one of the . . . friends that tried to jump me . . . She had just came from my house eating my food, then she think she going 'round the corner and start talking 'bout me." Early rejection weakened bonds with her caregivers and left her susceptible to subsequent threats of abandonment. Stating "I don't believe nobody would listen to me at home," Jackie resorted to violence as a way (albeit problematic) to diffuse the pain of her broken attachments and to provoke another to stay in relation. Similarly, the actions of both Alona (kicked out of her foster home at the request of the mother's new boyfriend and after she was subsequently moved out of a group home, robbed the facility) and Lisa (from a family of 10 children, when unexpectedly left to babysit a neighbor's children for a weekend, without parental relief, scalded the children's hands) were retaliation against adults who "didn't wanna listen to me," who "didn't even come [back] in, she didn't even call." The need to stay attached, to be counted—and intolerance for addi-tional losses—was strong, provoking both anger and despair in the face of powerlessness. Traumatic childhood experiences and the perceived lack of other models at their disposal may have predisposed girls to see violence as a solution to the problems they faced.

IMPLICATIONS

Nationally, there is much concern and debate about girls' violence. The real-ity is, however, that adolescent girls are themselves at great risk for exposure to violence in their homes and in their communities. As a result, many are growing up with a deep sense of adult betrayal and alienation. While the juvenile justice system, researchers, and the general public continue to classify violence by offense, this analysis found such legal distinctions of little help in understanding girls' actions. Official designations of robbery and assault are unable to recognize the manifestations of maltreatment, although these emotional effects are often central to adolescents' violent relationships.

An examination of the interpersonal and context-dependent nature of girls' violence suggests that extensive losses and violent experiences disrupted or prevented girls' attachment to their caregivers, and these experiences were disregarded or inadequately addressed. The resultant social detach-ment, mixed with childhood fears and anxieties, initiated a pathway that increased the likelihood of antisocial behaviors, including violence (Sroufe et al., 1999; Greenberg et al., 1997; Smith & Thornberry, 1995; Crimmins, 1995). Interviews with this group of violent offenders not only affirm much of what is known about links between female victimization and offending, but the girls' stories also begin to reveal how that process unfolds. The girls had a sensibility about violence that differed from that of mainstream, adult norms. Such differences may signify not only age, race, and class differences, but because these girls grew up saturated by trauma, they often could not "see" their own violence or that which surrounded them. The girls tended to "normalize" and minimize traumatic experiences, even as such events increased their susceptibility to developmental harm and post-traumatic stress. Thus, when we speak of *girls' violence* it is important to look through a wide lens, and to include violence enacted against girls, particularly violence within the context of primary caregiver relationships. Attachment theory helps explain how under adverse conditions in which primary bonds are disrupted, violence may be a reenactment of violence previously experienced, as well as a means of reestablishing connections with others.

For adults to intervene in girls' lives effectively and in a supportive manner, we need to first come to know who these girls are, what has been done to them, and why they are hurt and angry. Overlooking trauma and victimization, or depicting girls solely as either victim or offender, fails to recognize the significance of violence in their everyday lives, beginning at a very early age and often within the context of supposed caregiving relationships. As part of our social responsibility we must seek to understand the perspectives and internal logic of girls and to change the conditions that foster this social problem we call violence. If what "counts" as violence in their lives is different than in mainstream society, prevention and intervention programs must determine the distinctions and begin there. Otherwise, all our programming efforts are likely to be ineffective at best.

NOTES

1. Pseudonyms are used throughout the chapter.

2. The data are from a larger study of youth violence and drug involvement. See Crimmins et al., 1998. A total of 51 girls completed the interview. Two of these interviews were missing substantial amounts of information from the Instant Offense section and were dropped from the analyses comparing assaults and robberies.

3. Respondents were asked to specify race or ethnic background. Ten categories were offered as probes and responses were recoded black (57%), Hispanic/Latina (18%), white (12%), and biracial/multiracial (12%).

4. The girls ranged in age from 12 to 17 years old. Educational level was measured by the last grade completed. During the study young women age 18 and over residing in juvenile facilities were moved to the adult Department of Correctional Services.

5. The study used the officially designated Instant Offense to identify offenders but analyses were based on girls' narrative descriptions of the events.

6. It is important to note that this refers to the number of trauma items that the girls *reported* ever experiencing, not the actual number of events they experienced.

7. The analyses of childhood traumatic events are based on 24 respondents; the narrative data of 27 respondents were lost in the World Trade Center attack in 2001.

REFERENCES

Ainsworth, M. (1972). Attachment and dependency. In J. L. Gewirtz (ed.), *Attachment and Dependency* (97–137). Washington, DC: Winston.

Ainsworth, M. (1979). Infant-mother attachment. *American Psychologist* 34: 932–937.

Arnold, R. (1995). Women of color: Processes of victimization and criminalization of Black women. In B. Price & N. Sokoloff (eds.), *The Criminal Justice System and Women: Offenders, Victims and Workers*, Second Edition (136–146). New York: McGraw Hill.

Baskin, D., & Sommers, I. (1998). *Casualties of community disorder. Women's careers in violent crime.* Boulder, CO: Westview Press.

Batacharya, S. (2004). Racism, "girl violence," and the murder of Reena Virk. In C. Alder & A. Worrall (eds.), *Girls' Violence: Myths and Realities* (pp. 61–80). Albany: State University of New York Press.

Batchelor, S. (2005). 'Prove me the bam!': Victimization and agency in the lives of young women who commit violent offences. *Probation Journal* 52(4): 358–375.

Batchelor, S., Burman, M., & Brown, J. (2001). Discussing violence: Let's hear it from the girls. *Probation Journal* 48(2): 125–134.

Begum, S. (2006, May 5). Girl 'gangsta' siege on family. *The Asian News.* http://www.theasiannews.co.uk/news/s/513/513554_girl _gangstas_siege_on_family.html (accessed 5 September 2008).

Bowlby, J. (1969–1980). *Attachment and Loss* (Vols. 1–3). New York: Basic Books.

Bowlby, J. (1988). *A secure base: Parent child attachment and healthy human development.* New York: Basic Books.

Brown, L. M. (2003). *Girlfighting: Betrayal and rejection among girls.* New York: New York University Press.

Burman, M. (2004). Turbulent talk: Girls' making sense of violence. In C. Alder & A. Worrall (eds.), *Girls' Violence: Myths and Realities* (81–103). Albany: State University of New York Press.

Burns, D. (2007, February 19). Girl fights on the rise as women turn to violence. http://cbs2chicago.com/topstories/girl.fights. fist.2.335339.html (accessed 5 September 2008).

Chesney-Lind, M. (1989). Girls' crime and woman's place: Toward a feminist model of female delinquency. *Crime and Delinquency* 35(1): 5–29.

Collins, P. H. (1990). *Black feminist thought: Knowledge, consciousness, and the politics of empowerment.* Boston: Unwin Hyman.

Crimmins, S. (1995). Early childhood loss as a predisposing factor in female perpetrated homicides. (Unpublished doctoral dissertation, City University of New York).

Crimmins, S., Brownstein, H., Spunt, B., Ryder, J., & Warley, R. (1998). Learning about violence and drugs among adolescents. Final report to the National Institute on Drug Abuse. Grant No. R01 DA08679. Washington, DC: National Institutes of Health.

Daiute, C., & Fine, M. (2003). Youth perspectives on violence and injustice. *Journal of Social Issues* 59(1): 1–14.

Flores, R. (2006). Adolescent girls speak about violence in their community. *Annals of the New York Academy of Sciences* 1087: 47–55.

Gaarder, E., & Belknap, J. (2002). Tenuous borders: Girls transferred to adult court. *Criminology* 40(3): 481–517.

Greenberg, M., DeKlyen, M., Speltz, M., & Endriga, M. (1997). The role of attachment processes in externalizing psychopathology in young children. In L. Atkinson & K. Zucker (eds.), *Attachment and Psychopathology* (196–222). New York: The Guilford Press.

Harding, S. (1987). Is there a feminist method? In S. Harding (ed.), *Feminism and Methodology* (1–14). Bloomington: Indiana University Press.

Hartsock, N. (1996). Theoretical bases for coalition building: An assessment of postmodernism. In H. Gottfried (ed.), *Feminism and Social Change: Bridging Theory and Practice* (256–274). Urbana: University of Illinois Press.

Hayslett-McCall, K., & Bernard, T. (2002). Attachment, masculinity, and self-control: A theory of male crime rates. *Theoretical Criminology* 6(1): 5–33.

Herman, J. (1997). *Trauma and recovery*. New York: Basic Books.

Hirschi, T. (1969). *Causes of delinquency*. Berkeley: University of California Press.

Hussain, Y., Berman, H., Poletti, R., Lougheed-Smith, R., Ladha, A., Ward, A., & MacQuarrie, B. (2006). Violence in the lives of girls in Canada: Creating spaces of understanding and change. In Y. Jasmin, C. Steenbergen, & C. Mitchell (eds.), *Girlhood: Redefining the Limits* (53–88). Montreal: Black Rose Books.

Jones, N. (2004). "It's not where you live, it's how you live": How young women negotiate conflict and violence in the inner city. *The Annals of the American Academy of Political and Social Science* 595: 49–62.

Kruttschnitt, C., & Carbone-Lopez, K. (2006). Moving beyond the stereotypes: Women's subjective accounts of their violent crime. *Criminology* 44(2): 321–351.

Lopez, F. G., & Gover, M. R. (1993). Self-report measures of parent-adolescent attachment and separation-individuation: A selective review. *Journal of Counseling and Development* 71: 560–569.

Lovett, K. (2004, January 21). Infamous N.Y. "baby-faced butcher" free. *New York Post*. 7.

Maher, L. (1997). *Sexed work: Gender, race and resistance in a Brooklyn drug market*. New York: Clarendon Press.

Maher, L., & Curtis, R. (1995). In search of the female urban gangsta: Change, culture and crack cocaine. In B. Price & N. Sokoloff (eds.), *The Criminal Justice System and Women: Offenders, Victims and Workers*, Second Edition (136–146). New York: McGraw Hill.

Margolin, G., & John, R. (1997). Children's exposure to marital aggression: Direct and mediated effects. In G. K. Kantor & J. Jasinski (eds.), *Out of the Darkness: Contemporary Research Perspectives on Family Violence*. Thousand Oaks, CA: Sage.

Miller, J. (1998). Up it up: Gender and accomplishment of street robbery. *Criminology* 36(1): 37–66.

Moretti, M., Catchpole, R., & Odgers, C. (2005). The dark side of girlhood: Recent trends, risk factors and trajectories to aggression and violence. *The Canadian Child and Adolescent Psychiatry Review* 14(1): 21–25.

Ness, C. (2004). Why girls fight: Female youth violence in the inner city. *The Annals of the American Academy of Political and Social Science* 595: 32–48.

Phillips, C. (2003) Who's who in the pecking order? Aggression and 'normal violence' in the lives of girls and boys. *The British Journal of Criminology* 43 (4): 710–728.

Pollock, J., & Davis, S. (2005). The continuing myth of the violent female offender. *Criminal Justice Review* 30(1): 5–29.

Robinson, R. (2007). "It's not easy to know who I am": Gender salience and cultural place in the treatment of a "delinquent" adolescent mother. *Feminist Criminology* 2(1): 31–56.

Robinson, R., & Ryder, J. (2007, September 10). Fighting to survive: Understanding girls' violence through attachment and object relations theory. Conference paper, What Works with Women Offenders. Monash University, Prato, Italy.

Ryder, J. (2007). 'I wasn't really bonded with my family': Attachment, loss and violence among adolescent female offenders. *Critical Criminology* 15(1): 19–40.

Ryder, J., Langley, S., & Brownstein, H. (2008). "I've been around and around and around": Measuring traumatic events in the lives of incarcerated girls. In R. Gido & L. Dalley (eds.), *Women and Mental Health Issues across the Criminal Justice System* (45–70). Upper Saddle River, NJ: Prentice Hall.

Scelfo, J. (13 June 2005). Bad girls go wild. *Newsweek*. http://www.newsweek.com/id/50082 (accessed 9 July 2008).

Schaffner, L. (2004). Capturing girls' experiences of "community violence" in the United States. In C. Alder & A. Worrall (eds.), *Girls' Violence: Myths and Realities* (105–128). New York: State University of New York Press.

Schaffner, L. (November 2005). So-called girl-on-girl violence is actually adult-on-girl violence. A Great Cities Institute Working Paper. University of Illinois at Chicago Great Cities Institute Publication Number: GCP-05-03.

Shapiro, D., & Levendorsky, A. (1999). Adolescent survivors of childhood sexual abuse: The mediating role of attachment style and coping in psychological and interpersonal functioning. *Child Abuse & Neglect* 23(11): 1175–1191.

Shaw, C. (1930/1966). *The jackroller: A delinquent boy's own story*. Chicago: University of Chicago Press.

Shaw, C. (1936). *Brothers in crime*. Chicago: University of Chicago Press.

Shengold, L. (1989). Soul murder: The effects of childhood abuse and deprivation. New York: Fawcett Columbine.

Siegel, J., & Williams, L. (2003). The relationship between child sexual abuse and female delinquency and crime: A prospective study. *Journal of Research in Crime and Delinquency* 40(1): 71–94.

Simmons, R. (2003). *Odd girl out: The hidden aggression in girls*. New York: Harvest Books.

Smith, C., & Thornberry, T. (1995). The relationship between childhood maltreatment and adolescent involvement in delinquency. *Criminology* 33: 451–477.

Snyder, H., & Sickmund, M. (2006). Juvenile offenders and victims: 2006 national report. Washington, DC: U.S. Department of Justice, Office of Juvenile Justice and Delinquency Prevention.

Sroufe, L., Carlson, E., Levy, A., & Egeland, B. (1999). Implications of attachment theory for developmental psychopathology. *Development and Psychopathology* 11(1): 1–13.

Steffensmeier, D., Schwartz, J., Zhong, H., & Ackerman, J. (2005). An assessment of recent trends in girls' violence using diverse longitudinal sources: Is the gender gap closing? *Criminology* 43(2): 355–405.

Sullivan, M. (1989). *Getting paid.* Ithaca, NY: Cornell University Press.

SEVEN

REDUCING AGGRESSIVE BEHAVIOR

IN ADOLESCENT GIRLS

BY ATTENDING TO SCHOOL CLIMATE

Sibylle Artz

Diana Nicholson

Where we live, study, work, and spend our time, and the relationships that are a part of our everyday lives, affect us deeply. The characteristics, climate, and tone of social contexts and locations such as schools and communities frame the dynamics of our interpersonal relationships and contribute to our behavior in ways that serve either to support or discourage the use of aggressive and violent behavior (see Magnuson, 2002; Porter, 1991; Powell, 2003; Whitmer, 1997). The connection between behavior and context is important not only to explaining how girls may become aggressive and violent, but also to our understanding of how we might create environments that undo and change established patterns of aggressive and violent behavior (Morash & Chesney-Lind, 2009).

The literature on school climate shows that students who feel a sense of belonging at school are less likely to exhibit problem behaviors (Resnick et al., 1997), and schools in which teacher-student interactions are respectful and caring, and that employ positive, proactive disciplinary methods rather than punitive, exclusionary measures (e.g., zero-tolerance policies and school suspension or expulsion), tend to have lower school drop-out rates (Christle, Nelson, & Jolivette, 2004). Dropping out of school is usually preceded by poor academic performance and low feelings of competence and acceptance by teachers and peers and for females, often involves getting pregnant and becoming a teen mother (Lan & Lanthier, 2003).

Payne, Gottfredson, and Kruttschnitt (2009), in their recent review of the literature entitled "Girls, Schooling and Delinquency," note that student bonding elements, that is, those structural and interpersonal factors that foster school attachment, assist in protecting girls from engagement in delinquent behavior. Payne and colleagues also point out that communally organized schools (schools that emphasize collaboration, cooperation, social relations) report higher student achievement and lower levels of student involvement with delinquency (see also Sanders & Phye, 2004). Competitive social conditions contribute to the use of aggression and violence (Artz, 2004; Johnson & Johnson, 1989, 1998; Magnuson, 2002), and classrooms and schools where teachers favor certain students and exclude others on the basis of academic performance and other markers like race, class, and gender, are more violent (Morash & Chesney-Lind, 2009). We may therefore have reason to conclude that schools where competitive social conditions prevail and students experience little in the way of support and cooperation among peers and bonding between students and teachers, may also be conducive to students engaging in higher levels of aggression and violence.

The past relational experiences of students, including their familial and social histories, contribute to the interpersonal climate of schools. Evident in the literature on girls' use of aggression and violence are links between relationship-based victimization and poor school experiences (Artz, 1998; Levene, Madsen, & Pepler, 2004; Serbin et al., 1998). As well, a personal history of victimization through sexual harassment has been linked to school-based difficulties such as sustaining attention, inhibited classroom participation, getting into trouble at school, and skipping school (AAUW Educational Foundation, 2001). Victimization is also related to emotional distress, poor school achievement, low self-confidence, and behavior problems (Paul & Cillessen, 2007). Additionally, "aggressive victims" (i.e., children and youth who have a history of harsh discipline and abuse, and themselves use aggression), tend to be rejected by their peers, respond more aggressively to being victimized, struggle in school (Schwartz, 2000), and are at higher risk for disengaging from school (Graham, Bellmore, & Mize, 2006). Further, such disengagement can be exacerbated for those who have experienced multiple forms of victimization (Holt & Espelage, 2007). Victimization tends to predict an increased dislike for school over time (Card, Isaacs, & Hodges, 2007), especially if such victimization continues to be a part of everyday life at school. Finally, especially for girls and women, the relationship between strain and victimization, especially sexual victimization and involvement in delinquency, criminality, and the use of violence over the life course has been well established (see Katz, 2004, for an in-depth discussion of victimization and revised strain theory).

Given the strong connection between victimization and the use of aggression and violence in schools, and the importance of a supportive and cooperative school climate to lower school-based aggression and violence and to retaining students, our study[1] examined several identified relationships as discussed in the literature including: (a) the victimization experiences of our participants and their use of aggression and violence in schools, (b) various components that contribute to their schools' interpersonal climates, and (c) our participants' experiences of feeling supported and connected to their schools. We based our inquiry on data gathered in two schools, a small alternative high school for high-risk girls including pregnant and parenting teens and a public high school that identified itself as a "community school." These schools are located in two different school districts within a mid-sized Canadian city.

PARTICIPATING SITES

Alternative program. The alternative program serves high-risk adolescent females in grades 9 to 12. The program was launched in the 1970s and currently functions in a small facility that was formerly an elementary school. One large classroom has been converted into a lounge with comfortable couches for group sessions. A well-staffed daycare center is located within the school. An onsite kitchen makes it possible for the girls to prepare food and learn about nutrition. The program supports up to 40 high-risk girls, including pregnant and parenting girls, in an integrated learning environment in which staff model caring, respectful interactions and nurturing collegial adult relationships. The school staff includes a director, two teachers, and a youth and family counselor who interact with the students on a daily basis and spend lunch and break times with the students so that a strong adult presence contributes to the feelings of physical and emotional safety experienced by the students. The counselor works with the girls individually and as a group on life issues such as substance use, abusive relationships, birth control, depression, and grief and loss. Pregnant and parenting girls also attend additional support and education groups, and learn about caring parenting and attachment through modeling by the daycare staff. Recreational and cultural activities are combined with academics to offer further opportunities to practice and exchange feedback on social skills and appropriate behaviors. Conflict resolution is an important part of the program's curriculum. Any conflict that arises between students or between a student and a staff member either inside or outside the program is dealt with in facilitated conflict resolution sessions. Students are also supported to employ their conflict resolution skills without staff intervention.

Public high school. The coeducational high school is a comprehensive community school with approximately 650 students in grades 9 to 12. The school operates in a relatively new facility, built in the mid-1990s, and serves students during the day and the community in the evening and on weekends. The school has a modern auditorium and theater space as well as a gymnasium and playing fields that are made available to the community. About half the students in the school travel by bus, some from smaller communities as far as an hour away. A number of students commute to school in their own cars. The average class size in the high school is between 23 and 24 students. These classes contain a range of learners with a number of different learning needs but only one teacher for the full complement of students. The requirements of students with special needs are met outside the classrooms and homerooms to which these students are attached.

PARTICIPANTS

A total of 83 female students enrolled in the two schools described here volunteered as participants in the study: 64 from the high school and 19 from the alternative program. The alternative program participants included 9 girls who were neither pregnant nor parenting, 6 young mothers, and 4 pregnant teens. The mean age of the participants varied somewhat: 17.0 years, for the girls from the alternative program, and 15.1 years for girls in the pubic high school.

DATA COLLECTION

Data was obtained from a survey and individual interviews with students. Quantitative data on the use of aggression, victimization, and school climate was obtained using The Survey of Student Life (SSL),[2] an instrument adapted from Artz and Riecken (1994a&b). The survey was eight pages long, in scanable format, and consisted of 181 questions and space at the end of the survey for comments.

Life histories of victimization were examined through questions asking for a "yes" or "no" response to having previously been physically abused at home, physically attacked at school, beaten up by more than one person at a time, talked into sex with a boyfriend or girlfriend against one's will, sexually harassed, or sexually assaulted.

Use of aggression and violence was assessed in two ways. First by asking how many times in the past year respondents had beaten up another kid (e.g., "never," "once or twice," "several times," or "very often"). Second, by asking participants how often in the past month (e.g., "never," "1–3 times," "4–9 times," and "10+ times") they had been aggressive toward both boys and girls by using various behaviors (called someone a name, used obscene language on others, threatened others, sexually harassed others, damaged others' personal property deliberately, stole something, blackmailed someone, spread rumors, shunned or excluded someone, and put someone down for being, or by calling someone, gay or lesbian). School climate was assessed by asking a series of questions related to students' experiences with teacher encouragement, school discouragement, classroom cooperation, classroom competition, and school connectedness (see tables 7.4–7.8 for the questions).

All items in the survey were measured for internal consistency and Cronbach's alpha values were above the .75 cut-off, on every comparison. Aside from examining the frequencies reported by our participants (which we report here as percentages given the variation on the number of participants in each site[3]) we also examined the relationship between aspects of school climate and staying away from school because of fear and the most extreme form of physical violence that we queried: that of having beaten up another kid in the past year. Table 7.9 shows the correlation results on these domains.

Additionally, once we had collected and analyzed our survey results and uncovered some quite unexpected findings in our data from the alternative school girls, we conducted qualitative individual interviews with all the girls in the alternative program who wished to be interviewed (15 of the 19 participants) that further probed our findings. In the interviews, we asked girls about their definitions of aggressive behavior, their experiences including their earliest memories of their own and others' use of aggression and violence, their explanations for their own use of aggression and violence, and their experiences with teachers and fellow students in terms of inclusion, exclusion, and participation in their schools. Each interview was approximately an hour to an hour and a half long. We analyzed the interviews by first reading each interview in its entirety and then reading the interview again in order to identify emergent themes in the participants' responses to each question and charted these responses across questions to allow comparisons for similarities and differences.

QUANTITATIVE FINDINGS

In order to investigate whether the girls in the public high school and the alternative program were similar or different with regard to their victimization experiences, use of aggression, and perceptions of school climate within their respective schools, we applied chi-square analyses to their responses on each of the survey questions (df 1, N = 19, N = 64 on every calculation).

Past Victimization Experiences

Given the strong connection in the research literature between victimization and the use of aggression and violence, we looked first at our participants' past victimization experiences and learned that the young women attending the alternative program have pasts characterized by significantly higher victimization rates for having *ever* been attacked at school, beaten up by more than one person at a time, physically abused at home, and talked into sex against their will. They also reported higher levels of staying away from school because of fear than the girls from the public high school (see table 7.1). Although the alternative school girls reported levels similar to the public high school girls for having been attacked on the way to and from school and for being sexually assaulted, overall these girls reported significantly greater levels of experience with victimization. We then turned our attention to the participants' self-reported levels of their use of aggression and violence and expected that these would also be significantly higher for the alternative school girls.

Use of Violence

Contrary to the expectations based in the literature on the relationship between victimization and the use of aggression and violence, the participants' responses to our survey question about the most serious form of aggression—beating up another kid in the past year—yielded quite similar prevalence rates for the girls in the high school and the alternative program although this interpretation depends on the value at which we set our significance level (see table 7.2). We set the significance value at p > .05, the most common cut-off level for these kinds of comparisons, and believe our data indicates very little if any difference between the groups with respect to beating up others in the past year even though we expected to find significantly higher self-reported use of violence in the significantly more victimized alterative school girls.

We then examined the participants' self-reports regarding their most recent use of aggression, that is, their use of pushing and shoving, sexual

Table 7.1. Past Victimization Experiences

Have you *ever* . . .	Alternative program Gr. 9–12 (N = 19)	Public high school Gr. 9–12 (N = 64)	Chi-square (df = 1)
. . . been attacked on the way to or from school?	3 (16.7%)	6 (9.4%)	.55 (ns)
. . . been attacked at school?	5 (27.8%)	4 (6.3%)	6.10*
. . . been beaten up by more than one person at a time?	6 (33.3%)	2 (3.1%)	13.62***
. . . been physically abused at home?	7 (38.9%)	4 (6.3%)	12.41***
. . . been sexually assaulted?	7 (38.9%)	14 (21.9%)	1.94 (ns)
. . . been talked into sex by your boyfriend or girlfriend against your will?	8 (44.4%)	3 (4.7%)	17.84***
. . . stayed away from school because of fear?	6 (33.3%)	7 (10.9%)	4.70*

Table 7.2. Beaten Up Another Kid in the Past Year

	Alternative program Gr. 9–12 (N = 19)	Public high school Gr. 9–12 (N = 64)	Chi-square (df = 1)
Have you, at least once or twice in the past year beaten up another kid?	7 (36.9%)	11 (17.7%)	3.33 (ns)

harassment, and relational victimizing behaviors at school during the past month. We found significantly higher use of pushing and shoving and sexual harassment among the public high school girls, but no difference between the two groups with regard to relationally victimizing others (see table 7.3). So again, contrary to expectations, the alternative school girls, despite their significantly greater experiences with victimization, reported significantly lower or similar levels of recent aggression when compared with the less victimized high school girls. These findings certainly peaked our interest with regard to what might be countering the expected effects of victimization. We then examined our data on school climate.

INTERPERSONAL SCHOOL CLIMATE

As noted earlier, interpersonal school climate was assessed in our survey by asking a series of questions relating to teacher encouragement, school discouragement, classroom competition, classroom cooperation, and school

Table 7.3. Recent Use of Aggression

In the *past month at school*, have you, at least once or twice . . .	Alternative program Gr. 9–12 (N = 19)	Public high school Gr. 9–12 (N = 64)	Chi-square (df = 1)
. . . pushed/shoved someone?	5 (26.3%)	35 (54.8%)	4.72*
. . . sexually harassed someone (called them gay/lesbian, or put them down for being gay/lesbian)?	1 (5.6%)	18 (27.4%)	4.34*
. . . relationally victimized someone (excluded/ shunned, spread rumors, sworn at, threatened, or blackmailed someone)?	12 (61.1%)	53 (82.3%)	3.33 (ns)

Table 7.4. A Comparison of Self-Reported Levels of Experiencing Teacher Encouragement

Survey item	Alternative program Gr. 9–12 (N = 19)	Public high school Gr. 9–12 (N = 64)	Chi-square (df = 1)
My teachers think it is important to support me	19 (100%)	33 (52%)	14.69***
My teachers want me to do my best	19 (100%)	47 (74%)	6.35*
The teachers like everyone equally	19 (100%)	42 (65%)	9.26*
The teachers care about my feelings	19 (100%)	35 (54%)	13.23***

connectedness. Table 7.4 shows the survey results for items related to teacher encouragement.

In table 7.4 we see that the high-risk females in the alternative program unanimously reported feeling highly supported by their teachers, while the public high school girls report levels of support significantly lower than those of the alternative school girls.

Furthermore, as table 7.5 shows, although the alternative school girls and the high school girls reported similar levels of being afraid they will fail when they participate in class, finding it hard to express their thoughts clearly, and often feeling lonely in school, the alternative school girls reported significantly lower levels of getting discouraged and of never getting the chance to ask questions in school.

Table 7.5. A Comparison of Self-Reported Levels of Feelings of School Discouragement

Survey item	Alternative program Gr. 9–12 (N = 19)	Public high school Gr. 9–12 (N = 64)	Chi-square (df = 1)
When I participate in class I am afraid I will fail	6 (33%)	16 (25%)	.33 (ns)
I find it hard to speak my thoughts clearly in this school	2 (11%)	20 (31%)	3.23 (ns)
I often get discouraged at this school	0 (0%)	12 (19%)	4.16*
I have a lot of questions I never get a chance to ask in this school	1 (6%)	22 (35%)	6.20*
I am often lonely in this school	0 (0%)	8 (12%)	2.58 (ns)

Table 7.6. A Comparison of Self-Reported Levels of Engagement in Classroom-Based Competition

Survey item	Alternative program Gr. 9–12 (N = 19)	Public high school Gr. 9–12 (N = 64)	Chi-square (df = 1)
I like the challenge of seeing who is best	1 (6%)	25 (39%)	7.78**
I don't like to be second	3 (18%)	26 (40%)	3.98*
I am happiest when I am competing with other students	1 (6%)	17 (27%)	3.90*
I like to be the best in my classes (ns)	7 (39%)	22 (35%)	.04

In addition to experiencing significantly higher teacher encouragement, significantly lower school discouragement, and having chances to ask questions, the alternative school girls, aside from liking to be the best in their class and liking to help others learn at levels similar to those reported by the public high school girls, reported strongly preferring a school climate characterized by low competition and high cooperation. Tables 7.6 and 7.7 show the responses for the respondents' preferences and assessments with regard to classroom competition and cooperation.

Table 7.7. Classroom Competition and Cooperation among Students

Survey item	Alternative program Gr. 9–12 (N = 19)	Public high school Gr. 9–12 (N = 64)	Chi-square (df = 1)
Other students care about my feelings	18 (95%)	29 (46%)	14.57***
In this school we learn more when we work with others	15 (78%)	32 (50%)	5.0*
All the students in this school know each other well	19 (100%)	31 (49%)	16.26***
I like to share materials with other students	17 (88%)	22 (53%)	17.86***
I can learn important things from other students	18 (94%)	38 (60%)	8.35**
I like to help other students learn	17 (88%)	45 (70%)	2.85 (ns)

Table 7.8. School Connectedness

Survey item	Alternative program Gr. 9–12 (N = 19)	Public high school Gr. 9–12 (N = 64)	Chi-square (df = 1)
I am proud to tell others where I go to school	19 (100%)	42 (65%)	8.89*
I like going to this school	19 (100%)	49 (76%)	5.44 (ns)
It would take a lot to want to leave this school	19 (100%)	27 (42%)	19.82***
If I had a problem outside of school, I know I could ask someone at school to help me with it	19 (100%)	37 (58%)	11.88**
I share a common vision and sense of purpose with others at my school	19 (100%)	34 (53%)	13.95***
I feel like I belong here at this school	19 (100%)	36 (57%)	12.54***
At this school, I can influence decisions that affect me	18 (95%)	40 (62%)	17.23**

Table 7.8 examines school connectedness and shows that the alternative school girls report significantly higher levels of school connectedness than the public high school girls. These girls, who had dropped out of school and reentered school in an alternative program, often under difficult circumstances like being pregnant or parenting, to a person, reported being proud of their school, liking to attend, not wanting to leave, believing that they can ask for help within their school and feeling that they belong and share a common vision and purpose with others even to the degree that they can influence decisions that affect them. The public high school girls match the alternative school girls' sense of school connectedness only with respect to liking to attend their school.

INVESTIGATING THE RELATIONSHIPS BETWEEN SCHOOL CLIMATE AND "BEATING UP ANOTHER KID"

In addition to looking at experiences related to elements of school climate, we were also interested in examining the correlations between school climate and the girls' self-reported involvement in the most serious form of violence, "beating up another kid." In order to do this, we correlated mean scores (as a total for all the items shown in the table for each domain described in the previous section) for "teacher encouragement," "school discouragement," "classroom competition," "classroom cooperation," and "school connectedness" with students' responses for having "beaten up another kid" in the past year. We also calculated a correlation between "beating up another kid" and positive responses for "staying away from school because of fear." Table 7.9 shows the correlation results on these domains.

We see in table 7.9 that for public high school girls, lack of teacher encouragement, low classroom cooperation, low school connectedness, and having stayed away from school because of fear are significantly correlated with having beaten up another kid in the past year. We see no such correlations for the alternative school girls.

INTERPRETING OUR QUANTITATIVE FINDINGS

Our quantitative data yielded the unexpected finding that despite having reported significantly higher levels of victimization strain than the public high school girls, the alternative school girls reported significantly lower use of aggression on the majority of items that we scored. The alternative school girls also reported significantly higher levels of all aspects of teacher encouragement and classroom collaboration along with significantly lower levels of school discouragement and classroom-based competitiveness, and significantly higher school connectedness. These findings, and the significant negative correlations for teacher encouragement, classroom cooperation, school connectedness, and the significant correlation for staying away from school with the public high school girls' recent use of aggression, suggested to us that we needed to learn more about the school climate in the alternative school and its effects on the girls who attended this school. We did not ignore our findings that the alternative school girls still used aggression and violence, but we did want to understand why the girls that we would have expected to use more aggression and violence than girls who have experienced less victimization overall did not do so. We therefore turned to interviews with the alternative school girls to help us make sense of our findings.

Table 7.9. Correlations between School Climate and Use of Physical Violence

School climate domain	Alternative program Gr. 9–12 (N = 19)	Public high school Gr. 9–12 (N = 64)
Teacher encouragement	−.297	−.334**
School discouragement	.200	−.105 (ns)
Classroom cooperation	−.054	−.235*
Classroom competition	.271	−.189 (ns)
School connectedness	−.076	−.276*
Stayed away from school because of fear	.326	.259*

QUALITATIVE FINDINGS

When we examined the alternative program girls' use of aggression and violence further through the interviews we learned that under certain circumstances aggression and violence were seen by them as perhaps wrong but still necessary for self-defense. As they explained it:

> I can't say that I don't, but I can't say that I do [use aggression]. I guess I do sometimes, but I don't know . . . I don't believe in fighting, it's hurting the other person but it's more hurting you for hurting the other person . . . I haven't used violence for about 2 years now . . . The other person actually hit me first, so it was all self-defense.
>
> I've never used those [aggression and violence] before . . . I've been in fights, but that's just defending myself.
>
> I don't use violence on people unless they use it on me.

Two females in the alternative program acknowledged that they tend to use aggression only when they are drinking.

> I've had problems with aggression before . . . I've never really been a violent person, like never ever . . . I use violence sometimes, if I'm drinking.
>
> I'm usually aggressive when I'm drinking . . . I kind of feel that maybe I'm like, not "better" but like I can [do it] . . . and some of the stuff I say when I'm drunk I wouldn't say [when sober].

When asked whether it is okay to hit someone when you're mad at them or if you're having an argument, all the girls in the alternative program said clearly that it would be wrong, and most stated that the only time when it is okay to hit someone is in self-defense. However, as previously noted, we also heard the girls say that sometimes they just lashed out when they didn't know what else to do or they couldn't control themselves because they were drunk. As they saw it,

> It's never okay to hit someone unless it's like self-defense . . . if they're being attacked or something.
>
> Nobody deserves to get physically abused like unless the person hit you first and you're just trying to defend yourself; then so be it.

Still, they also acknowledged that aggression has its uses:

> Nothing will come from punching someone in the face, you'll feel a little bit better and a little bit tougher but afterwards you'll feel like shit.
>
> I don't think it's right [to use threats] but I do it to get what I want . . . Since I was younger, I'd be like, 'tough tactic' a lot and I just realized it worked, I guess, so I use it.

I try not to use [aggression]. I think it's a really bad thing, but sometimes, I don't know, I find it's a really good way to get it out, but I try not to use it towards other people . . . It depends. It has to be pretty bad to hit them but sometimes it helps and it might not be good but if they deserved it then maybe it's a good thing . . . it helps you feel good.

Depends on what they did, but I don't think they deserve to be beaten up; they deserve to get punched or hit. Oh, no, it's not really teaching them a lesson but it gets your emotions out.

We learned from the alternative school girls that they had several reasons for engaging in the use of aggression and violence: acting out of self-defense, drinking alcohol and losing control, feeling good after punching someone in anger especially if the other person "deserved" it, and the fact that aggression works in that it gets them what they want. These explanations for the use of aggression and violence serve to hold in place behavior that even those using it see as wrong, and are reminiscent of explanations that we have heard many times in the past (Artz, 1998, 2000, 2004; Artz, Blais, & Nicholson, 2000). These explanations seem to offer an instrumental understanding of violence ("I do it to get what I want") or a reactive understanding of violence connected for some to the disinhibiting effects of alcohol and the temporary, but nevertheless good feelings of release that accompany punching someone, especially someone who one sees as deserving it (i.e., violence as a moral necessity provoked by the behavior of others).

Ahmed and Braithwaite (2006) explain the notion of violence as a moral necessity brought on by the behavior of others as a response to strain that assists with dealing with shame. According to Braithwaite (1989), Katz (2002), and Ahmed and Braithwaite (2006), people experience shame in response to an absence of community attachments, parental abandonment, abuse, and feelings of hopelessness, and act to displace that shame by blaming others for their own wrongdoing much as our alternative program participants did. When shame is displaced, a young person dissociates his or her personal actions from the consequences of the action. When social disapproval for a young person's wrongdoing is expressed in disrespectful ways (e.g., social ostracism), the experience of wrongdoing becomes stigmatized and the likelihood that a young person will engage in shame displacement (i.e., blaming others) in the future increases. It is in this way that denial of forgiveness and opportunities for reconciliation by adults can effectively increase aggressive behavior in children and youth. Thus, rather than reacting to misbehavior with exclusionary practices that cause a child to feel stigmatized and lose social ties, a child needs to be "enmeshed in a web of positive social influence" (Ahmed & Braithwaite, 2006: 365) that facilitates their ability to change their behavior. In order to be able to manage shame in an integrative manner and effectively self-regulate against the use of aggression, a young person needs access to emotional support and needs adults in their world to express trust in the young person's abilities and hope for their future.

The alternative program girls' experiences with past victimization and violence seemed to support their current thinking about how aggression and violence work and could certainly be characterized as shame-based as the following excerpts from our interviews will show. Most of the girls in the alternative program reported their first experiences or memories of aggressive and violent behavior involved their families and happened when they were very young:

> I was maybe five or six and my mom was just out of the divorce with my dad and she was going out with this new guy and they moved into his house and . . . after they got married, it was like a week after they got back from their honeymoon or something and he's just shaking her or something like that and I remember seeing that . . . I didn't understand what was going on . . . but I knew he was beating her.
>
> My mom and my dad . . . just yell at each other.

In addition to witnessing aggression and violence between their parents, some of the girls also spoke about being the victims of their parents' aggressive and violent behavior:

> My first mom, she was very abusive to me, and then my grandmother got me.
>
> I was really young and I was chewing gum and it fell out of my mouth and I couldn't find it anywhere and . . . I gave up and . . . went to bed. Like this was like at four [years of age] when I lost the gum, and I went to bed, I get woken up by my stepdad grabbing my neck, lifting me up, bringing me into the living room, throwing my face into the couch and then showing me the gum that was squished on the couch and made me pick it up. And my sister tried to get a fork to like help me pick it out or something, and he got really mad at her and pushed her away.
>
> When I started being aware of violence is when I first saw my foster mom hit my sister. And I didn't like it so I bit her . . . I was like two years old and my sister was like not even one.

One girl in the alternative program explained that she had practiced self-harm by cutting herself for years after having been sexually abused by her stepfather.

Physical fights with siblings were also part of many of the girls' childhoods. In some instances, parents would also participate in physical fights between siblings:

We were trying to beat each other up and he [brother] shut the door on my hand and I'd kick him . . . I was ten or thirteen. He'd be mean or say something, get in my face or like "Oh, you little wussie," taking a shot with me. And I'd try to prove him wrong and push him down and get it a few times . . . I pushed her [sister] . . . She [sister] put me in the hospital . . . Cause I read her diary so she kind of choked me . . . until I passed out . . . I was around nine and she was fifteen or sixteen.

I remember with my mom, I used to fight with her so bad. We used to fight physically too so that was really draining. And my sister, me and my sister used to fight so bad. She was a big girl and I was like one hundred and ten pounds and really skinny and she used to sit on me and suffocate me with pillows and stuff and my mom used to punch me in the face. I never get to punch her back ever . . . It's not fair. And that would really frustrate me is that they could hurt me but I couldn't hurt them back.

For some, like this girl, aggression and violence came to pervade their view of the world:

I've experienced fights over everything. Money, drugs, girls, boys, just objects . . . Everywhere you go. I see violence in everything, right? You can look out the window and watch the kids play at recess and you can see violence.

Aggression and violence in many forms were also pervasive in the alternative school girls' previous school experiences:

I know how it feels to be picked on. Other schools are really racist . . . towards a family life, how you act, how you dress; it's not really the color of your skin, it's who you are . . . Friends can be nice to you then they go back to being rude . . . I was so confused . . . It was usually one of my friends would take my other friend away . . . I got excluded from them all the time . . . it hurt a lot.

I hated elementary school . . . I didn't like how the other girls were treated better than me. Like that's mean . . . The popular, bitchy, prissy girls that get chosen for everything . . . I never got to do anything . . . And it was hard being a third daughter and wearing cast-me-downs constantly so you got people making fun of you.

Like at regular schools everybody is so judgmental. [At most schools] girls don't get along with girls . . . Like it's a competition [for] guys. If you're not dressed to the style, they shun you . . . If you're slower than other students too, you really get judged on that . . . You know, 'Ah ha, you're stupid.'

[If you] walk into a room with like five girls that you don't know, they're not going to just be friendly most of the time. They're going to be like, "Okay, who are you and why are you here?"

There was one girl in [my old school]; she bothered me for a good year and a half and finally it just build up and I snapped . . . Like with her, she was just irritating me and throwing me in a happy circle . . . a huge group of people . . . you get pushed around, shoved around every time you stand up you're pushed around and ninety percent of the time you get thrown into a locker.

The alternative school girls described past school experiences where they almost uniformly felt excluded or neglected by teachers in their prior schools:

[If] you weren't participating in class, they [teachers] didn't ask you what was wrong, they just assumed that you were like all the kids and you just didn't want to [learn].

[At other schools] some kids are really like good with the teacher and other students the teacher just kind of looks over you, kind of ignores you.

I wasn't as likely to ask [questions]. I felt like I was bothering the teacher. I didn't care enough to ask.

She [teacher] used to make fun of me in class, in front of all the other students. She made me feel like a total shit, so I would just hide in the corner and not do anything.

I went to kind of like a hippy [elementary] school . . . I never saw any violence . . . We weren't classrooms, we were called "families" . . . So going to high school was totally shocking. I didn't like the way I was being treated by the teachers because I went from being like twenty kids to a teacher to being like forty kids to a teacher and them not even knowing your name . . . The teachers didn't know you and the different learning styles.

The alternative school girls' past experiences seemed in all ways to set them up for the ongoing use of aggression and violence that they were still, to some degree at least, using in everyday life, but something was also different. Despite everything that they had thus far experienced, they also seem to be in the midst of making a change at least insofar as their school experiences are concerned. As already noted, unlike the girls in the regular high school who participated in this study, the alternative school girls reported high teacher encouragement, low school discouragement, low classroom competition, high classroom cooperation and high school connectedness. It may well be that the approaches of the staff and teachers at the alternative school are providing other options for dealing with interpersonal difficulties for the girls who attend the program.

Interviews with the girls in the alternative program provided details about the elements of support within the program that may well be making a difference. As the girls explained in their interviews, the staff and teachers in the alternative program assisted them with conflict resolution and problem solving at every turn:

> If we have a problem with somebody, then we can tell them to their face and then we don't ever get angry with each other for being honest. I think it all begins with [this school], so we all kind of learn how to be like that with each other . . . They have a way of making you feel like you can really support yourself. Like I found when I wasn't here, I was doing what other people wanted me to do and feeling like I had to kind of put on a mask so I could hide my true self so people wouldn't judge me. When I came here I felt so welcome. And like we have different groups and stuff, like self-esteem groups, and it really helped me to explore my own mind, my own soul.
>
> [Counseling] was through here . . . being able to talk to someone whether it was like going out with my friends or dealing with an issue at home or something like that. It was just like someone who didn't really take sides, like listened.
>
> I was so like shitty and never happy and stuff and I'd be just like fighting all the time in my life . . . I treated people badly yeah. They treat me badly too so it goes both ways . . . My life has totally changed in the past month . . . What really helped me was this school . . . They just helped me to get through stuff and give me advice on how I can go about it and tell me like, what I need to take care of myself.
>
> We do conflict resolution . . . It always works. That's why we get along so well in this school.
>
> It's a lot easier to [defend your beliefs] here, in this community, in this school. [Here] no matter what, you're allowed to say what you want . . . what you believe in . . . and everyone will respect you for saying that.
>
> This is a school where I feel safe. I've never had this kind of help anywhere else that I've gone to.

The theme of feeling cared about was predominant in the girls' descriptions of relationships with the staff and teachers in the alternative program:

> This school is like a home, like a special environment, and I can't describe it, it's just a good place. Like in other schools it's like we're the students and they're the teachers. Like here, the teachers are our friends.

[In my old school] the teachers just want to get paid; here they actually want to get to know you and help you.

At first I wasn't really willing [to participate] because I thought it was the same old shit . . . I kind of came in here with my guards up, and then after a while, I just loved to participate . . . The teachers talk to you and know more about what's going on in your life and they have more of an understanding and they just genuinely care, pretty much . . . If I'm off for a day, someone will ask, "Oh, you weren't here yesterday. What's wrong?"

Kids may make them [teachers] mad, but they [teachers] don't show it at all.

We sit in the same room but we all go at our own pace . . . It's what you want to do when you want to do it kind of thing. But they still have that structure you know like A [teacher] will sit there and be like, "Come on, I know you can do this. You've just got to get yourself going," and she's good about getting people to work.

The girls' interviews highlighted how a sense of belonging and school connectedness were nurtured by the cooperative atmosphere in the alternative program:

We all know each other so well. I think that helps a lot. And we all feel very comfortable talking to each other about everything . . . They know they're not judged . . . This school is the best program I've ever heard of.

You come here and it's like some people are behind you, right where you are, and some people are ahead of you, and they all like help out. They don't laugh at you for not knowing something . . . It helps you open up . . . I wish more schools were like this. I wouldn't be able to go back to a regular school. I tried and I couldn't.

I love it here, so cozy and I know all the girls and I know they don't have a problem with me and they make me feel involved. From day one, they were like "Oh yeah, . . . we'll help you." I like working as a group because you all learn from each other, like especially their opinions. I can't work alone because I have a learning disability. I can't be in normal classrooms, I can't learn. So it's really one-on-one assistance and even some of the girls do that . . . they come over and teach me.

The girls in the alternative program also revealed that part of feeling connected to school derives from having a say in how things are done in the school:

We have a lot of say in how things are done. It's comforting that they care what we think.

We have a lot of say here, 'cause it's smaller, so you get your words out faster. It's a tight-knit community.

We can decide on a lot . . . they have a suggestion box or you just put up your hand, "Oh, I think this," and they'll write it down on the board and if everyone agrees [it gets done].

Here there's lot of different choices and if some of them aren't working for you, you can always tell them. You know they'll get looked at, at least.

The alternative program also helped the girls learn about how to deal with and respect their emotions. The girls told us that the program taught them that emotions are natural and very important sources of information that can be used to help determine one's own personal boundaries. They pointed out that it's important to acknowledge emotions but also to not get overwhelmed by always trying to understand them:

[Emotions] are what people do; humans cry, they get angry, they get sad, they get depressed. It happens . . . You can't really do much about it . . . [just] relax yourself or take that time out that you need . . . I never used to know my boundaries.

[It is important to understand your emotions] or else you're just confusing yourself more and more and you never know what to do . . . you need to be in tune with your emotions or you're going to get screwed up actually.

Emotions mean a lot. Never hold them back, because you'll feel better inside [if you allow emotions] . . . But don't always think about it.

Emotions are really important. I can usually identify what I'm feeling . . . I used to get in a lot of fights with my mom . . . I never really understood that you have to go through another emotion to get to anger . . . I learned that here . . . I can usually pick up on my first emotion and realize that I'm getting to the angry point and I need to calm down, I need to take a break, or I need to get out of the situation right now.

Emotions are very real and you shouldn't ignore them or try to make them go away. You should just feel your emotions . . . [Emotions help] you know how to stop yourself from getting angry or aggressive because you can feel yourself and you can either choose to be violent or choose not to . . . Before, when I was younger, I'd just blame everyone else . . . You've got to own your own shit.

The girls in the alternative program noted that learning about emotions helped them to avoid hurting other people:

> You can never really tell what other people are feeling, you should always ask.
>
> Before, I used to push them [emotions] aside. Now I'm starting to like identify my emotions and I've learned to respect them . . . and it started me looking at how I treat other people.
>
> You can't really *understand* other people's emotions but you can respect them and how they're feeling on different things.

Those girls in the program who were pregnant acknowledged learning about the role that hormones during pregnancy played on their emotions. The young mothers in the program spoke about how learning about their own emotions helped them to learn to identify and respect their child's emotions and also helped them to be better parents:

> I think it's really important to understand a child's emotions because they're not sure of them yet. Like they're just learning them and they get frustrated and stuff and you have to try to help them so that they know it's okay to feel that way.
>
> I think it is really important to understand how he [son] is feeling. If he is upset, I don't want to try to play with him, you know, like if he's crying.
>
> I think that it's very important to understand your child's emotions because otherwise you . . . can't possibly act on them . . . If he [son] is upset because he's hungry and I give him Tylenol because I believe it's his teeth, well that's not helping him. And he has different cries, different emotions.

One young mother acknowledged aloud that parents can hurt their children "by not taking care of themselves." Another young mother told us that she recognizes that her son can sense when she is angry or upset:

> He can feel it in my heartbeat and he can feel it in the tone of voice I use . . . I'll go have a glass of water or have a cigarette or whatever, calm down, give myself a couple of minutes to breathe, and then I'll go pick him up and he's happy.

The clear and often evocative statements provided by the alternative program girls certainly assisted us with understanding why these girls who, given their past victimization experiences might have been expected to score much lower on teacher encouragement, school discouragement, classroom cooperation, and school connectedness, responded as positively as they did to our survey questions.

DISCUSSION

In tying our findings to current research we theorized that what is different for the alternative school girls who participated in our study is that the strain of victimization experienced by these girls is buffered by the practices of their staff and teachers. The alternative school girls had, as they told us in their interviews, been subjected to an absence of community, and a variety of abusive experiences at the hands of teachers, parents, other family members, and intimates in their lifeworlds, and in the process, been shamed and had learned to perpetuate the cycle of abuse by blaming their victims for their own aggressive and violent behavior. But these girls were also moving toward a different understanding of how anger and conflict could be dealt with. Robbers (2004) stated that social support—the network of people who one turns to in times of stress—can act as a buffer to strain. When a person feels valued, cared for, loved and belongs to a network of emotional support, she or he is more likely to respond in socially adaptive ways to experiences with stress and strain. The types of strain often experienced by females include gender discrimination, sexual, emotional or physical abuse, restrictions on activities, and excessive demands from family. All of these forms of strain can create obstacles to forming meaningful interpersonal relationships that decrease opportunities for the buffering effect of social support, effectively exacerbating experiences of strain. Robbers (2004) investigated gendered responses to strain and found that for females, the likelihood of delinquent behavior decreases when they have high levels of social support.

While having the potential for turning around the shame-based cycle of aggression and abuse, the supportive practices of the alternative school staff and teachers also seem to be just what Moretti, DaSilva, and Holland (2004) call for with respect to how we might positively intervene with aggressive and violent girls. As Moretti and colleagues state, "interventions [with aggressive and violent girls] are most likely to be effective when they assist girls to better meet their needs for interpersonal connectedness in ways that are neither hurtful to themselves or others" (52). The alternative program, by offering a cooperative, encouraging atmosphere that supports the girls' feelings of belonging and connectedness in the program also provides a context in which the use of aggression is not required[4] even if the respondents still believe aggression and violence are required elsewhere. Opportunities for education, achievement, personal growth, and connectedness to a community are protective factors against girls' aggressive and violent behavior (Artz & Nicholson, 2002). When working to create a supportive school climate, it is important to create a cooperative milieu, and ensure that students feel encouraged at and connected to school. A considerable research literature states that the development of a sense of school belonging depends upon a cooperative school environment (Battistich et al., 1997; Natvig, Albrektsen, & Qvarnstrøm, 2003; Schaps, 2002). Other research attests to the importance of taking students' concerns seriously, providing them with opportunities to experience competence, respecting them as individuals, and ensuring that they have a voice in decision-making (Baker & Bridger, 1997; Fallis & Opotow, 2003).

We argue that it is important in research and practice to not underestimate the power that school context has to influence the use of aggressive and violent behavior (Powell, 2003). When aggression is viewed as an interactive social issue rather than a problem that exists within individuals (Whitmer, 1997), it becomes possible to envision how social contexts can inform the sense-making that goes into determining action, especially among youth who have, in their pasts, existed in contexts that make the use of aggression and violence viable behavioral options. Encouraging prosocial over aggressive behavior largely depends on a school's ability to create an interpersonal climate wherein even youth who have been highly victimized can feel safe, supported, valued, and able to participate in learning.

This research suggests that investigations into aggressive behavior can benefit from considering the contextual conditions that inform decision-making for action. Schools like the alternative school described here can serve as exemplary models for the creation of contexts that support high-risk girls to take positive steps toward pursuing and achieving their goals in life.

NOTES

1. This study was part of a five-year (2002–2007) Canadian Institutes of Health Research (CIHR)-funded New Emerging Team longitudinal research project entitled *Aggressive and Violent Girls: Contributing Factors, Developmental Course and Intervention Strategies*. The principal investigator on the team was Dr. Marlene Moretti; the co-investigators were: Dr. Marc LeBlanc, Dr. Candice Odgers, Dr. Nadine Lanctôt, Dr. Bonnie Leadbeater, and Dr. Sibylle Artz. Each co-investigator was responsible for independently conducting research that contributed to the overall findings of the project.

2. A copy of the survey can be obtained by contacting the authors.

3. We acknowledge that even though some differences are not statistically significant, there appear to be large mean differences between the two groups. However, our small sample sizes make our results suggestive rather than definitive.

4. The emphasis on conflict resolution skill development and practices in the alternative program also contribute to the girls being able to respond in non-aggressive ways to perceived threats or the misbehaviors of other students which, in another context might be seen as fodder for aggressive responses.

REFERENCES

AAUW Educational Foundation. (2001). *Hostile hallways: Bullying, teasing and sexual harassment in school*. Washington, DC: American Association of University Women. www.aauw.org (accessed 15 October 2008).

Ahmed, E., & Braithwaite, V. (2006). Forgiveness, reconciliation, and shame: Three key variables in reducing school bullying. *Journal of Social Issues* 62(2): 347–370.

Artz, S. (1998). *Sex, power, and the violent school girl*. Toronto, ON: Trifolium.

Artz, S. (2000). Considering adolescent girls' use of violence: A researcher's reflections on her inquiry. *B.C. Counselor* 22(1): 45–54.

Artz, S. (2004). Revisiting the moral domain: Using social interdependence theory to understand adolescent girls' perspectives on the use of violence. In M. Moretti, M. Jackson, and C. Odgers (eds.), *Girls and Aggression: Contributing Factors and Intervention Principles* (101–114) New York, NY: Kluwer/Plenum.

Artz, S., Blais, M., & Nicholson, D. (2000). Developing Girls' Custody Units, Phase 1 Report to Justice Canada, Ottawa, ON.

Artz, S., & Nicholson, D. (2002). *Aggressive girls: Overview paper*. National Clearinghouse on Family Violence, Health Canada, Family Violence Prevention Unit, Ottawa, Ontario.

Artz, S., & Riecken, T. (1994a). *A study of violence among adolescent female students in a suburban school district*. Ministry of Education, Research & Evaluation Branch, and Gender Equity Programs.

Artz, S., & Riecken, T. (1994b). *Final report: A study of violence among adolescent female students in a suburban school district*. For Gender Equity Programs, Ministry of Education and Ministry Responsible for Multiculturalism and Human Rights.

Baker, J., & Bridger, R. (1997). Schools as caring communities: A relational approach to school reform. *School Psychology Review* 26(4), EBSCOHOST (accessed 24April 2002).

Battistich, V., Solomon, D., Watson, S., & Schaps, E. (1997). Caring school communities. *Educational Psychologist* 32(3): 137–151.

Braithwaite, J. (1989). *Crime, shame and reintegration*. New York, NY: Cambridge University Press.

Card, N., Isaacs, J., & Hodges, E. (2007). Correlates of school victimization: Implications for prevention and intervention. In J. Zins, M. Elisa, & C. Maher (eds.), *Bullying, Victimization and Peer Harassment: A Handbook of Prevention and Intervention* (339–366). New York, NY: Haworth.

Christle, C., Nelson, C. M., & Jolivette, K. (2004). School characteristics related to the use of suspension. *Education and Treatment of Children* 27(4): 509–526.

Fallis, R., & Opotow, S. (2003). Are students failing school or are schools failing students? Class cutting in high school. *Journal of Social Issues* 59(1): 103–119.

Graham, S., Bellmore, A., & Mize, J. (2006). Peer victimization, aggression, and their co-occurrence in middle school: Pathways to adjustment problems. *Journal of Abnormal Child Psychology* 34(3): 363–378.

Holt, M., & Espelage, D. (2007). A cluster analytic investigation among high school students: Are profiles differentially associated with psychological symptoms and school belonging? In J. Zins, M. Elisa, & C. Maher (eds.), *Bullying, Victimization and Peer Harassment: A Handbook of Prevention and Intervention* (85–102). New York, NY: Haworth.

Johnson, D. W., & Johnson, R. T. (1989). *Cooperation and Competition: Theory and Research*. Edina, MN: Interaction Book Company.

Johnson, D., & Johnson, R. (1998). Cooperative learning and social interdependence theory. In *Social Psychological Applications to Social Issues*. www.cooperation.org/pages/SIT.html (accessed 16 August 2005).

Katz, R. (2002). Re-examining the Integrative Social Capital theory of crime. *Western Criminology Review* 4(1): 30–54.

Katz, R. (2004). Explaining girls' and women's crime and desistance in the context of their victimization experiences: A developmental test of revised strain theory and the life course perspective. In M. Chesney-Lind & L. Pasko (eds.), *Girls, Women and Crime: Selected Readings* (24–41). Thousand Oaks, CA: Sage.

Lan, W., & Lanthier, R. (2003). Changes in students' academic performance and perceptions of school and self before dropping out of schools. *Journal of Education for Students Placed at Risk* 8(3): 309–332.

Levene, K., Madsen, K., & Pepler, D. (2004). Girls growing up angry: A qualitative study. In D. Pepler, K. Madsen, C. Webster, & K. Levene (eds.), *The Development and Treatment of Girlhood Aggression* (169–190). Toronto, ON: Lawrence Erlbaum.

Magnuson, D. (2002). Qualities of moral experience under cooperative, competitive and individualistic conditions. Unpublished manuscript, Cedar Falls, Iowa, School of Health, Physical Education and Leisure Services, University of Northern Iowa.

Morash, M., & Chesney-Lind, M. (2009). The context of girls' violence. In M. Zahn (ed.), *The Delinquent Girl* (182–206). Philadelphia, PA: Temple University Press.

Moretti, M., DaSilva, K., & Holland, R. (2004). Aggression in adolescent girls from an attachment perspective: Research findings and therapeutic implications. In M. Moretti, C. Odgers, & M. Jackson (eds.), *Girls and Aggression: Contributing Factors and Intervention Principles* (41–56). Boston, MA: Kluwer.

Natvig, G., Albrektsen, G., & Qvarnstrøm, U. (2003). Methods of teaching and class participation in relation to perceived social support and stress: Modifiable factors for improving health and well-being among students. *Educational Psychology* 23(3): 261–274.

Paul, J., & Cillessen, A. (2007). Dynamics of peer victimization in early adolescence: Results for a four-year longitudinal study. In J. Zins, M. Elisa, & C. Maher (eds.), *Bullying, Victimization and Peer Harassment: A Handbook of Prevention and Intervention* (29–47). New York, NY: Haworth.

Payne, A., Gottfredson, D., & Kruttschnitt, C. (2009). Girls, schooling and delinquency. In M. Zahn (ed.), *The Delinquent Girl* (147–163). Philadelphia, PA: Temple University Press.

Porter, E. (1991). *Women and moral identity*. North Sydney, NSW: Allen & Unwin.

Powell, L. (2003). On (not) "coloring in the outline." *Journal of Social Issues* 59(1): 197–211.

Resnick, M., Bearman, P., Blum, R., Bauman, K., Harris, K., Jones, J., Tabor, J., Beuhring, T., Sieving, R., Shew, M., Ireland, M., Bearinger, L., & Udry, R. (1997). Protecting adolescents from harm: Findings from the National Longitudinal Study on Adolescent Health. *JAMA* 278: 823–832.

Robbers, M. (2004). Revisiting the moderating effect of social support on strain: A gendered test. *Sociological Inquiry* 74(4): 546–569.

Sanders, C., & Phye, G. (2004). *Bullying: Implications for the Classroom*. San Diego, CA: Elsevier Academic Press.

Schaps, E. (2002). Community in school: Central to character formation and more. Paper presented at the White House Conference on Character and Community, 19 June 2002, Washington, DC. [electronic source] http://www.ed.gov/admins/lead/safety/character/schaps.pdf. (accessed 18 June 2004).

Schwartz, D. (2000). Subtypes of victims and aggressors in children's peer groups. *Journal of Abnormal Child Psychology* 28(2): 181–192.

Serbin, L., Cooperman, J., Peters, P., Lehoux, P., Stack, D., & Schwartzman, A. (1998). Intergenerational transfer of psychosocial risk in women with histories of aggression, withdrawal, or aggression and withdrawal. *Developmental Psychology* 34: 1246–1262.

Whitmer, B. (1997). *The violence mythos*. Albany, NY: State University of New York Press.

EIGHT

NEGOTIATIONS OF THE LIVING SPACE

Life in the Group Home for Girls Who Use Violence

Marion Brown

SETTING THE CONTEXT

Ruth was 17 years old when she moved into the group home where I was working. She had experienced horrendous abuse and violence in her family home, woken in the mornings by her stepfather's hands around her throat. She was running away from home, struggling in school, and feeling desperate. I was certain that she was better off living at the group home; I was sure we could provide a safe and comforting space to live, support her in school, and work with her on the layers of hurt in her life.

Six months later, the previously drug-free Ruth was coming home stoned each day. She was arrested for shoplifting on her eighteenth birthday. When she was suspended from school after several incidents of beating up other girls, my unease reached its peak. Not enough that I struggled with the tension of the care and control aspects of my role, I now struggled with the increasing experience that the very setting that had promised to heal from the past had paved an equally troubling future.

Working in group homes, I have met many young women like Ruth, and have had many anxious discussions with colleagues about how to balance

175

the potential harms of the residential context with the potential helps that it could provide, conversations that continue today. This chapter is based on research with girls who live in groups homes and their use of violence, an interest spurred on by the nagging concern that the group home's structural need for compliance, in combination with early experiences of violent subcultures and the societal culture of compulsory heterosexuality and hegemonic femininity, might perpetuate a climate within which girls engage in violent behavior as a means of experiencing personal power. I wondered if the group home might be a site for the evidence of these tensions and I wanted to learn from the girls about how they make sense of their lives.

INTRODUCTION

Over the past ten years, media attention in Canada has constructed an interest in and focus on sensational events involving girls' engagement with violent behaviors, from harassment and bullying, to assault and murder, contributing to a sense of moral panic on the part of the public. The formal code for responses to criminal charges in Canada, the Youth Criminal Justice Act, mandates a move toward community-based placements and programs rather than incarceration for crimes by both male and female youth (Department of Justice, Canada, 2002). This chapter draws on research with girls who live in group homes because of their use of violence, seeking to understand how the girls make sense of the rules, the roles, and the requirements of a range of socially controlled settings. The historical origins of residential care settings are reviewed before contextualizing violence in the early lives of the girls. Listening to the stories of the girls led to the development of a conceptual framework for understanding the dynamics of context and behavior, drawing on Foucault's work on discipline and punishment (1979).

RESIDENTIAL SETTINGS: PURPOSES AND PROGRAMMING

Children's residential facilities began to be developed in industrial times, when children moved from rural to urban settings for work and therefore became more visible to the public eye. Increased mobility and opportunities for labor led to the separation of many children from their parents, a situation considered to have weakened parental oversight and authority (Rutman, 1987). In Canada, private charity merged with governmental responsibility to establish a range of services for children's welfare, leading to the passage of the Industrial Schools Act of 1874 (Rutman, 1987). This Act encouraged the opening of residential, custodial, and educational settings for youth under the age of 14 who were considered "out of control" or without appropriate parental supervision.

Although the Canadian literature is silent on the history of placing *girls* in surrogate care sites, examples of correctional and training facilities in the United States are instructive. For example, in the United States, the response to girls' behavior through the juvenile court system and training schools has historically been associated with anticipated precocious sexual expression (Abrams & Curran, 2000). Training schools and reformatories sought to realign girls with traditional prescriptions for femininity, believing complete immersion was required. The girl was removed from society's temptations immediately upon signs of "trouble," to be returned to society equipped to become a wife and mother: domesticity was the goal. Chastity, compliance, and compassion were considered central to the progress of humanity, and the moral fibre of girls, then as now, was considered a cornerstone to the preservation of families, the social order, and the caring contract (Abrams & Curran, 2000; Reitsma-Street, 1998).

Literature on programming within residential youth care began to emerge in the 1950s, with the publication of Bruno Bettelheim's *Love Is Not Enough* (1950) and Redl and Wineman's *Children Who Hate* (1951) and *Controls From Within* (1952). The latter of Redl and Wineman's books focused attention on the residential milieu as the central therapeutic influence for change. While this concept of milieu had been in the literature since August Aichhorn's work in the 1920s (cited in Trieschman, Whittaker, & Brendtro, 1969), Redl and Wineman developed a framework for therapeutic programming and the role of the residential child and youth care worker based on the context of the shared living space. Expanding upon these ideas further, Trieschman et al. (1969) wrote of *The Other 23 Hours* outside the psychotherapy office and the growing legitimacy of the "lifespace" of youth as the primary site of therapeutic influence. The use of daily life events for therapeutic purposes was developed as the core intervention principle in the lifespace (Garfat, 1998).

Organizational theory cites that "the central characteristic of residential settings for youth is their relative separation from the outside world" (Arieli, Beker, & Kashti, 2001: 404), a position congruent with the early purposes of placing delinquent girls in reformatory schools. At the same time, the ultimate goal is reentry to the family and community schooling so that progression into adult correctional institutions is less likely. A further component in milieu programming/residential care is the premise of normalization, wherein ordinary experiences are created and shared so that boys and girls in residential care feel less differentiated and marginalized under the community labels of being "troublesome" or "delinquent" (Whitaker, 1981).

Programming in residential youth care facilities has undergone significant philosophical shifts over the years (Garfat & Mitchell, 2000). In the 1970s and 1980s the provision of basic care in group homes was the norm, in the belief that a safe and steady home-styled setting could provide the guidance and structure necessary for growth toward social citizenship. More recently, through the 1990s and into the 2000s, residential facilities are expected to provide treatments and interventions to *resolve* the difficulties that precipitate a youth entering the residential care system. Emphasis shifted to creating a therapeutic milieu with a focus on behavioral, emotional, and psychological change through simplified behavior modification approaches (Garfat & Mitchell, 2000).

As the field of youth care has developed its philosophies of treatment and intervention, practitioners in the field now advocate moving away from behavior modification to a relationship- and process-based approach for work with troubled youth and their families (Garfat, 1998; Krueger, 1988, 1998). Relationship-based approaches are founded upon John Bowlby's attachment theory (Bowlby, 1979; Snow & Finlay, 1998; Steinhauer, 1991). Attachment theory is based on the notion that nurturance, stimulation, structure, and security are required for the normal, healthy development of all children (Bowlby, 1979). The nature and intensity of the infant-caregiver(s) bond (most often with the mother) determines the degree to which these primary needs are met (Bowlby, 1979). Best practices in residential programming currently advocate the child or youth being placed geographically close to the family of origin, with collaboration of service personnel "wrapping around" the young person in order to provide comprehensive planning (VanDenBerg & Grealish, 1996). Intervention planning is based on establishing meaningful relationships between youth and practitioners and analysis of the needs underlying problematic behaviors (Garfat, 1998; Snow & Finlay, 1998).

Like many helping professions, the field of residential child and youth care struggles to negotiate the competing demands of care and control (Carniol, 2000; Heinonen & Spearman, 2001; Mullaly, 1997, 2002), and working with girls who use violence brings this dialectic into sharp focus. For example, rooted in gender essentialisms, care professionals anticipate that boys will *externalize* their pain, and expect and prefer girls to *internalize* their pain and/or reveal it clearly by communicating in relationships. When they do not, two difficulties must be "managed": the externalized behaviors, for example, the thrown furniture, the property damage, or the assaulted person; and the ideological contradiction: the girl who is not only non-compliant in her behavior, but also in our understanding of her as a young woman.

This level of analysis is absent from the existing residential child and youth care literature. First, there is a homogenization of "youth" in the residential care field, such that, for example, an article detailing a "framework for understanding client violence in residential treatment" (McAdams & Foster, 1999) does not differentiate between male and female clients (or workers, for that matter). Arieli et al. (2001) reviews the "opportunities and risks" of the residential setting as a socialization context and no mention is made of opportunities and risks associated with gender socialization, identity, or performance. Ward (2004) writes of the need for a theoretical framework to guide analysis and planning of "every detail, function and interaction of daily group care practice with young people" (209) and yet leaves out the "details" of sex, gender, and race. Consistent throughout the narrow literature on residential child and youth care is the muting of sex, gender, masculinities and femininities, race, class and ability. The result is that "youth in care" become characterized as a single population, and in the absence of intersectional analyses, the template for normalcy based upon the Eurocentric, hetero-normative, white, able-bodied male, already in evidence throughout the West, remains dominant.

The absence of gender analyses in the child and youth care literature means that the corollary issues of sexism and objectification, heterosexism, racism, classism, and ableism are also absent. Thus the material conditions that shape young people's lives beyond the isolated milieu of the residential setting are ignored. Micro analysis of interaction and relationships is pursued without situating these within the material realities of the macro world. One such example is the way non-compliance by girls is conceptualized and understood. Gendered socialization prescribes that girls are raised to care for others and define themselves in terms of relationships with others, and are often socially punished for not doing so (Reitsma-Street, 1998; Underwood, 2004). Residential group home sites typically prioritize compliance with the organizational routines of the setting and individualized development plans for each resident, without analysis regarding how compliance is uniquely situated for girls. The girl that resists, swears, hits, and otherwise refuses to "go along" with standard expectations is "a problem." However, just at the moment when violent and non-compliant girls in residential care seem to be a thorough challenge to the construction of femininity, one person emerges toward whom the essentialized notions of girlhood are directed: the boyfriend. Here is where non-compliance turns to compliance, primarily in regard to romanticized notions of heterosexual relationship. Here is where the persona of defiance and non-compliance is subjugated, and here is where the greatest danger lies in the mutual reinforcement of compulsory heterosexuality and hegemonic femininity. At long last, here is the compliance that is sought, yet in a context where the young woman is most vulnerable to exploitation, violence, isolation, and distress (Tolman et al., 2003).

OVERVIEW OF THE RESEARCH

This qualitative research study asked 22 young women what it means to them to be female, to use violence, and to live in group homes. Conversations unpacked each of these facets of their lives as well as detailed their interrelations and correlations. Their stories suggest that girls are continually negotiating the terms of what it means to be female, shaping and being shaped by gender stereotypes, role models, interactions with boys, and the ongoing scrutiny of other girls as extensions of themselves. These girls talked of fighting each other based on principles of loyalty and morality, in short, fighting when they "had to." They also fight each other to convey specific messages about boys, being verbally maligned and having their belongings stolen. Finally, and centered in this chapter, the narratives of the girls told that navigating the living space is an ongoing and intricate process, one that begins with understanding the formal and informal rules and comes to life amid the shifting dynamics among and between staff and residents in ways that keep them forever on their toes.

SITUATING VIOLENCE

It is important to contextualize the violence by girls within the geographic area of central Nova Scotia, Canada, to situate it within the subject of youth violence so steadily in the media across Canada and beyond. Parameters are required so the reader has a sense of the scope of the definitions, incidences, and their impact on the communities involved. All the girls in this research had fought physically with other girls, as well as at least one of the following: siblings, parents, teachers, foster parents, and group home staff. All defined violence as physically hurting another person. While we discussed verbal harassment and relational aggression as violence, the girls were clear that there is a vast distinction between these and what they consider violence, both in terms of the nature of contact and the degree of impact. They defined violence as the physical striking or manipulation of another person's body with some part of their body. Hand-to-hand fights were the norm, with little mention of use of weapons and no talk of involvement in gangs.[1] All the girls self-defined as violent in this way, though more than half spoke of these as *past*, not current, behaviors. At the same time, all the girls acknowledged that they would fight again if they "needed to."

Further, the girls' familiarity with violence began when they were small children. It was part of the scenery, an accustomed contributor to daily life. As Zoe[2] (15, Aboriginal) said, "It was all around me." There was no demarcation point signaling when violence entered the lives of these girls. Mothers, fathers, stepmothers, stepfathers, uncles, aunts, brothers, sisters, cousins, relatives, friends, boyfriends, and school experiences provided models for violent behaviors. Violence pervades the lives of these girls, in their homes and neighborhoods, on television, in music, movies, and video games, such that they are all intimately familiar with it. Thus there is a porous boundary between having perpetrated violence and having been victimized by violence. Some overtly reflected on their childhoods as a frightening time. Bobbi (14, white) said,

> All the violence and stuff happened around me and it was mostly because of everyone drinking . . . Family, friends, like my family's friends, [when I was] five, six, seven, eight, nine, ten. [I felt] bad, scared, not safe.

Others readily rhymed off concrete messages of violence in their midst. For example Hanna's (15, white) mother's tattoos said "fighting bitch." Erin (17, white) was chased by her siblings with a knife, and Shannon (20, white) watched her parents "practically kill each other." Sylvie (15, Aboriginal) said,

> My sister and I, we would play fight, where our version of play fight basically would be pulling out each other's hair, punching each other in the guts, you know, really beating each other up, pushing each other down stairs, slamming each other's head into doors, people slamming each other to the floor, full nelsons, half nelsons, you know, and that was our play fighting (laughing) . . . We basically . . . try to break your nose first so you'll hold your nose up and [then] get . . . punched in the stomach, so you know, you go down faster. So once you're down you kick, like a few times, in the stomach, and if you're really violent you kick them in the head . . . Yeah, my uncles taught me how to fight.

Jodi's (15, African Nova Scotian) words *imply* harm rather than name it explicitly when she spoke of her mother:

> I'm not allowed to see her. If she comes to see me she'll be in jail. I don't know why. I never got to talk to her yet.

Inside the home and out in the neighborhood, violence is indeed "all around" these girls. Natasha (15, African Nova Scotian) reflected on the region where she grew up:

> Where I lived . . . violence every day, just the area I lived in . . . Finding people getting shot, people getting stabbed, people getting drownded [sic], people getting ganged.

Description soon led to thoughts on coping and surviving in the setting. Shannon (20, white) spoke to her means for coping with her early environment when she said, "That's just how I was brought up. If someone wants to fight ya, it doesn't matter if you're gonna win or lose, you just gotta stick with it and try your hardest." Alex's (18, white) strategies led toward one outcome: "Don't come home and say you got beat."

In this pervasive *context* of violence, *use* of violence is so normalized that there is a closer proximal step to its enactment. The girls did not cross a line one day, moving from victim to perpetrator. Their use of violence was not retold according to a catalyst event. The move was seamless, between being witness to and living in an environment of violence to using violence to protect or express oneself. Further, the "violent" label was at once both situational and integrated. To be violent depends on one's assessment regarding the requirements of the context. Violence emanates from the conditions and circumstances, rather than from whom one is as a person. At the same time, the requirements for violence are intimately experienced and persistently reinforced, shaping the actions and behaviors of these girls.

NEGOTIATING THE LIVING SPACE

The living space figures prominently in the lives of these girls, given that context both shapes and is shaped by the people in its midst, and group homes are sites where girls both use and experience aggression and violence. The girls in this study had lived in a range of residential settings and systems, including hospital inpatient units, foster homes, assessment facilities, homeless shelters, short-term receiving centers, secure facilities and, as the common denominator, long-term group homes. While not all had been incarcerated, it was clear that all these girls experienced degrees of custody, considering their experiences in out-of-home placements.

Negotiating the living space of the group home is an ongoing and intricate process. It begins with concrete understandings about the written rules and moves to figuring out the unwritten expectations, unspoken norms and codes of relationships within the program. There are always girls (or in coed facilities, boys as well) moving in and out, continually shifting the relationship dynamics in the facility. Staff members come and go on their shifts, with different combinations of staff also altering dynamics. The living space is always in flux, shuffled daily, hourly, and moment by moment, with many disparate personalities and roles in the mix. Becoming adept at managing the shifting relations becomes an unarticulated yet required skill. Ultimately, strategies are required in order to survive in that milieu. Reading the physical setting, the codified rules and the people within, and managing as much as possible the reading others have of you, is necessary to just get by.

CHOICE AND CONSTRAINT

The first order of business upon moving into a group setting is to learn the written, formal rules, such as curfews, chores, phone and television time, regulations regarding contact with family and friends, bed times, and expectations regarding school and programming. Given the range of mandates among the facilities, the rules vary considerably. Representing opposite ends of a continuum, independence-oriented homes were consistently more highly valued by the girls than those with strict rules and secure care facilities. For girls in independence-oriented group living settings, choice was highlighted as a defining and prized feature. However, recognition of choice was not conflated with appreciation for it: girls living with individualized routines were clear that they had earned it through their current choices and record of compliance with the structured expectations of social workers and youth care facility workers. They were *entitled to it*, as opposed to *grateful for it*. Jackie (16, white) spoke to what it takes to maintain her independence-oriented placement:

> It's an awesome house. I love it. I wouldn't want to be at any other group home. To tell you a matter-of-fact I probably wouldn't go to another group home. If they tried to send me, I (tsk), I don't know where I'd go but I wouldn't go because I'm not one for group homes. It's pretty laid back; it's pretty much "do what you want to do." You know go out first thing in the morning, just come back by your curfew. That's it. You don't have to come home for supper, whatever. This house is an independent living house, so your stay is up to you. If you want to live in Samuel House and not follow through and not go to school and not do what's expected of me, you get kicked out—point blank. They'll give you a couple of chances but you get kicked out.

At the other end of the spectrum is the province's secure care facility, where a family court judge has suspended the civil liberty of freedom and ordered a secure care certificate for 30 days (Children and Family Services Act, 1990, Sections 55–59). Although sometimes refuting the reasons for being placed in the secure facility, while placed there the girls seem to recognize that being in secure care cannot be argued. Emily (16, Aboriginal) reported that she recommends anyone living in secure make good use of the time: "You just take what they give you, learn it, and don't do it to just do it, actually learn what you're supposed to be learning; then you can get out of here faster."

Looking back on being in the secure facility, however, can be a different story. Tonya (16, African Nova Scotian) talked about the windows that can't be open or broken: "Full of windows . . . you're in there looking out at where you want to be." Emily (16, Aboriginal) echoed the same thought when she said, "They give you this room and all you do is look out the window and there's nothing there, you need space. You can't lock a kid up in a small room when they're mad, then you just think." Jackie (16, white) expanded on the concern:

> [Being in the secure facility] is not a sensible experience for kids I don't think. . . . I just disagree with the whole situation [because] you've gotta know if you want to change. . . . Someone can't make that decision for them. [Being in the secure facility is] going to kind of make them more pissed off and more aggravated and that's going to lead to anger for someone making that decision for that

person. . . . They have to have a slap in the face of reality to not want to continue fighting.

In the middle of the continuum, what seems most difficult is living in community group homes, with unlocked doors and windows but with strict expectations regarding curfew, contact and activity. Jodi (15, African Nova Scotian) said,

> I think it's like pretty strict [here]. Like they're telling me they want me to stay in, that they want the girls to stay in. Like how are we going to do that if you've got strict, strict rules? Here, when I say "I'm going over town," they say "Where over town?" "Down the Block." "Where in the Block?" Like you have to tell them which street you're going to walk on. They're too strict. I dunno—they like need to change their system bad. Cuz I'm like, ok how am I going to stay here? If you guys are always strict that's what makes me want to leave . . . Like girls like being free and they don't like people being right in their business . . . cuz, like that's not a normal life, no, that's not freedom at all. They said we're mostly, we're more, we're more stable having them rules in place. I think that's false.

In contrast, the same young woman, when I saw her while living in the secure facility two months later, said,

> Whatcha gonna do? I gotta be here, I was here before and I know what I gotta do. Ain't nothin' I can do but do my 30 days. (Jodi, 15, African Nova Scotian)

Sometimes the rules make no difference to the choices of the residents. At times the girls plan on serving their consequences when they decide to stay out all night, as in the case of Carly (14, white) who said that "weekends are my time," and after going to school and complying with other expectations for the week, she would do what she wanted on the weekends, including being "gone without permission." She knew she would incur consequences, and she would serve them, but they were not going to deter her from spending her free time the ways she chose. In other cases, regardless of the rules, as Tonya (16, African Nova Scotian) said,

> the girls did whatever they wanted, we'd go out, stay out all night, we didn't go to school, do chores . . . it might have been the expectation that we do those things but they [staff] didn't do nothin' if we didn't.

While sorting out the material setting and its expression through rules, the girls also embark on an unspoken process of dissecting the *unspoken* realms of choice and constraint: the tone and the atmosphere that underscore the house dynamics. First among these, for Bobbi (14, white), is assessing trust:

> It's kinda different though, because like . . . there's this whole group of people that you can't, some of them you can't really trust. And it's hard to get close to those [new] people cuz you didn't know them for a long time, you're just moving around from group home to group home, so it's hard to talk about things. Total strangers. That takes a while to build a relationship.

There is also the discursive adjustment to make, in addition to the material, that this is where one is now living. Shannon (20, white) named this explicitly when she said,

> The first time I went in it was really scary cuz I never been in anything like that . . . I'd never been away from my mom. It was really weird, and there was all these people in there, and like one of my good friends I'd known forever, she was in too, she was like "oh, you're living here now?" I was like "*Living? What?*"

The subtext to this feature of living in group settings is one of choice and constraint, and assessing one's situation against that continuum. Personal behaviors and decisions as well as rights and entitlements are assessed according to expectations and experiences of choice and constraint. Questions of responsibility are weighed as well: to what degree is it my responsibility to comply with the (structural) expectations? Self-assessment reigns over the assessment of social workers and facility staff, whose evaluations are considered partial (Aja,14, white said, "They never know the whole story"), biased (Jodi, 15, African Nova Scotian said, "They only see what they wanna see"), and/or unreasonable (Tonya, 16, African Nova Scotian said, "They can't expect me to do that"). The only authentic judge is oneself. Upon this self-assessment rests the degree to which the girls *accept* the terms of their choices and constraints.

"MAKING ME WORSE"

The very behaviors that social workers, family members, school personnel, youth care workers, and therapists want to interrupt and extinguish were often developed, enhanced, and subversively encouraged while living in group care settings. Aja (14, white) said, "I swear to God this place is just making me worse." Techniques for stealing were learned, different drugs tried, new accomplices met, networks for selling stolen goods established, and the ever-present peer audience prompted, cajoled, cheered, and endorsed engagement in violence and all things forbidden. Given these experiences, some girls expressed surprise this model of care is promoted by the state. Others such as Carly (14, white) voiced that "if they're so stupid to put us all together, then oh well." Jodi (15, African Nova Scotian) detailed her experiences relative to behaviors and their consequences:

> Like, group homes, I don't think they should even exist . . . cuz I never used to take off. I never . . . like I wasn't as bad as I am now. Now, I'm starting to do drugs because of group homes. I take off every day, I don't do as good as I used to at school. Like, group homes just mess up your life I think . . . Because there's so much negativity around. There's so much pressure, you don't even know. I try, I've been in group homes for two years now . . . and I've been trying to fight it off all those months and all those years. I would try to fight it off so bad and . . . I was doing good but sometimes you can't be around negativity and pressure all that time. You just end up like fucked. I'm not that fucked up yet, but I'm gonna if I don't stop myself. And I am trying to stop myself. I am trying to get myself help and stuff. Just uh, it's not like working.

Shannon (20, white) described the connection between group norms and decision-making:

> I don't know why but everyone else was egging me on: "Come on Shan, come fight her, come fight her." [I was] like "Okay, let's go." I wanted to show people that I wasn't weak, that I could do it.

Carly (14, white) corroborated that "fights are always worse in group homes, because there's always a crowd there, always someone wanting you to fight." Ciara (16, Aboriginal) said that the group can influence how long a fight continues: "It depends, like if the person thinks they're done with you they'll stop but sometimes people will be like 'oh, come on, continue, continue' or they'll just pull people off and they'll say 'okay, I'm done, I'm done.'" According to Shannon (20, white), fights in group homes are

> way more likely to happen because like, you don't always get along with someone in the house. Then the group is like "fight, fight, come on," [and] you just wanna like knock her out, and it's like . . . all these people are really yelling and then you're in trouble . . . And like, it's, if you're in a fight it's on purpose. Normally there's one person in the house that nobody likes [and then a fight is] way

more likely to happen, cuz . . . if you're the person fighting the one
that nobody likes and you actually get hurt, then everybody else
is in on the fight, then you just have to stage house war, which
happens in this house a lot.

Zoe (15, Aboriginal) locates the power in the hands of the incoming resident
in the dynamic that has affected her:

New kids come there, right, and then everyone looks up to them
and you want to look up to them too so you do whatever they're
doing and makes people get in trouble and stuff, depending on
what they're doing and I find that happens in a lot of group
homes from the stuff I did . . . I loved going to school and stuff
and when I went to Connexion all that went down the toilet, I
don't know. Then when I started living at Atlantis I wanted to
fit in with the other girls, like. [That meant] like running away,
doing drugs, sleeping around, not following rules, being plain ole
sassy and bitchy, and . . . then I got use to being like that . . . cuz I
saw other people doing it.

With ample group encouragement to follow the norms and to establish
oneself in a particular way, these girls make their decisions. Hanna (15,
white), who had been living in group homes for 8 months, reflected on the
changes in her behavior:

I used to be like a normal kid but now I'm starting to act hard
too . . . acting big for everybody else, and picking up on other peoples'
stuff like. Me, I don't like people staring at me. If someone stares
at me for too long, I'll tell them, like "stop staring at me." Before
[living in group homes] I'd just walk by and I wouldn't care. Before
[living in group homes] I didn't say stuff like that, right, I wouldn't
tell nobody, I'd just keep it to myself because I didn't want to mess
with people. But now, I just tell people and I basically pick fights
for myself and I actually win . . . And now it just kinda grew on
me and I'm getting in trouble all the time and getting charged all
the time and stuff like that.

These stories suggest that the other residents as well as the new
acquaintances and involvements that have resulted from moving into the
group setting contribute to decisions and behaviors that the girls consider
unhealthy, unlawful, or "just a very unacceptable thing for me to do" (Jessie,
16, white). In the group home, girls need to assess what the setting demands
and strategize how these demands can be managed. The consequences for
not falling in line with the influences of the group home subculture include

social ostracism and the violence that frequently accompanies it. That their decisions in these circumstances may result in "making me worse" should then hardly be surprising.

NAVIGATING STAFF

Among these ingredients of choice, constraint and becoming "worse," the staff team is experienced by the girls as a body of both care and control. For the most part, the girls refer to "the staff" as a single body rather than as a number of individuals. "It," not "they," is seen as representing unified rules, with little internal variation; though with practice, one can learn to identify discrepancies. The staff team is at once known and unknown: their role as purveyors of the basic care (housing, food, personal care items, and log writing) is known and they are known to have power to give and take privileges and consequences, both within and beyond the house, via contact with social workers and teachers. Yet the girls know there are layers of inter-pretation, discretion, bias, values, and unique personality that surround the concrete, known parameters. Staff members can be both friend and foe.

The girls reflected in detail on the approaches and specific interventions of the staff of group homes, from their vantage point of experience in the living space. They know this space acutely well and their reflection on the staff's role is always active. Tonya (16, African Nova Scotian) is clear that "Staff at the group home, they all get paid, they get money for it. They don't care, they can't help you with nothing . . . They didn't get through to me, they were nothing to me." At the other extreme, Melissa (18, white) spoke of feeling isolated in her current independent living situation compared to the sense of support she felt while living in a succession of group homes:

> Well it's just cuz you're used to like being in group homes and stuff and they're always wanting to know like everything—in a good way too, like I'm not putting them down—but I mean when you're so used to that and then just it goes, like you really miss it hey, cuz it shows . . . that they do really care, right?

Ciara's (16, Aboriginal) evaluation of the staff offered some of each:

> Some of them [the staff], me and my friends think they're just there for all the money. Some of them we think they're there to take care of us, like to look after us and try and help us get outta there and make better choices in our life.

The girls clearly expected the staff to keep the peace within the living space, through means ranging from tightened admission criteria, to giving the girls time and space to address their concerns without interfering.

Jackie (16, white) said, "This house is supposed to be [ages] sixteen and up and that's what I agree with. There's some girls here that are younger but I totally disagree with it, because they're not at the same maturity level." Alex (18, white) reported that when girls in the house are in conflict, the best thing for the staff to do is,

> listen in on it, but don't try to directly involve yourself and don't suggest anything. It just gets you really, really heated. It makes you think about everything, because you're both firing at each other's face when you hear that.

The range of preferred interventions appears to be an expression of what each girl has found personally helpful or meaningful in her own life. That was their frame of reference. Tonya (16, African Nova Scotian) provided such an example:

> I don't know how they can say "don't use your body for money" and then not give them [the girls] money. There's no other way to get it. Money is important because otherwise you're bumming cigarettes and who wants to do that? You want to go out to eat, buy clothes at the mall, and go to the movies, so you have to steal or feel shitty. How can you feel mature when someone's controlling your money?

The girls talked of staff having significant control over their daily lives, in both the material and discursive realms. The material control is manifested through curfews, privileges, chores, and access to money. Discursive control begins with feeling scrutinized: the girls know they are watched and evaluated. The eyes of the staff are always upon them, an experience that fits squarely into the choice and constraint balance always at hand. They know that monitoring and control are central features of living in group care settings, as determined by the mandate of the program, and they bristle under the watchful evaluation of the staff, in general and specific incidents. Reflecting broadly, Alex (18, white) spoke of knowing about being watched throughout her two years living in group homes:

> I don't need that shit anymore ... It's just too much. Staff are always right up in your business ... [T]hey know everything, like you know what I mean, we live here. It's like, how long can they sit there and write logs for us? I've been doing this for two years, I don't want them to do that anymore. I'm tired of it. I just want to be able to walk around.

Recalling a specific incident, Bobbi (14, white) said,

One time I was on the computer and someone else put pornographic things on the computer so I went on the computer and I tried to get it off and then staff said that I put it on the computer . . . I was on the computer when I was trying to help so they misjudged me and that makes me mad.

Jackie (16, white) talked about her strategy for coping with the constant scrutiny, saying she is "the type that would just say what they want to get them off my back but not apply it," something Alex (18, white) calls "therapeutic bullshit."

The girls think that the staff know what will and will not be helpful for the girls in terms of responses and interventions, and believe that the staff make conscious decisions accordingly. The girls know that the staff's job is to assess their needs, behaviors, emotions, relationships, potentials, and risks. Staff members are expected to get their assessments "right," which to the girls generally means congruence with the assessments of the girls themselves. The girls believe the staff have the skills necessary to perform their assessments, thus when the staff intervene in ways that aggravate the girls, they are considered to be doing so *willfully*, deliberately undermining the wishes, interests, even safety and health, and ultimate growth away from violence, of the girls. The frustration of the girls toward the staff in these times is remembered in detail, felt intensely, and analyzed by each of the girls according to this construction of the staff person's responsibility.

For example, Raylene (16, African Nova Scotian) spoke of living in a facility where she was physically restrained by the staff: "If someone comes on top of me, grabs me, that just makes me want to be more violent, like you know what I mean?" According to Raylene's frame of reference, physical restraint is contraindicated in the goal of decreasing violent behavior. Tonya (16, African Nova Scotian) shared that

I went to Fundy Centre [secure facility] because they thought I was at risk of prostitution, which was bullshit. I was so angry I assaulted anyone, girls and staff . . . I picked up a phone and chucked it at their face, kicking the doors, sayin' "you guys are child abusers!"

Jodi (15, African Nova Scotian) told a lengthy story about the staff at her group home thinking that she had homemade knife in her possession (a "shank") and therefore calling the police to come to the group home and remove her:

Staff changed the story. Staff said that I said that . . . I had a knife and . . . I was going to do something. But I didn't tell them what I was going to do. So . . . I couldn't do nothin' about it cuz the police got all the, all the power in the world. Like I couldn't—I'm only little—I can't do nothing about it. I was so mad out of my mind . . . I was like, I was just out of my mind. I was saying "how can you say, tell me you care about me and then change my words? Like seriously get the hell out of my—." Like I was like going crazy. I was saying " 'Bye, I do not want to talk to you guys." They were saying "Oh just take care." *Take care?* Like don't fucking talk to me, seriously! If you have the guts to sit there and call the police on me and say I said something that I did not say then first of all I'm chucking my whole room and then I'm chucking me.

On these occasions the girls are clear that the staff could have prevented the incident, had they been more reasonable, more understanding, or more inclusive in hearing the girl's testimony. Tonya (16, African Nova Scotian) referred to her sense of staff responsibility when she said, "They were all up in my face making me this fucking angry." Here Tonya hones in on a key element in this process: the staff are *making her* this angry. It is an intentional act on the part of the staff. She reacted to the watchful eye of one particular staff member, whom she said, "was always checking on me, coming in my room, turning the lights off and on, checking my closets in case I snuck someone in there. One day she came in and was checking all through my room and I punched her in the fuckin' eye." Alex (18, white) reflected on the approach taken by a staff person in one incident:

> Yeah she [the staff member] pissed me off. She told me I was in a state of mind from my stepmom [dying]. I was all upset and I was freakin' out man . . . So, she said, "I'll give you a quarter to go outside and call." I said "Um, it's long distance otherwise I wouldn't ask you to dial the number for me, I could call on the resident's line. Like, think about it, you work here, you should know that." And she said, "Well you're not in the state of mind . . ." and I said "*Fuck* my state of mind" . . . She could've calmed me down . . . but fuckin' you don't tell me no, I can't talk to my family.

The girls reported that the staff ought to "know better" than to intervene or respond in the ways that escalate anger. Their resulting anger is thus understandable, because they have been provoked.

As much as the staff is considered a unified body, their interventions and responses are not uniformly cast as surveillance, scrutiny, and aggravation. There are significant accounts of staff as supportive and encouraging, playing important roles in moving toward the future. Natasha (15, African Nova Scotian) contrasted her experiences of living with a foster family and living in a group home, preferring the group setting because "you see that there's more people that care about you . . . They won't sit there and tell everybody your business . . . That's why I like group care cuz I can trust these guys." Shannon (20, white) said, "They just encourage you to be the best that you can, just work your heart out and all that . . . they want you to be like a lady, not like a little kid fighting," a comment that connects the staff role with messages sent and received about femininity. Suzanne (16, white) specifically appreciated the long-term investment of her community group home staff over a series of placements:

> I was amazed . . . that I was running and running and running for a, usually, um, I'd run every day but then there, because I went for a month at a time and then after that I got up here and then . . . like they'd still keep my placement and then, like I'd come here and I'd call them up and be like "Am I going back there?" And they'd be like "Ya, you're coming back." At first, I took it for granted but then I really sat down and thought about it, like wow like, you know, they must really want to help me and care for me or they would just kick me out. That made me smarten up a little bit and be like "okay, I gotta settle down now and think about what I really want in life and why I'm running and why I should stop."

Feeling supported by the staff often hinges on reflected praise: hearing from the staff that they think one is moving forward in healthy and productive ways. Jackie (16, white) said,

> Heidi, the staff here, said to me yesterday, she said, "Jackie, I was iffy about you coming back but you . . . for the past month you have done excellent." Everybody said they know that I was capable of doing it but I just never applied myself . . . Some of the things that the staff say don't, haven't really stuck with me because I've heard it too many times before, but them saying, "Jackie do it for you, don't do it for others" and "you're smart and you're capable and you're—you can do so much," stuff like that I hold on to.

Zoe (15, Aboriginal) learned from staff that she holds admirable qualities, specifically trustworthiness:

> I love the staff there. The staff are good . . . They cared for me and they trusted me and everything, like I was allowed being with their kids and all that stuff and at their homes, some of them let me see their homes and stuff, and ya, one time I was with one staff and she had to go with her husband to the store . . . and I would actually like go with her, her husband, and her two kids. So some people actually trusted me a little bit which felt good.

The support and commitment from the staff boosted the ongoing appraisal of self in the group living context. Positive reviews by the staff are contingent upon the qualities and efforts of the girls themselves, and thus feels doubly satisfying: it is encouraging to hear positive words, and the positive words rest on the being and doing of the young woman herself.

SYSTEMS OF SURVEILLANCE

Living in group homes is living on a fulcrum, with the host of external demands teetering on one side and the concomitant internal demands tottering on the other. Foucault's conceptualization of surveillance, developed in his 1979 publication *Discipline and Punish*, provides a useful framework for broadening the analysis, helping us to move beyond the individualist interventions that pathologize girls and their emotional development.

In his historical accounting of the treatment of criminals, Foucault noticed the move from public tortures and executions, undertaken to deter illegal behavior, to the sequestering of inmates in institutions away from the public eye. Although shrouded from the public view, the new system relied heavily on visibility *within* the system as the central means through which the person remains socially disciplined (Foucault, 1979). Inmates were visible at all times through the layout of the physical structures, often with one guard monitoring many men. Foucault's analysis was that over time, the expectation of visibility itself becomes regulatory, the threat of consequences becomes internalized and the need for external control decreases. Social processes and relations are refined to ensure that the inmate—or group home resident—becomes and remains complicit with the social machinery for compliance.

Surveillance is the continual interplay among watching what the other is doing, watching oneself and watching the other watch oneself, all of which derive from the concept of the "looking-glass self" (Cooley, 1918). The premise is that part of my process of figuring out what I want to be involves wondering what you see, and want to see, as you look at me. My assumptions of your perceptions of me are woven into my current self-configuration. Surveillance ranges from noticing and watching, to scrutinizing and commenting, to regulating and policing; these dimensions apply to the self as well as other audiences, and there is always an audience. In the group home the audience is comprised of staff, whose role is to watch, record, convey, and often accord benefits or demerits on the basis of that watching, and whose case notes and planning decisions are the means through which the girls' lives are made visible and public. Girls in group homes are also regularly surveilled by the other girls in their midst: the girls watch, listen, wonder, learn, assume, judge, and police each other. Outside the group home there are social workers, whose purpose is to watch, record, and convey; teachers; family members, and all layers of community interactions and the cultural landscape. And there are the boys, whose actions and intentions are well concealed under heterosexism's protection. Across all audiences, there is the unstated knowledge that one will be "read" according to one's actions and reactions in the group home setting. These "readings" become internalized, as self-regulation and self-surveillance become ingrained and the girls form their own self-audience as they practice and perform in private. Jackie (16, white) invoked some of the layers of audience and its role in regulation when she described,

> I find most girls now, they dress to impress other people, but they don't dress to impress themselves . . . It comes from your parents. It comes from your own self being. It comes from the men you deal with or you meet. It comes from not knowing any better.

Each audience employs "micro-technologies" of surveillance (Foucault, 1979). For example, the staff utilizes curfews, chores, and programming content and process to surveil the girls. The daily log writing of youth care workers can enact a more powerful dynamic in the behaviors and decisions of the girls than the provincial legislation of the Children and Family Services Act. Lisa (15, white) referred to logs written about her as "gonna make . . . or break" any plans she wants to pursue in the near or distant future. Jodi's (15, African Nova Scotian) words reflect the power of the log in maintaining surveillance:

> My other group homes didn't say that [they thought she was prostituting] but they gave me hints, like that is what they are tryin' to say. They don't think I know but I do. I bet it's even in my logs.

IMPLICATIONS FOR PRACTICE

Group homes—their structures, staffing and programs—exist within the broader social fabric, which is woven of capitalism, consumerism, and neo-liberalism. This weaving upholds freedom and autonomy as limitless opportunities and creates the individual as fully responsible for both success and failure (Ife, 1997; Mullaly, 2002; Swift et al., 2003). The individual alone, or at most, her family, is responsible for all manner of difficulties that play out in the social sphere (Gonick, 2004). It should not be surprising then that much of the experience of the girls living in group homes parallels the assumption of personal responsibility for "making good choices" and "turning one's life around." Both praise and condemnation are visited upon the girl, depending on *her* decisions given *her* situation.

The injustice of locating the problem of violence within the individual is that it decontextualizes experience, psychologizes and individualizes what are fundamentally social experiences and obscures the vested interests of social structures that perpetuate all manner of social inequities. Emphases on individual fortitude and intrapsychic resilience—central tenets of the neoliberal discourse—encourage this devolution, as do stories of incredible personal triumph over adversity. These foci also prevent diligent critique of material inequities and social structures (Aapola, Gonick & Harris, 2005; Walkerdine, Lucey, & Melody, 2001). The conundrum is that it is well nigh impossible to step outside this discourse: it is invisible and omnipresent. Thus the structures, staffing, and programming of group homes are contributing to the discourse as they are being shaped by it. What are we to do?

Although structuralist explanations for social problems are sometimes critiqued for targeting action high above local impact, I argue that the discourses that contextualize the lives of girls who use violence and live in group homes are accessible for us to enter into and reshape on a daily basis. Opportunities and resources for influencing racism, classism, heterosexism, and hegemonic femininity—key themes throughout the stories of the girls of this research—are available to all people living and working in the midst of these girls. Practice approaches in group homes must resist individualism, pathology, and the abdication of collective, social responsibility for these daily life experiences. At the same time, it is recognized that practitioners in group homes are operating within the same discursive contexts as the girls themselves. It will take a sustained collective effort to shape and be shaped by a different discourse, built on structural analysis of, and collective responsibility toward, girls who use violence.

According to the pathologizing and individualizing discourses that pervade Western neoliberalism, girls who use violence are considered failures at accomplishing culturally prescribed expectations of girlhood. Theorizing surveillance suggests that the regulation of social performances *requires* discourses of failure, in order to ensure that the girls continually monitor and scrutinize themselves and other girls. This analysis clearly points to understanding issues of violence as a transitory confluence of factors wherein context is the pivot point. The problem of violence, then, is neither essential to the girl, nor static within the girl. This conceptualization is critical to progressive interventions for practice in community-based group homes.

Insofar as use of violence is an indicator that something is wrong, we need to listen to the stories the girls offer, mired as they may be in contradiction, ambivalence, and confrontation. Focusing only on the control or extinction of violence and aggressive behaviors silences the voice that is suppressed in her use of violence and does not attend to nor help to reauthor the underlying story (Brown, 2006).

Interventions with girls who use violence must probe deeply beneath the surface layers about how, when, and where violence is used and how girls, including the self, are conceptualized. These stories must be explored line by line for their myriad meanings and for what they can reveal of the cultural discourses of regulation. For example, we need to hear the accounts, as I did with these girls, of the distrust toward and situational distaste for other girls. We cannot shy away from the contradictory feelings and messages that girls receive and absorb about each other. To silence those stories is to reinscribe the gold standard that to be female is to be sugar and spice and all things nice, and that "nice girls" can only act in particular ways, which do not include feeling, speaking, and behaving negatively toward each other. At the same time we also cannot leave intact these reinscriptions of damning portrayals of each other. Rather, we need to stay in these conversations and seize the opportunities to talk about the "cultural logic" (Brown, 2006) of misogyny and sexism in ways that make sense to girls. Solidarity among girls and women is a legitimate possibility when the mechanics of misogyny and sexism are made transparent and understood. These conversations can explore what it would take to see other girls as allies, through whom support and kinship can be grown.

Extending from the conceptualization that power exists not as a tangible entity but as an energy that can be enacted in multiple ways, interventions and programs need to explore a broad array of means through which girls can feel power, control, and responsibility within their constructions of themselves. Use of violence can be interpreted as one such means, a stance I posit is required to counterbalance the prevalent messages that a girl who uses violence is a failure at girlhood. Second, if fighting is a means through which girls feel some power in an otherwise dispossessed existence, as these data suggest, we can work with girls to discover additional means through which they can feel power. We cannot assume that the ways in which girls feel power are through relationships, as the ethic of care argument contends. A basic implication from this research is that specific interventions with girls who use violence must not subscribe to gender-essentialized assumptions and biases. These girls seek power and strength valued in the same ways that power and strength are valued for boys, thus program development must begin with listening to the stories of girls to hear how they experience power and strength among "contradictory social demands" (Walkerdine et al., 2001, 212).

Finally, the accounts of surveillance reviewed herein suggest that these girls are always assessing and evaluating how and who they want to be and how others expect them to be. Both the content of these evaluations and their processes lie beneath manifestations of violence. They will be different for everyone. If, as Foucault suggests, discourse is a violence done to all things (1979), we need to understand that systems of surveillance and discourses of failure will continue in the lives of girls and to continue to explore their implications with the girls themselves leading the way.

CONCLUSION

I often think of Ruth, that girl I knew when she was 17 years old. I think about how my interactions with her provoked my thinking and I wonder how her experiences in our group home have influenced her later life. I question if she experienced any healing while with us and how she would now reflect back on those first few years outside her family home. I have no way of knowing. But I have an understanding, of what some of her struggles might have been, and I am clear that our role as practitioners working in residential settings is not to dilute the complex lives of girls who are struggling to find their way in a world that seeks to individualize and pathologize their social experiences, that continues to construct girls according to dichotomies as either sugary sweet or calculatingly cruel, and to be (hetero)sexually restrained either way. I am clear that as practitioners, parents, and the public, it is our responsibility to build new discourses of what it means to be a girl and that doing so will lead to collaborative programs and responsive communities. There is no single recipe for what constitutes the girl who uses violence and lives in group homes, therefore there is no single recipe for how best to understand and work with her. Yet listening closely, hearing the promises, pitfalls, and possibilities, ensures that we are centered on her life and her context as we move forward to respond.

NOTES

1. These parameters mark this study as distinct from the sensational media coverage of recent shootings and stabbings among boys within school settings in Canada and the U.S. literature on girl violence that centers on participation in gangs.

2. Throughout this chapter, all names for persons, locations, agencies, and facilities have been replaced with pseudonyms.

REFERENCES

Aapola, S., Gonick, M., & Harris, A. (2005). Young femininity: Girlhood, power, and social change. Houndmills, UK; New York: Palgrave Macmillan.

Abrams, L. S., & Curran, L. (2000). Wayward girls and virtuous women: Social workers and female juvenile delinquency in the progressive era. AFFILIA 15(1): 49–64.

Arieli, M., Beker, J., & Kashti, Y. (2001). Residential group care as a socializing environment: Toward a broader perspective. Child & Youth Care Forum 30(6): 403–414.

Bettelheim, B. (1950). *Love is not enough: The treatment of emotionally disturbed children*. Glencoe, IL: Free Press.

Bowlby, J. (1979). *The making and breaking of affectional bonds*. London: Tavistock.

Brown, C. (2006). Discipline and desire: Regulating the body/self. In C. Brown & T. Augusta-Scott (eds.), *Narrative therapy: Making meaning, making lives* (105–131). Thousand Oaks, CA: Sage.

Carniol, B. (2000). *Case critical: Challenging social services in Canada*. Fourth Edition. Toronto: Between the Lines.

Cooley, C. H. (1918). *Social process*. New York: C. Scribner's Sons.

Department of Justice, Canada. (2002). *Youth criminal justice act*. http://laws.justice. gc.ca/en/Y-1.5/ (accessed 25 November 2005).

Foucault, M. (1979). *Discipline and punish: The birth of the prison*. New York: Vintage Books.

Garfat, T. (1998). The effective child and youth care intervention: A phenomenological inquiry. *Journal of Child and Youth Care* 12(1–2): 1–178.

Garfat, T., & Mitchell, H. (2000). Recommendations from a review of the Association for the Development of Children's Residential Facilities. Unpublished program evaluation. Dartmouth, Nova Scotia.

Gonick, M. (2004). The 'mean girl' crisis: Problematizing representations of girls' friendships. *Feminism & Psychology* 14(3): 395–400.

Heinonen, T., & Spearman, L. B. (2001). *Social work practice: Problem solving and beyond*. Toronto: Irwin Publishing.

Ife, J. (1997). *Rethinking social work*. Australia: Addison Wesley Longman.

Krueger, M. A. (1988). *Intervention techniques for child/youth care workers*. Washington, DC: Child Welfare League of America.

Krueger, M. A. (1998). *Interactive youth work practice*. Washington, DC: CWLA Press.

McAdams, C. R., & Foster, V. A. (1999). A conceptual framework for understanding client violence in residential treatment. *Child & Youth Care Forum* 28(5): 307–328.

Mullaly, B. (1997). *Structural social work: Ideology, theory, and practice*. Second Edition. Don Mills, ON: Oxford University Press.

Mullaly, B. (2002). *Challenging oppression: A critical social work approach*. Don Mills, ON: Oxford University Press.

Redl, F., & Wineman, D. (1951). *Children who hate; the disorganization and breakdown of behavior controls*. Glencoe, IL: Free Press.

Redl, F., & Wineman, D. (1952). *Controls from within: Techniques for the treatment of the aggressive child*. Glencoe, IL: Free Press.

Reitsma-Street, M. (1998). Girls learn to care; girls policed to care. In C. Y. Baines, P. M. Evans, & S. M. Neysmith (eds.), *Women's Caring: Feminist Perspectives on Social Welfare*, Second Edition (106–137). Toronto: McClelland & Stewart.

Rutman, L. (1987). J. J. Kelso and the development of child welfare. In A. Moscovitch, & J. Albert (eds.), *The Benevolent State: The Growth of Welfare in Canada* (68–76). Toronto: Garamond Press.

Snow, K., & Finlay, J. (1998). *Voices from within: Youth speak out*. Toronto: Office of the Child and Family Services Advocacy.

Steinhauer, P. (1991). *The least detrimental alternative*. Toronto: University of Toronto Press.

Swift, J., Davies, J. M., Clarke, R. G., & Czerny, M. (2003). *Getting started on social analysis in Canada*. Fourth Edition. Toronto: Between the Lines.

Tolman, D. L., Spencer, R., Rosen-Reynoso, M., & Porche, M. V. (2003). Sowing the seeds of violence in heterosexual relationships: Early adolescents narrate compulsory heterosexuality. *Journal of Social Issues* 59(1): 159–178.

Trieschman, A. E., Whittaker, J. K., & Brendtro, L. K. (1969). *The other 23 hours; child-care work with emotionally disturbed children in a therapeutic milieu*. First Edition. Chicago: Aldine.

Underwood, M. K. (2004). Girls and violence: The never ending story. In M. M. Moretti, C. L. Odgers, & M. A. Jackson (eds.), *Girls and Aggression: Contributing Factors and Intervention Principles* (239–248). New York: Kluwer Academic/Plenum Publishers.

VanDenBerg, J., & Grealish, E. M. (1996). Individualized services and supports through the wraparound process: Philosophy and procedures. *Journal of Child and Family Studies* 5(1): 1–13.

Walkerdine, V., Lucey, H., & Melody, J. (2001). *Growing up girl: Psychosocial explorations of gender and class*. New York: New York University Press.

Ward, A. (2004). Towards a theory of the everyday: The ordinary and the special in daily living in residential care. *Child & Youth Care Forum* 33(3): 209–225.

Whitaker, J. (1981). Major approaches to residential treatment. In F. Ainsworth & C. Fulcher (eds.), *Group Care for Children: Concepts and Issues* (89–127). London: Tavistock.

PART III

GIRLS' VIOLENCE:
EXPLANATIONS AND IMPLICATIONS

NINE

"IT'S ABOUT BEING A SURVIVOR . . ."

African American Girls, Gender,
and the Context of Inner-City Violence

Nikki Jones

"It's about survival!"
—Tracey, Philadelphia

"It's about being a survivor, and we have to survive."
—Kiara, San Francisco

Tracey and Kiara, African American women in their early twenties,[1] shared these strikingly similar remarks with me during the course of my field research in Philadelphia (2001–2003) and San Francisco (2005–present). Despite coming of age on opposite coasts of the country, the two young women expressed a concern with "survival" that has become a defining feature of inner-city girls' adolescence since the 1980s.[2] Typically, the experiences of young women like Tracey and Kiara are overshadowed by the moral panic surrounding "mean girls" in the suburbs or the "crisis of the young black male" in urban settings. Yet, as I've discovered over the course of field research in neighborhoods marked by concentrated poverty and its associated social problems, both boys *and* girls who come of age in distressed urban neighborhoods develop a preoccupation with survival. In contrast to the lives of many middle-class, suburban adolescents, African American inner-city girls and their parents, grandparents, or caretakers must make "hard choices" (Richie, 1996) about how to manage the various challenges associated with coming of age in today's inner city, including threats of interpersonal violence and exposure to lethal violence.

In this chapter, I describe the characteristics of the neighborhood settings in which African American, inner-city girls come of age, the "situated survival strategies" (Jones, 2010) girls develop to navigate these settings, and the *gendered* consequences of their doing so. I then draw on the narratives of Tracey and Kiara to illustrate how girls reconcile the gendered dilemmas of inner-city adolescence. I conclude the chapter with a final adolescent girl's narrative (Terrie) that highlights the limitations of these strategies when it comes to girls' vulnerability to gender-specific violence—a prevalent threat for adolescent girls who grow up in distressed urban neighborhoods.

RACE, GENDER, AND INNER-CITY VIOLENCE

The concern for survival that is revealed in Tracey and Kiara's comments is informed by the settings in which inner-city girls come of age. Tracey, who worked as a violence intervention counselor in Philadelphia when I first interviewed her in 2001,[3] grew up in a predominantly black neighborhood in the southern part of the city that has been shaped by various social forces. A large, post-industrial, northeastern city, Philadelphia has experienced many of the same structural and economic changes that have impacted cities across the U.S. over the last 30 years, including deindustrialization, the concentration of poverty, and hypersegregation of its inner-city areas (Wilson, 1980, 1987, 1996; Massey & Denton 1999; Anderson, 1999). In some respects, Philadelphia's central city population has been hit harder by these changes than residents in comparable metropolitan areas. Philadelphia's poverty rate in 2000, the year before I began my field research, was 22.9%—almost double the national rate of 12.4 percent. Rates of concentrated poverty increased in Philadelphia during the 1990s as they leveled or declined in other metropolitan areas across the United States. In some South and West Philadelphia neighborhoods (where I conducted much of this study), between 30 and 40% of the resident population live in poverty (Brookings Institution Center on Urban and Metropolitan Policy [BICUMP], 2003;Pettit & Kingsley 2003). It is now well known now that this combination of poverty and segregation tends to concentrate crime, violence, and other social ills in poor communities of color (Peterson & Krivo, 2005; Wilson, 1980, 1987, 1996; Massey & Denton, 1999; Anderson, 1999; Lauritsen & Sampson, 1998; Sampson & Wilson, 1995).

Kiara grew up in a similarly distressed neighborhood in San Francisco. In the mid-1900s, the Fillmore neighborhood of San Francisco where Kiara was "born and raised," as she says, was home to a vibrant African American community. During this time, the neighborhood was often referred to

by locals as "the .Harlem of the West." After World War II, as the ship-
ping industry and many of its African American workers moved away, city
government officials declared the area a slum and large portions of the
neighborhood were razed and replaced by housing projects. As inner-city
conditions worsened across the country, the predominantly black Fillmore
also experienced the various consequences of the increased concentration
of poverty, including increased crime, rapidly deteriorating schools, and an
increase in drug trafficking and the violence associated with the drug trade
(Wilson, 1980, 1987, 1996; Anderson, 1999; Massey & Denton, 1993). For
many who are familiar with the city, including the residents of the nearby
and gentrifying Lower Pacific Heights, Alamo Square neighborhoods, and
smaller Japantown neighborhoods, the Fillmore is largely considered a "bad
neighborhood" marked by crime and violence. Newspaper reports of shootings and gang activity often reinforce such assumptions (Van Derbeken and
Lagos, 2006; Martin, 2006; Van Derbeken, 2005).

Much of the violence that takes place in neighborhoods like the ones
Tracey and Kiara grew up in is governed by a hypermasculine "eye-for-an-
eye" ethic that urban ethnographer Elijah Anderson describes as the "code
of the street": a system of accountability that governs formal and informal
interactions in distressed urban areas, especially interpersonal violence. At
the heart of "the code," Anderson writes, is a battle for respect and manhood
(1999). In Black Sexual Politics (2004), Patricia Hill Collins writes that as
black men embrace "the code," they embrace a hegemonic masculinity that
is based on the coupling of strength with dominance—white men with wealth
and power are able to demonstrate such masculinity through economic or
military dominance (in addition to physical dominance), while poor black
men in distressed urban areas must rely primarily on physical domination,
which makes themselves and others in their community more vulnerable
to violent victimization.[4]

Inner-city girls may have no manhood to defend, yet, as Tracey and
Kiara's remarks suggest, girls do have reason to be preoccupied with their
own survival. Like adolescent, inner-city boys, inner-city girls have stories
to tells about peers who get "rolled on" or "jumped," or were involved in a
"fair one" gone bad. Like their male counterparts, inner-city girls can often
name someone who has been shot, robbed, or stabbed. During the course of
field research in Philadelphia, I encountered girls who witnessed this violence
directly. Inner-city girls understand at early ages that stray bullets do not
discriminate between young and old, guilt and innocence, or boys and girls.
They know that the settings of inner-city life, whether school buildings or
row houses, neighborhood street corners or porch stoops, do not come with
a special girls-only pass to live beyond the reach of violence. The need to
avoid or overcome dangers throughout their adolescence presents a uniquely
gendered challenge for girls who grow up in these neighborhoods.

BETWEEN GOOD AND GHETTO: AFRICAN AMERICAN GIRLS, GENDER, AND VIOLENCE

As a system of accountability, gender reflects widely held beliefs, or normative expectations, about the "attitudes and activities appropriate for one's
sex category" (West & Zimmerman, 1987: 127). During interactions and
encounters with others, children and adults evaluate themselves and others
in light of these normative gender expectations in ways that reinforce or
challenge beliefs about the natural qualities of boys and girls, and especially
the essential differences between the two (West & Zimmerman, 1987; West
& Fenstermaker, 1995). Generally, women and girls who are able to mirror
normative expectations of femininity during their interactions with others—for
example, by assuming a passive demeanor and presenting an appearance that
does not significantly deviate from the standards of mainstream culture or
local preferences—are evaluated by adults (e.g., family members, teachers,
counselors) and by peers as appropriately feminine girls or *good* girls. Meanwhile, girls or women who seem to violate perceived gender boundaries by
embracing stereotypically masculine behaviors (e.g., strength, independence,
and an outwardly aggressive demeanor) often are disparagingly categorized
as "unnaturally strong" (Collins, 2004: 193–199).

The intersection of gender, race, and class further complicates the
degree to which girls measure up to gender expectations. African American, inner-city girls in the United States are evaluated not only in light of
mainstream gender expectations but also in light of the expectations of black
respectability: the set of expectations governing how black women and girls
ought to behave. These expectations are reflected in images of "the black
lady"—think Claire Huxtable from the popular 1980s sitcom *The Cosby
Show*—the middle-class, black woman who reflects many of the expectations
of white, middle-class femininity (Collins, 2004: 139–140). Black ladies
distance themselves from behavioral displays of physical aggression or overt
sexuality that are commonly associated with poor or working-class black
women. Black women and adolescent girls whose shade of skin color, body
size, attitude, or demeanor deviate even slightly from mainstream expectations of femininity or black female respectability are especially vulnerable
to the formal and informal sanctions that accompany such gender violations
(Cole & Guy-Sheftal, 2003; Collins, 2004; Richie, 1996).

Inner-city girls who live in distressed urban neighborhoods face a *gendered dilemma*: they must learn how to effectively manage potential threats
of interpersonal violence—in most cases this means that they must work the
code of the street as boys and men do—at the risk of violating mainstream
and local expectations regarding appropriate feminine behavior. This is an
especially difficult dilemma for girls, since the gendered expectations surrounding girls' and women's use or control of violence are especially constraining.
Conventional wisdom suggests that girls and women, whether prompted by

nature, socialization, or a combination of the two, generally avoid physically aggressive or violent behavior: girls are expected to use relational aggression and fight with words and tears, not fists or knives. Inner-city girls, like most American girls, feel pressure to be "good," "decent," and "respectable." Yet, like some inner-city boys, they may also feel pressure to "go for bad" (Katz, 1986) or to establish a "tough front" (Anderson, 1999; Dance, 2002) in order to deter potential challengers on the street or in the school setting. They too may believe that "sometimes you do got to fight"—and sometimes they do. In doing so, these girls, and especially those girls who become deeply invested in crafting a public persona as a tough or violent girl, risk evaluation by peers, adults, and outsiders as "street" or "ghetto."

Among urban and suburban adolescents, "ghetto" is a popular slang term that is commonly used to categorize a person or behavior as ignorant, stupid, or otherwise morally deficient. Inner-city residents use the term to describe the same kinds of actions and attitudes Elijah Anderson termed "street orientation." Analytically, the pairs "ghetto" and "good," or "street" and "decent," are used to represent "two poles of value orientation, two contrasting conceptual categories" that structure the moral order of inner-city life (Anderson,1999,: 35). In inner-city neighborhoods, the decent/street or good/ghetto distinctions are powerful. Community members use these distinctions as a basis for understanding, interpreting, and predicting their own and others' actions, attitudes, and behaviors, especially when it comes to interpersonal violence (Anderson, 1999). There is also a gendered dimension to these evaluative categories: good or decent girls are "young ladies" while "ghetto chicks" are adolescent girls whose "behaviors, dress, communication, and interaction styles" contrast with mainstream *and* black middle-class expectations of appropriate and respectable femininity (Thompson & Keith, 2004: 58).

The branding of adolescent girls as ghetto is self-perpetuating, alienating the institutional forces that protect good girls and forcing adolescent girls who work the code of the street to become increasingly independent. Girls who are evaluated by adults or peers as ghetto, as opposed to those evaluated as good, ultimately may have the code as their only protection in the too often violent inner-city world in which they live. Their efforts to protect themselves puts them at risk of losing access to formal institutional settings like schools or the church, where girls who mirror normative gender expectations—girls who are perceived by others as good—can take some refuge. Yet, even for those good girls, this institutional protection is inadequate—they are aware that they may become targets in school or on the street and they too feel pressure to develop strategies that will help them successfully navigate their neighborhoods. Thus, inner-city girls find themselves caught in what amounts to a perpetual dilemma, forced by violent circumstances to choose between two options, neither of which offers the level of security that is generally taken for granted in areas outside of urban poverty.

Of course, real people—and perhaps especially adolescents—do not fit neatly into only one of two conceptual categories. My conversations with girls about their experiences with violence, along with my observations of their actions and conversations with others, revealed that girls astutely worked the code in between the *equal and opposing* pressures of good and ghetto. From this social location, girls are able to challenge and manipulate the constraining social and cultural expectations embedded in gender and the code, depending on the situation. Elijah Anderson defines the activity of adapting one's behavior to the set of rules that govern a situation—decent or street, good or ghetto—as "code switching." Inner-city families and youth, most of whom strive for decency, put a "special premium" on the ability to "switch codes and play by the rules of the street," when necessary (Anderson, 1999: 36, 98–106). Of course, this act is complicated for girls whose working of the code is likely to challenge expectations regarding appropriate feminine behavior. Inner-city girls work the code with the understanding that they are always accountable to these gendered expectations and that gender violations are likely to open them up to a series of public or private sanctions. Girls' lives seemed to be defined by this everyday struggle to balance the need to protect themselves with the pressure to meet normative expectations associated with their gender, race, and class positions. Girls' accounts of how they manage these expectations, including how they work the code, defy any simple categorizations or stereotypical evaluations of girls as *either* good or ghetto. Instead, girls' accounts of violent incidents reveal that they embrace, challenge, reinforce, reflect, and contradict normative expectations of femininity and black respectability *as* they work the code. Girls' accounts of navigating inner-city adolescence are characterized by this *fluidity*.

SITUATED SURVIVAL STRATEGIES

As urban, adolescent girls navigate a difficult and often unpredictable urban terrain, they develop a set of what I describe as *situated survival strategies*: patterned forms of interpersonal interaction, and routine or ritualized activities oriented around a concern for securing their personal well-being. The knowledge of threats to their safety shapes their daily lives. Urban, adolescent girls craft their situated survival strategies within the context of inner-city life, and between the extreme and oftentimes unrealistic physical and behavioral expectations of the good African American girl, who will grow up to be a respectable black lady, and the behavioral expectations of the code, which encourage the adoption of aggressive postures or behaviors that are typically expected of boys and men, yet are essential to managing threats in this context.

I call the two common strategies teenaged girls use to reduce the likelihood of encountering serious threats to their well-being on the streets or in school settings *situational avoidance* and *relational isolation*. The concept of situational avoidance captures all of the work teenaged girls do to avoid social settings that pose threats to their well-being and situations in which potential conflicts might arise. In contrast to girl fighters, who feel confident spending time on the street and in places where others hang out (what Anderson [1999] terms "staging areas"), situational avoiders confine themselves to the home, spending the majority of their time reading books, doing schoolwork, watching television, or daydreaming about being somewhere—anywhere—other than in their homes or neighborhoods. When they are outside, the same girls will rely on their own mental maps of areas and people to avoid. They restrict their movement in public spaces; they are reluctant to explore new areas of the city or to alter their daily routines outside their home in any significant way. In the most serious cases, girls who have had repeated conflicts at school may avoid going to school altogether, choosing to remove themselves from the place where fights are most likely to occur.

The concept of *relational isolation* illuminates the work girls do to isolate themselves from close friendships, especially those with other adolescent girls. The ties of loyalty and affection that accompany friendships increase the likelihood that girls will come to the defense of one another, if the need arises. Thus, by avoiding close friendships, girls can reduce the likelihood of their involvement in physical conflict. Among the young women I spoke with, the most common strategy was to divide relationships with other girls into two categories: friends and associates. Often, when I asked girls about their friends, they would correct me, pointing out, "I don't have friends. I got associates." In settings governed by the culture of the code, friends and associates connote two distinct status positions, which in turn reflect one person's degree of loyalty to another. Friend indicates a strong loyalty link; associate indicates a weaker link. Generally, it is expected that you will fight for a friend, but there is no equivalent requirement to fight for an associate. Designating other members of one's peer group or social network as associates instead of friends thus limits the likelihood of becoming involved in interpersonal conflicts on the grounds of loyalty. This strategy of insulating themselves from potential conflicts by limiting the strength of their social relationships may have serious long-term consequences for inner-city girls. Some girls are deliberately stunting the growth of their relational networks at a stage in adolescent development typically associated with the creation of healthy, trusting, and loving relationships. The way the culture of the code of the street alters patterns of adolescent development may be particularly significant for young girls, who are generally believed to be more relational-based than young men.

"IT'S ABOUT BEING A SURVIVOR"

In many ways, Tracey and Kiara exemplify African American, inner-city girls' efforts to reconcile the good/ghetto dilemma described in this chapter. In sharing stories about their lives, both young women suggest that the strategies they developed to navigate inner-city adolescence, including situational avoidance and relational isolation, helped them to "survive." As a violence reduction counselor serving youth who live in neighborhoods regularly exposed to violence, Tracey passes on the lessons she learned during her childhood to girls who are actively managing potential threats of interpersonal violence. Her advice reflects an underlying effort to maintain a level of respectability and an awareness of the importance of proving to potential challengers that you are an able fighter (Jones, 2004). Kiara also expresses an appreciation of the importance of displaying a "tough front" as a way to deter future challengers (Anderson, 1999). Kiara's narrative also illustrates how she engaged in gendered code-switching by actively embracing, rejecting, recreating, or recombining elements of mainstream and local masculinities and femininities to not only "become" a particular sort of girl or woman but also to "survive," as she says, in a setting where girls' safety is never guaranteed.

TRACEY AND KIARA

Tracey shares many similarities with the young people she visits as a violence reduction counselor. The block Tracey grew up on looks a lot like the blocks she visits regularly for meetings with girls injured in intentional violent incidents. On one corner of her childhood block stands an empty shell of an apartment house. On another corner sits an old tavern. Opposite the tavern stands a rib joint that has been out of business for as long as Tracey can remember. "The corner," the place where the local drug dealers conduct their business, is just a couple of blocks down from the old, abandoned restaurant. Tracey's childhood memories are punctuated by her grandmother's warnings to avoid that corner and its potential violence. Tracey tried to heed her grandmother's warnings as a young girl. Like some of the girls she now counsels, Tracey tried to avoid the corner altogether. When she couldn't avoid walking past the corner, she quickened her pace and averted her eyes in an effort to discourage any verbal or non-verbal interaction from the group assembled there.

Tracey describes her grandmother as her primary caretaker during her childhood, although she lived in the South Philadelphia row home with her grandmother, grandfather, mother, and younger brother. As a teenager she chaffed at her grandmother's efforts to restrict her mobility, much like the girls she counsels. "I lived with my grandmother all my life," she tells me, "and I know how it is when she, they don't want you to go anywhere, but you go anyway. And they don't want you to do this but you do that, and like nobody could tell me nothing, anything, you know?" Tracey was not a "fighter" as an adolescent girl although, she says, she was the type of girl who often aroused "jealousy" in other teenaged girls: "Like, I was part of that group in school, like . . . there were girls dressing in dresses and skirts and stuff, just sitting in class looking in magazines when you're supposed to be doing work." Tracey also remembers thinking that she was more "grown" than she actually was as an adolescent girl. "I just thought I knew everything," she recalls. When she advises girls who are just a few years her junior, she is careful to help them first consider non-violent responses to ongoing conflicts. At the same time, her familiarity with the code of the street that the drug dealers on the corner live by, and others in her neighborhood understand well, compels Tracey to send a message to her young charges that middle-class observers might find troubling. She instructs girls to adopt some of the strategies she learned as an adolescent girl: *first* try to talk a conflict out or, if possible, ignore a potential challenger. If these efforts fail, *then*, she says—not as a violence reduction counselor but rather as a young woman who has survived the challenges faced in urban schools and streets—you fight.

Like Tracey, Kiara grew up in a neighborhood that has been shaped by the structural changes to urban life in the late twentieth century. As she tells me when I first met her on a June afternoon in San Francisco (in 2005), she was "born and raised" in the Fillmore and came of age during some of the most violent periods in the neighborhood. Kiara is well aware of the lingering effect that this violence has left on the neighborhood. On an impromptu tour after a sit-down interview, Kiara led me down Fillmore Street, past the local police station and a McDonald's, one of several fast food restaurants in the neighborhood and a hub of local activity. As we passed by the police station Kiara yelled: "They don't give a fuck!" Her remark reinforced a comment she shared with me during her interview. I had asked Kiara if she felt like the police were on her side when she was growing up and she responded in a way that echoed the isolation and alienation felt by both male and female respondents I encountered during my field research in Philadelphia: "I know they weren't [on my side]. They'd shoot me if they got the chance. They scared of us [neighborhood residents]." Kiara's demeanor changed from hard to reflective a block later. "People be getting shot up here," she says as she points to the housing complex facing us from across the street: "this is where a lot of the trouble happens." She tells me that if I look closely I can see "RIP" scratched into the concrete or painted on sidewalks. Local residents leave the markings out of respect for friends or family members who have been lost to the violence of the street. "It's like a modern-day hieroglyphics," she says.

Like Tracey, Kiara's grandmother took on primary responsibility for raising her, albeit for more tragic reasons: Kiara's mother was shot and killed by her father, who she tells me was a big-time drug dealer in the neighborhood before he was sent to prison. As a child, Kiara tells me, she "was always really cheery bright, imaginative, questioning child without a mother." The combination of these personality characteristics—"cheery" and "imaginative"—and tragic circumstances—a girl child without a mother—would, according to Kiara, draw people toward her who were interested in taking care of her. Yet, Kiara also garnered a level of respect, even as a child, because of the street reputation of her father; people would "cater" to her because her father "used to sell a lot of drugs" in the neighborhood. Kiara sums up her appreciation of the importance of being able to move between good and ghetto, depending on the situation, when she reveals to me that, as a child: "I had the street element and I was aggressive for the streets, pretty for the pictures."

During my interview with Kiara, I asked her how she came to develop the sense of independence that seemed to characterize her responses. I was curious, in part, because her remarks echoed the same sort of individualism and independence that ran through some of the stories that I listened to in Philadelphia. She replied, "Umm because, if your mother's on crack or dead and your daddy is a hustler or in jail it's like you are forced to only see through the eyes of your own because no one is cultivating or teaching you therefore you draw your own conclusions. *You learn to trust yourself* opposed to trusting your parents . . . it's a way of life, nature teaching you [instead of] your parents teaching you" (emphasis mine). Like Tracey and many of the girls she counseled, Kiara also emphasized the importance of presenting a tough demeanor as a way to discourage potential challenges from others: "We have to be aggressive and growl and bite," she says, "(even though my bark is worse than my bite) but its like you get a warning and that's the warning." Again, she refers to how young people like herself come to this realization through observation and experience: "This is nature teaching us cause mama's at work and daddy's in the pen or out hustling. And cause I think since we eighties babies and that's when crack hit it fucked up . . . the community . . . crack killed everything, people were chasing money cause it controlled everything." Kiara finally sums up her lengthy response to my initial question in language that echoed both the strength and vulnerability I observed during my field research among African American, inner-city girls in Philadelphia: "It's about being a survivor, and we have to survive. We are going to thrive by any means necessary, even though they trying to kill us."

In order to "survive" inner-city adolescence, Kiara manages her presentation of self in a way that she considers protective: she orients her demeanor and behavior in an effort to send a preemptive message to others that she is not one to be challenged—a message that is well understood by others in her neighborhood. As a violence reduction counselor, Tracey sometimes encourages her adolescent girls to adopt similar strategies to manage threats of interpersonal violence. This preoccupation with managing potential threats of violence permeates the lives of adolescent, inner-city girls and their caretakers; decisions about which routes to take to school or home, where to shop, or how to spend one's free time are all impacted either directly or indirectly by considerations of where violence is likely to take place. For many African American inner-city girls and their mothers, grandmothers, and other-mothers, survival is an all-encompassing project.

The strategies that girls develop to successfully navigate their troubled public school hallways and neighborhood streets may prove to be useful when negotiating threats of interpersonal violence, however, my conversations with inner-city girls revealed the limits of these strategies in the face of gender-specific violence and especially sexual assault. The final short narrative highlights how even "tough" girls who are skilled at fighting and winning remain vulnerable to violence against women and girls in distressed urban neighborhoods and the rather limited resources that are available to help adolescent, inner-city girls respond to such violence when it occurs.

TERRIE'S STORY

Terrie was just completing her junior year at a local public high school when we first met. She stands about 5'8" and weighs about 165 pounds. She lives in an older row home with members of her immediate and extended family including her mother, her mother's fiancée, her Uncle Slim, and a collection of real and adopted sisters. Terrie hasn't seen her biological father, who is currently serving time in one of the state's prisons, in years. However, the man she terms her "real" father (her mother's ex-boyfriend) who Terrie believes "chose" to be her father (a lineage that she defines as far more significant), remains a stable presence in her life. During the day, Terrie is charged with taking care of her little sisters. Terrie's mother, who Terrie says is like her best friend, works two jobs and is home just two nights of the week. In addition to the role of caretaker that Terrie occupies within the home, she is often seen as a counselor for most of the younger kids in the neighborhood, who often come to her with questions and concerns.

Terrie's neighborhood is only blocks from the invisible yet well-known cut-off point that extends around the university area where I began most of my days in the field. A walking bridge that crosses over a set of regional railroad tracks bound a somewhat integrated neighborhood populated with working-class African Americans and an ethnically diverse mix of university students. Quite literally on the other side of the tracks is Terrie's neighborhood, populated by a mix of residents whose income levels range from little to none to steady; often the homes these residents inhabit share a wall with abandoned or condemned houses. Drug dealers, teenagers, and grandmothers share the space within the neighborhood boundary. At the end of the block is a house that is a center for a variety of illegal hustles, including drug selling and arbitrary violence. On the opposite end of Terrie's block is a corner, which is a center of open-air drug trafficking and thus the locus of much of the violent activity that occurs in the neighborhood. Terrie can quickly recall several young men who have been shot on the corner in recent years, including her own cousin. She explains to me that whenever she walks by the corner all the guys say "Hi" to her. "See," she explains, "they all know me." Everybody knows Terrie because, after living in the neighborhood for 15 years, she has built a reputation for being what she describes as a "violent person." The stage for her fights is often the public high school and by her account she is always the victor. As Terrie explains to me over a series of conversations, the fights she gets into serve in some way to protect her reputation and the associated authority and respect that enables her to navigate the neighborhood and school setting (Jones, 2004).

As I listened to Terrie describe her fights and encounters with other girls it became clear that much like other girls I interviewed who were committed to proving that they were able fighters, Terrie derived several benefits from her public battles with other girls. Each time she takes on a challenger in public and wins she does so in front of an audience that stands ready to reaffirm her reputation as a fighter, as someone not to be challenged by others. She is committed on some level to maintaining a reputation as "a violent person," as she says, and that reputation remains intact with each public victory. I also realized that Terrie's ability to fight and win allowed her to continue on with other activities and commitments that were important to her. Terrie's displays and occasional use of aggression and violence, which helps to facilitate her mobility through both her neighborhood and school, is just one of the ways that Terrie can trade on her prowess and the reputation that is associated it. Terrie can also trade on her reputation as a fighter in other ways; for example, she can come to the aid of people she sees as vulnerable. Finally, Terrie's commitment to maintaining her reputation not only allows her to walk the halls in school or the streets in her neighborhood as someone who "everybody knows" and respects but she can also continue to attend her Advanced Placement classes and plan for a future that might allow her to move beyond her neighborhood upon graduation. Terrie attended a course for gifted students at a local university over the summer and planned to attend college and hoped to be the first in her family to graduate from high school.

It is important to note that while the use of violence can ensure a degree of respect, freedom, and protection, for some young women like Terrie and those she deems worthy, this same reputation is essentially meaningless in the face of other threats young women face, particularly the threat of sexual assault. Terrie's tough front was shaken during a recent visit to a corner store in her new boyfriend's neighborhood. After she stepped into the store and began walking down a short aisle, the male store clerk made his way to the front of the store and locked the door. As Terrie recreates this scene for my benefit, I can see something in her face that I have not seen during our previous conversations: fear. Terrie pauses for a moment and I share her silence, imagining all the terrible things that could have happened to her; sexual assault—rape—is, of course, at the top of that list. I suspect, by the worried look on her face, that this is Terrie's primary imagined horror as well. She continues the story, telling me that after seconds that seemed like an eternity, a customer appeared at the store's glass entrance door. The clerk, startled by the customer's abrupt arrival, unlocked and opened the door, and Terrie slipped out, unharmed.

When Terrie returned to her boyfriend Derrick's house, it took her a few moments to calm down. After she got herself together, she told Derrick what happened and he became furious. Derrick's response is shaped by the masculinity resources that are most accessible to him within the culture of the code: anger and physical violence. He threatens to go to the store immediately and shoot the clerk. Terrie convinces Derrick not to do so. In recounting her plea, though, she reveals a hole in the protective buffer her tough front typically provides. If she wanted the clerk to be seriously injured—to be shot—she would not need to rely on Derrick. Neither, though, would she need to take action herself. "I have brothers to do that," Terrie says.

Terrie's experience at the corner store exposes the limitations of her carefully constructed tough front. That front does not convey the same sort of meaning to the male store clerk as it does to other teenaged girls in a school setting. To the clerk, Terrie is simply a potential sexual object. Terrie's reputation gives her an edge at school, and her skill as a fighter may be protective in a shoving match with a boyfriend. In the case of sexual assault, however, her ability to define the situation fades quickly, as does her power to fight back. Terrie's relative powerlessness in responding to a potential rapist is further illuminated by her comment that she would call on her *brothers* if she needed to retaliate against the store clerk. This response makes clear the limited set of resources available to inner-city girls who are raped or beaten by boyfriends or strangers. Terrie does not mention even considering calling the police—a decision that reflects her neighborhood's tenuous relationship with law enforcement. Neither does she mention calling a rape crisis hotline, or any other sort of community-based organization. Instead, Terrie relies on those elements of the code that obligate her brothers to defend her honor, along with their own.[5]

CONCLUSION

There are a number of lessons to be learned from young women like Tracey, Kiara, and Terrie, whom I have come to think of as "ghetto survivors" after my interview with Kiara. Ghetto survivors are adolescent, inner-city girls who develop innovative and effective strategies to ensure a basic need—survival—that many of their middle-class counterparts take for granted. These adolescent girls learn at early ages how to navigate the troubled terrain of distressed inner-city neighborhoods. In doing so, these girls reflect what Kiara describes as the more positive aspects of "ghetto." "I think that there are good elements to ghetto," Kiara told me during our interview, "like improvising for what you don't have." While their counterparts who come of age in more stable urban or suburban settings may take survival for granted, inner-city girls like Tracey, Kiara, and Terrie improvise for what they don't have: a reasonable level of personal security in neighborhood and school settings. As Kiara states so succinctly, African American girls who live in distressed urban neighborhoods feel social pressure to be not only "pretty for the pictures" but also "aggressive for the streets." Yet, as protective as the various situated survival strategies that inner-city girls employ in response to real or imagined threats of interpersonal violence may be, such strategies do little to decrease girls' vulnerability to threats of gender-specific violence, including sexual assault. Over time, inner-city adolescence can take an exacting toll on girls, as "survival" becomes an exhausting, all-encompassing project with especially high stakes. A concern for this survival project is revealed in the strikingly similar remarks shared by Tracey and Kiara who, as a consequence of shared circumstances, have developed similar understandings about their social worlds, and the inherent dangers that come along with being young black women in their neighborhoods.

Currently, it is in vogue to lament the rise of the violent girl (as discussed in earlier chapters in this book; see also Chesney-Lind & Eliason, 2006), however, the lessons learned from Tracey, Kiara, and Terrie suggest that our time would be better spent not in developing new reasons to punish girls but rather in examining more deeply the settings in which African American, adolescent girls come of age, the various strategies they develop to navigate these settings, and the consequences of their doing so.

NOTES

Sections of this chapter are drawn with permission from previously published works, including: "Working 'the code': Girls, gender, and inner-city violence," *The Australia and New Zealand Journal of Criminology* 41, 1 (2008): 63–83; *Between Good and Ghetto: African American Girls and Inner City Violence* (New Brunswick: Rutgers University Press, 2010), and " 'I was aggressive for the streets, pretty for the pictures': Gender, difference, and the inner city girl," *Gender & Society* 23, 1 (February 2009): 89–93.

1. Kiara described a multiracial identity during our interview, but she also identifies as a black woman. I use the terms African American and black interchangeably.

2. In *Perceived Collective Efficacy and Women's Victimization in Public Housing*, DeKeseredy et al. report: "In the qualitative interviews, many women reported that they were concerned with 'survival' and their main strategy is to mind their own business and refuse to acknowledge problems or report crime" (15–16).

3. The city hospital based violence reduction project targeted youth aged 12 to 24 who entered the emergency department as the result of an intentional violent incident and lived in one of several zip codes in South and West Philadelphia.

4. Anderson's and Collin's analysis are consistent with other masculinity studies that describe how the lack of access to economic resources encourage poor men of color to "become men" through displays of physical strength and violence.

5. In NO! The Rape Documentary, Aishah Simmons provides a compelling account of black women's experiences with rape and the complexity of black women's responses to sexual assault. For resources on sexual assault, see http://notherapedocumentary.org/

REFERENCES

Anderson, E. (1999). Code of the street: Decency, violence, and the moral life of the inner city. W.W. Norton.

Brookings Institution Center on Urban and Metropolitan Policy (BICUMP). (2003). Philadelphia in focus: A profile from Census 2000. Living Cities: The National Community Development Initiative.

Chesney-Lind, M., & Eliason, M. (2006). From invisible to incorrigible: The demonization of marginalized women and girls. Crime, Media, Culture 2(1): 29.

Cole, J. B., & Guy-Sheftall, B. (2003). Gender talk: The struggle for women's equality in African American communities. New York: One World. Ballantine Books.

Collins, P. H. (2004). Black sexual politics: African Americans, gender, and the new racism. New York and London: Routledge.

DeKeseredy, Shahid Alvi, W. S., & Tomaszewski, E. A. (2003). Perceived collective efficacy and women's victimization in public housing. Criminology and Criminal Justice 3(5).

Fine, M., Freudenberg, N., Payne, Y., Perkins, T., Smith, K., & Wanzer, K. (2003). Anything can happen with police around: Urban youth evaluate strategies of surveillance in public places. Journal of Social Issues 59(1): 141–158.

Jones, N. (2004). 'It's not where you live, it's how you live': how young women negotiate conflict and violence in the inner city. Annals of the American Academy of Political and Social Science 595 (September 2004). Eds. Elijah Anderson et al. Sage Publications.

Jones, N. (2008). Working 'the code': Girls, gender, and inner-city violence. The Australia and New Zealand Journal of Criminology 41(1): 63–83.

Jones, N. (2010). Between good and ghetto: African American girls and inner city violence. New Brunswick: Rutgers University Press.

Lauritsen, J. L., & Sampson, R. J. (1998). Minorities, crime, and criminal justice. In M. Tonry (ed.), The Handbook of Crime and Punishment (58–84). New York: Oxford University Press.

Massey, D., & Denton, N. (1993). American apartheid: Segregation and the making of the underclass. Cambridge: Harvard University Press.

Peterson, R. D., & Krivo, L. J. (2005). Macrostructural analyses of race, ethnicity, and violent crime: Recent lessons and new directions for research. Annual Review of Sociology 31: 331–356.

Pettit, K. L. S, & Kingsley, G. T. (2003). Concentrated poverty: a change in course. The Urban Institute.

Philadelphia Police Department: Crime Statistics. http://www.ppdonline.org/hq_statistics.php 3-30-2006 (accessed 9 January 2009).

Richie, B. (1996). Compelled to crime: The gender entrapment of battered black women. New York and London. Routledge.

Sampson, R. J., & Wilson, W. J. (1995). Toward a theory of race, crime, and urban inequality. In J. Hagan & R. Peterson (eds.), *Crime and Inequality* (37–54). Stanford, CA: Stanford University Press.

Thompson, M., & Keith, V. (2004). Copper brown and blue black: Colorism and self-evaluation. In C. Herring, V. Keith, & H. D. Horton (eds.), *Skin Deep: How Race and Complexion Matter in the "Color Blind" Era*. Champaign: University of Illinois Press.

West, C., & Fenstermaker, S. (1995). Doing difference. *Gender & Society* 9: 8–37.

West, C., & Zimmerman, D. H. (1987). Doing gender. *Gender & Society* 1: 125–151.

Wilson, W. J. (1980). *The declining significance of race: Blacks and changing American institutions*. Chicago: University of Chicago Press.

Wilson, W. J. (1987). *The truly disadvantaged: The inner city, the underclass, and public policy*. Chicago: University of Chicago Press.

Wilson, W. J. (1996). *When work disappears: The world of the new urban poor*. New York. Vintage Books.

Zernike, K. (2006). Violent crime rising sharply in some cities. *New York Times*. National. February 12.

TEN

THE IMPORTANCE OF CONTEXT IN THE

PRODUCTION OF OLDER GIRLS' VIOLENCE

Implications for the Focus of Interventions

Merry Morash
Suyeon Park
Jung-mi Kim

Numerous studies have established that, throughout adolescence, girls are much less likely than boys to attack, fight, or hit other people (Wolfgang, Thornberry, & Figlio, 1987; Osgood, Johnston, O'Malley, & Bacherman, 1988; Elliott, Huizinga, & Menard, 1989; Maguire & Pastore, 1997; Snyder & Sickmund, 1999; McCurley & Snyder, 2004: 6). This finding holds for violence against peers and family members, the most common targets of adolescents' assaults. Consistently, in different settings and periods, compared to male gang members, girls associated with gangs are less likely to be involved in fighting (Joe & Chesney-Lind, 1995; Miller & Decker, 1999; Bjerregaard & Smith, 1993; Esbensen & Winfree, 1998; Fagan, 1990; Miller, 2001: 141). Even in dangerous neighborhoods, being a girl decreases the chances of violence (Sampson, Morenoff, & Raudenbush, 2005), and girls are less likely than boys to carry firearms (Molnar et al., 2004). Similarly, girls are less violent than boys toward their parents even if they have been severely victimized by parental physical, sexual, or emotional abuse (Browne & Hamilton, 1998). These findings do not justify ignoring those girls who are assaultive, particularly if they persist or manifest this behavior in late adolescence, and thus are vulnerable to continued involvement in the justice system as adults. Silverthorn and Frick (1999) concluded from their research that girls often began delinquency well into adolescence, but their illegal behavior continued into adulthood. Odgers and Moretti (2002: 112) documented an alternative pattern for girls, which was a shift from aggressive behavior to substance abuse. Both of these patterns point to the importance of understanding the influences on girls who are aggressive toward the end of their teenage years. Documenting the predictors of older girls' violence contributes to this understanding.

There is a dearth of quantitative research on girls who are violent in late adolescence, in part because their limited delinquency leads to ignoring girls, and in part because of the challenges involved in studying a rare behavior. The research described in this chapter takes advantage of one part of the National Longitudinal Survey of Youth that began with data collection on a sample of youth in 1997 (NLSY97), and which has produced data that can be used to shed some light on the predictors of older girls' violence. The research also is used to draw some conclusions about the appropriate interventions to address older girls' violence.

There are multiple levels of possible influence on girls' violence. Ignoring individual-level risk factors could lead to a failure to respond to violence-producing characteristics of particular girls. Alternatively, if research only considers individual predisposing factors, but late-adolescent girls' violence is a response to dangerous neighborhoods or schools, then programs grounded in such research could distract attention from interventions to remove or protect girls from negative contexts, or in the long run to improve those contexts. Helping individual girls (and boys) cope effectively with dangerous environments can have some positive effects, but the power of an individual-level intervention could be counteracted by strong and pervasive settings that support or even require girls' use of violence to survive.

THE DATA

With funding form the U.S. Department of Labor, after the first data collection for the NLSY97, subsequent interviews have been carried out with the same youth each year. The initial sample of 8,984 adolescents (age 12 through 16) overrepresented racial minorities and Hispanics, so for the analysis described in this chapter, weighting was used to produce estimates of statistical parameters that are nationally representative.[1] To allow for inference about time order, just the 1,394 girls who were age 12 and 13 in 1997 were included, predictors were based on data collected beginning in 1997 and extending through 2002, and assaults were indicated by data collected for 2001 and 2002. An advantage of the NLSY97 is that even with the restricted sample and after some sample dropout over the years, 1,265 girls could be included in the analysis. Another advantage is that theoretically relevant variables at different levels—individual, family, peer, ties to legitimate institutions (school, religion, and work), and perceived danger of the school and community environment could be included in a predictive model. The disadvantage is that the data were not designed to test any particular theory of girls' violence, and thus some important variables (especially childhood sexual abuse) were not measured. Yet, the large, nationally representative sample of girls, the range of variables that are available, annual measures of self-reported assault and other delinquency, and the longitudinal design make analysis of NLSY97 data a good starting point for a predictive approach to understanding older girls' assaults.

HYPOTHESIZED PREDICTORS OF OLDER GIRLS' ASSAULTS

Individual Differences

Early delinquency. Early antisocial and delinquent behavior of children and young teens has repeatedly been shown to predict later delinquency (e.g., Chamberlain, 2003). Specific to girls, Caspi, Lynam, Moffit, and Silva (1993) documented that childhood behavior problems predicted continued delinquency. Similarly, Hamalainen and Pulkkinen (1995) showed that peer and teacher ratings of 8- and 14-year-old girls as aggressive predicted later delinquency. A meta-analysis (Lipsey & Derzon, 1998) of research on girls and boys showed that a juvenile offense of any type between ages 6 and 11 was the strongest predictor of subsequent violence. Also a juvenile offense between ages 12 and 14 was the second strongest predictor of violence after age 14. In the present research, delinquency in early adolescence was indicated by responses to questions about frequency of stealing, assaulting others, selling drugs, and destroying property in the year before the first interview, and based on factor analysis results, factor scores were generated to reflect early delinquency. Early delinquency was expected to predict girls' assaultive behavior in late adolescence.

Early running away. It is well established that abuse in the family can lead girls to run away from home. Studies suggest that between 30% and 75% of runaway girls have been abused (McCormack, Janus, & Burgess, 1986; Tyler et al., 2001: 161). Girls who have been abused at a young age run away early and survive on the streets by trading sex, dealing and using drugs, and affiliating with people who break the law (Chen et al., 2004). Each of these survival strategies could create situational reasons for girls to use violence to protect themselves and to manage on their own, and early-age running away appears to be especially serious, signifying the possibility of multiple street survival strategies and the inadequacies and unavailability of families to meet girls' needs. At the first NLSY97 interview, girls were asked if they had ever run away, and an affirmative response was used to indicate being runaway at an early age.

Early puberty. Evidence that girls who reach menarche early in disorganized communities are prone to violence (Obeidallah et al., 2004) is discussed later in more detail in the section on community context. No literature could be located to shed light on whether the documented association of early menarche to violence continues to late adolescence. Girls were considered to have started puberty early if their first menstruation was before age 11; 14% of girls were in this group.

Hope for the future. Research suggests that girls in communities with concentrated disadvantage commit assaults in part because breaking the law cannot make things worse than they are. For instance, Ness (2004) described Philadelphia girls' perceptions of bleak futures no matter what they did. They were already alienated from legitimate institutions, so police and juvenile justice system contact could not add further to such problems. Just for the 2000 interview for the NLSY97, youths were asked to report their likelihood of being victims of crime and being arrested in the year after the interview, and to report the probability of both expected outcomes within five years. The answers to the four questions were combined to produce a composite measure of expected victimization and arrest, or low hope for the future (Cronbach's alpha = .85).

Family Characteristics

Household member incarceration. Parental criminality and related parental incarceration predict girls' and boys' delinquency and subsequent adult lawbreaking (for a review and analysis, see Dallaire, 2007; Murray, Janson, & Farrington, 2007). Phillips, Erkanli, Keeler, Costello, and Angold (2006) showed that the high prevalence of substance abuse and mental illness associated with parents' criminality and incarceration led to negative family conditions (e.g., financial strain) that became worse due to parental incarceration. Another hypothesized link of parent-to-youth behavior is that parents' illegal activity promotes social learning that supports youths' lawbreaking (Farrington, 2002). Since any household member could promote youths' illegal acts through social learning and creating family strain, the incarceration of any household member before 2001 was used as a predictor of girls' assaultive behavior.

Parental support and monitoring. Especially for girls, lack of parental support appears to promote delinquency, including violence (e.g., Saner & Ellickson, 1996). Consistent with this conclusion, California girls in trouble with the law told researchers (Acoca & Dedel, 1998: 43) that a negative relationship with parents was a much greater influence on their delinquency than substance abuse, school problems, and boyfriends. Highlighting the importance of another key family process variable, parental supervision, Bottcher's (1995) comparison of sisters and their highly delinquent brothers showed that restrictions on movement and monitoring by parents explained the girls' lower delinquency. Several studies have confirmed the importance of both supportive parent-child relationships (Baumrind, 1996; Steinberg et al., 1991) and monitoring (e.g., Cernkovich & Giordano, 1987; Broidy, 1995; Chamberlain, 2003) to girls' delinquency.

A measure of parental monitoring was derived from the girls' annual Likert-type ratings of the following items for both their mothers and fathers: "How much does he/she know about your close friends, that is, who they are?" "How much does he/she know about your close friends' parents, that is, who they are?" "How much does he/she know about who you are with when you are not home?" and "How much does he/she know about who your teachers are and what you are doing in school?" Responses were measured on a 5-point scale ranging from 0 = knows nothing to 4 = knows everything. A composite scale was created for each year from 1997 through 2000 using the highest parent's score for each item. These measures were combined for the four years to indicate level of monitoring throughout the period (Cronbach's alpha = .78).

In 1997, the girls were asked to rate the supportiveness of each of their parents from 1, "very supportive," to 3, "not very supportive." These ratings were used to code girls into one of three ordinal categories: low support from one or both parents, medium support from at least one parent, and high support from at least one parent. The numbers were reversed so that a high score indicated high support.

Grades completed in school. Saner and Ellickson (1996) found that for girls more than boys, violence was connected to low academic achievement. Qualitative research has provided some explanation. Three different studies have shown that when teachers exposed girls' academic limitations in front of peers, girls maintained their status by fighting with peers (Grant, 1984; Brown, 1998; Leitz, 2003). The NLSY97 indicator of academic achievement that was used was the school grade completed by 2002.

Religious activity. In addition to schools, religious institutions can provide involvement in and ties to legitimate activities and opportunities that might lead to lower levels of delinquency, including violence (Regnerus & Elder, 2003; Jang & Johnson, 2005). Particularly convincing evidence of the influence of religion was provided by a meta-analysis (Baier & Wright, 2001) finding that the higher the percentage of girls in the study, the more findings of negative effects of religion on delinquency. Religion may be especially important in communities marked by extreme disadvantage (Jang & Johnson, 2003, 2004, 2005; Johnson et al., 2000; Pattillo-McCoy, 1998; Regnerus & Elder, 2003). Girls participating in the NLSY97 self-reported the frequency of attending religious services for 2000 and 2001, and their self-reports were combined (Cronbach's alpha = .80).

Work activity. In a compelling piece of research, some years ago Sullivan (1989) showed that for boys, the availability of legitimate work activities interrupted adolescent delinquency and facilitated law-abiding behavior later in adolescence. In contrast, when youth could not find legitimate work, they turned to burglary and robbery to "get paid." This pattern has not been explored for girls, but work activity could provide legitimate income and keep girls out of settings where they would be exposed to violence and where they would use violence either instrumentally or in self-defense. Few girls worked when they were very young, and the questions to measure work activity were not comparable before 2001 and during or after that year. Thus, the measure of work activity was the combined number of hours worked in 2001 and 2002.

Involvement with gangs. Some girls with abusive and negative family experiences turn to gangs as family extensions or replacements, and in dangerous neighborhoods, to provide protection (Acoca & Dedel, 1998; Joe & Chesney-Lind, 1999). Social scientist Miranda (2003: 29) wrote that she had been a "situational" gang member to prevent threats, harassment, and assaults. Joe and Chesney-Lind (1999) and Campbell (1991) also found that girls joined gangs to prevent being attacked. Even if gang membership provides some protection, it could result in increased fighting to protect other members (Dietrich, 1998: 134; Portillos, 1999: 241; Miller, 2001; Laidler & Hunt, 1997) and maintain status in the group (Laidler & Hunt, 2001:. 675). Each year, the NLSY97 included questions about belonging to a gang. The variable to reflect gang membership was a count of the number of years beginning in 1997 that girls reported they belonged to a gang.

Neighborhood and school context. Several quantitative studies have shown a connection of living in a disadvantaged or violent community to girls' violence (Brooks-Gunn et al., 1993; Durant et al., 1994; Ingoldsby & Shaw, 2002; Molnar et al., 2005). The Project on Human Development in Chicago Neighborhoods (PHDCN) was specifically designed to identify and separate neighborhood and other influences on adolescents. That study found that a combination of early puberty and disadvantaged neighborhood was associated with girls' violence. Research has suggested some possible reasons. Early-maturing girls may get involved with older boys who model and encourage use of violence (e.g., Ge et al., 2002).

Sexual harassment may be pronounced in neighborhoods where males lack ways to positively define their masculinity (Benson et al., 2003). Furthermore, parents in dangerous neighborhoods may try to keep early-maturing girls at home to protect them, but this could actually lead to anger and assaults by the girls, who might become involved in gangs to escape parental controls, or who might fight to signal their anger at being confined to restrictive gender arrangements (see Haynie, 2003). The PHDCN researchers (Obeidallah et al., 2004) theorized that cumulative stress resulted from the negative neighborhood conditions and problems resulting from early menarche (being seen as deviant among peers or as mature by older boys and men). Based on the Obeidallah et al. (2004) findings, the interaction of the variable reflecting dangerousness of the neighborhood, and early menarche was considered in the analysis. To measure dangerousness of the area, each respondent was asked how many years she had been in a neighborhood with gangs and how many years her friends or siblings had been in a gang. These two items have been combined to form an indication of dangerous area (alpha = .60).

   Victimization through bullying. Being bullied in school can lead to aggressive and assaultive behavior (Haynie et al., 2001; Juvonen, Graham, & Schuster, 2003; Nancel et al., 2003). The outcome can result because victims learn the methods and attitudes that support attacking others (Baldry, 2003), or because victims join groups or act alone to stop their own victimization by assaulting others (Farrington, 1993). The analysis therefore included a predictor that reflected bullying. Girls indicated whether they were bullied before age 12 and after age 12, negative responses were coded as 0, affirmative responses were coded 1, and the responses relevant to the different times were added together into an index.

Analysis

The dependent variable was the count of self-reported assaults in 2001 and 2002. Negative binomial regression was selected as the method for statistical analysis because the most common value for number of assaults was 0, and only 8.9% of girls reported any assaultive behavior in the two-year period summarized in the independent variable. The distribution of assault is far from normal, making ordinary least squares regression (OLS) analysis inappropriate (Long, 1997; Long & Freese, 2003).

Findings

Descriptive statistics, calculated after the data were weighted, are presented in table 10.1 (next page). For subsequent analysis (correlations and regression), missing values were imputed. The bivariate correlations (table 10.2, page 227) show that girls who expected a future marked by their own victimization and arrest in 2000 reported committing assaults in 2001 and 2002. There were positive associations of the number of assaults with the variables, early delinquency, early running away, and household member incarceration. The number of assaults that girls reported in late adolescence was also positively related to the number of years they identified themselves as gang members and perceptions of their neighborhoods as dangerous. There were weak negative but statistically significant correlations between the number of assaults and grades completed in school, parental support, and monitoring by parents. Girls who finished more grades in school, with more parental support, and with more parental monitoring reported less assaultive behavior than others.

   The statistics for the three binomial regression analysis models show that the data have an acceptable fit to the models. However, the addition

Table 10.1. Descriptive Statistics for Dependent and Independent Variables Used in the Analyses

Variables	Mean	SD	Min.	Max.	N	% yes
Assault	.30	1.65	0	23	1265	
Early delinquency	-.11	.77	-.85	14.34	1394	
Early running away	.05	.22	0	1	1394	5%
Early puberty	.15	.35	0	1	1394	14%
Low hope for the future	10.43	14.24	0	93.75	1394	
Household member incarceration	.07	.26	0	1	1394	7%
Parental support	2.81	.43	1	3	1394	
Parental monitoring	42.16	8.58	9	64	1394	
Grades completed in school	12.29	1.19	0	16	1394	
Religious activity	3.66	1.97	1	8	1394	
Work activity	681.80	479.67	0	2848	1394	
Involvement with gangs	.03	.26	0	4	1394	
Black[1]	.16	.36	0	1	1381	16%
Other race[1]	.12	.32	0	1	1381	12%
Dangerous neighborhood context	1.39	1.63	0	8	1394	
Victimization through bullying	.07	.26	0	1	1394	7%

[1]White is the reference category.

Table 10.2. Correlation Matrix

	(1)	(2)	(3)	(4)	(5)	(6)	(7)	(8)	(9)	(10)	(11)	(12)	(13)	(14)	(15)	(16)
(1)	1.00															
(2)	.27**	1.00														
(3)	.13**	.33**	1.00													
(4)	-.01	.04	.05*	1.00												
(5)	.18**	.17**	.13**	.01	1.00											
(6)	.10**	.05	.05	.00	.04	1.00										
(7)	-.11**	-.17**	-.14**	-.01	-.14**	-.09**	1.00									
(8)	-.13**	-.19**	-.17**	-.01	-.19**	-.06*	.34**	1.00								
(9)	-.09**	-.11**	-.08**	.02	-.00	-.07*	.07*	.08**	1.00							
(10)	-.04	-.08*	-.07**	.00	-.11**	-.09**	.07*	.21**	.14**	1.00						
(11)	.02	.02	-.02	-.01	.01	.04	-.03	-.03	.05	-.05	1.00					
(12)	.15**	.28**	.22**	-.00	.10**	.05*	-.06*	-.11**	-.10**	-.06*	-.04	1.00				
(13)	.04	-.02	-.00	.13**	-.03	.02	-.04	-.06*	-.05	.13**	-.09**	.02	1.00			
(14)	.00	.03	.09**	.02	-.01	-.01	-.03	-.09**	-.00	-.03	-.08**	.06*	-.16**	1.00		
(15)	.22**	.20**	.22**	.05*	.19**	.09**	-.12**	-.21**	-.11**	-.05	.01	.27**	.12**	.16**	1.00	
(16)	.04	.13**	.10**	.04	.05	.08**	-.00	-.01	-.02	.02	-.06*	.11**	-.02	-.01	.09**	1.00

Key

(1) Assault
(2) Early delinquency
(3) Early running away
(4) Early puberty
(5) Low hope for the future
(6) Household member incarceration
(7) Parental support
(8) Parental monitoring

(9) Grades completed in school
(10) Religious activity
(11) Work activity
(12) Involvement with gangs

(13) Black[1]
(14) Other race[1]
(15) Dangerous neighborhood context
(16) Victimization through bullying

**P < .01, *P < .05, [1]White is the reference category.

of contextual variables did improve the fit of the model, suggesting the importance of context despite the limitations of indicators in the available data. The multivariate binomial regression analysis identified the non-spurious predictors of assaults. Then, exploratory analysis of interaction effects was done to understand the unexpected finding of a negative relationship of years in a gang to assaults.

Several findings about non-spurious predictors of assaults were similar to results of the correlation analysis. Being a runaway at a young age and seeing a future marked by one's own victimization and arrest in mid-adolescence predicted assaults in late adolescence. It is notable that compared to those who had never run away, girls who had run away at least once by the 1997 interview reported significantly more (376%) assaults during 2001 and 2002. Each unit increase in the ordinal scale variable that measures low hope for a future with no crime involvement equates to a small but statistically significant increase of 2% in total number of assaults. Household member incarceration was significantly associated with more assaults. Girls with family members incarcerated within the last five years committed 132% more assaults than other girls. Contrary to findings in other research, the one other individual-level difference, early puberty, was related to *lower* levels of assault in late adolescence.

Girls who were more heavily monitored by their parents committed fewer assaults. Years of school completed, but not religious and work activity, were related to assaults. Each year of school the girls completed lowered the number of assaults in late adolescence by 41%.

When contextual variables were added, early running away and low hope for the future still predicted more assaults. Parental monitoring, early puberty, and grades completed in school continued to predict fewer assaults. However, household member incarceration was no longer significantly related to assaults. Unexpectedly, gang membership was significantly associated with fewer assaults. Finally, the multivariate analysis showed that the more dangerous a girls' neighborhood, the more likely she was to engage in assaultive behavior.

When interaction terms were added, there was no shift in important predictors except for the early puberty variable. Inconsistent with PHDCN findings, early puberty was not predictive of older girls' assaultive behavior, and the combination of a dangerous neighborhood with early puberty was not predictive. Also, an analysis (not shown here) of one-third of the girls in neighborhoods perceived as most dangerous produced a result of not significant for early puberty as a predictor of assaults. It is recognized that the PHDCN findings did not focus on assaults in late adolescence.

To shed light on the unexpected finding that gang membership predicted fewer assaults, interaction terms between gang memberships and each of the other independent variable were added to the model one at a time. Only the interaction of being black and gang membership was significant, and is therefore included in table 10.3. The interaction term between gang

Table 10.3. Negative Binomial Regression Results for Assault

Variables	Model 1			Model 2			Model 3		
	b	SE	Exp(b)−1	b	SE	Exp(b)−1	b	SE	Exp(b)−1
Non–context variables									
Individual level									
Early delinquency	.01	.14	.01	.01	.14	.01	.02	.15	.02
Early running away	1.56	.47	3.76**	1.24	.44	2.46**	1.27	.44	2.56**
Early puberty	−.72	.32	−.51*	−.80	.33	−.55*	−.85	.63	−.57
Low hope for the future	.02	.01	.02**	.02	.01	.02*	.02	.01	.02*
Family level									
Household member incarceration	.84	.39	1.32*	.67	.40	.95	.68	.40	.97
Parental support	−.08	.29	−.08	−.12	.32	−.11	−.13	.32	−.12
Parental monitoring	−.06	.02	−.06*	−.06	.02	−.06**	−.06	.02	−.06**
Ties to legitimate institutions									
Grades completed in school	−.52	.18	−.41**	−.29	.13	−.25*	−.31	.13	−.27*
Religious activity	−.07	.08	−.07	−.11	.07	−.10	−.10	.07	−.10
Work activity	.00	.00	.00	.00	.00	.00	.00	.00	.00
Peers									
Involvement with gangs	.37	.38	.45	−.69	.34	−.50*	−1.14	.43	−.68**
Control variables									
Black[1]	.53	.34	.70	.39	.34	.48	.30	.35	.35
Other race[1]	−.20	.41	−.18	−.55	.42	−.42	−.55	.44	−.42

continued on next page

Table 10.3. Continued

Variables	Model 1			Model 2			Model 3		
	b	SE	Exp(b)−1	b	SE	Exp(b)−1	b	SE	Exp(b)−1
Context variables									
Dangerous neighborhood context				.41	.08	.51**	.40	.09	.49**
Victimization through bullying				.17	.33	.19	.12	.34	.13
Interaction term									
Black* Involvement with gangs							1.25	.58	2.49*
Other race* Involvement with gangs							.23	.63	.26
Early puberty* Dangerous neighborhood context							.02	.18	.02
Constant	6.84	2.17**		3.68	1.73*		3.92	1.76	
Log psuedolikelihood	−543.73			−528.76			−528.16		
Chi–Squared (df)	96.66 (13)**			120.18 (15)**			122.48 (18)**		
N	1253			1253			1253		

**P < .01, *P < .05
[1]White is the reference category.

membership and being black increased assaults by 249%. It appears that for black youth, being involved with gangs for more years is related to more assaults in late adolescence.

DISCUSSION AND CONCLUSION

Several of the significant predictors of girls' assaults in late adolescence implicate family and neighborhood contexts in the production of older girls' violence. Very early runaway behavior (before 13) but not early general delinquency was key in predicting which girls self-reported assaultive behavior between ages 16 and 17. This finding persists after controls for other family process variables, gang membership, ties to legitimate institutions, perceptions of the neighborhood as dangerous, and being bullied in school are considered, and it suggests the importance of running away at an early age and the precursors of running away (which are not available for study with the NLSY97) for predicting girls' assaultive acts in the long run. Alternatively, girls who were assaultive in late adolescence did not have a pattern of general, early delinquency.

The literature provides some reasons for the finding about running away. Youth who run away from home are typically escaping from negative conditions, not running to attractive and enticing living arrangements (Lindsey et al., 2000; Molnar et al., 1998; Tyler & Cauce, 2002; Sullivan & Knutson, 2000). A study of California girls involved in the juvenile justice system showed that they ran from parental conflict that included chronic verbal disagreements and physical fights among family members (Acoca & Dedel, 1998: 43). The introduction to this chapter cited key literature on girls' running from homes where they were abused sexually and in other ways. Once youths are on the run, "risk amplification" (Chen et al., 2004:. 1) occurs, as youths are victimized (Tyler et al., 2004) and turn to gangs and/or the use of violence for self-protection.

Consistent with the finding about early running away, the persistent statistical significance of "low hope" for avoiding future victimization and arrest further implicates girls' context as an influence on their violence. Before they were violent in 2001 and 2002, girls perceived themselves as probable victims of crime and as probable subjects of arrest. This suggests that the girls' defeatism that Ness (2004) described, that justice system involvement could not make things worse, combined with the expectation of victimization, might make the use of violence seem like a reasonable choice. Girls' expectations regarding their future victimization and arrest may be quite realistic. Thus, the challenge is to design an intervention that actually reduces girls' victimization and arrest, rather than one that gives them false hope.

The PHDCN research found that early puberty was an important predictor of girls' violence, but only in dangerous and disorganized neighborhoods. We considered whether the inability to reproduce this finding with the NLSY97 was because a different definition was used for early menarche. This did not seem to be the case. Based on earlier research and their own identification of natural breaks in the data, Obeidallah et al. (2004) defined early as the most extreme 20%, and used a cut-off point of less than 11 years old. The NLSY97 suggests the exact same age cut-off to identify the girls with earliest onset of puberty, and thus the age used to indicate "early" was the same in both studies. Perhaps the use of structural indicators of neighborhood conditions in the Obeidallah et al. (2004) study made a difference, since the present analysis used reports of household break-ins and gang activity. Also, the NLSY97 data were used to predict assaults in late adolescence, a point at which any initial effects of early puberty might be dissipated.

Household members' incarceration and girls' violence also were unrelated in the multivariate analysis of the NLSY97 data. Clear (2007) has written about how the most disadvantaged neighborhoods have the greatest number of individuals incarcerated, and the resulting weakening of the neighborhoods and the families in them. A connection of household member incarceration with dangerous neighborhoods may account for the inability to show a non-spurious and significant connection of household member incarceration to girls' assaultive behavior. The negative neighborhood conditions likely explain any predictive power of incarcerated household members.

It appears that just for black girls, more years in a gang predicted higher levels of late-adolescent assault. Being black is another variable that is intertwined with neighborhood disadvantage (Sampson & Morenoff, 1999; Wilson, 1987), since African Americans are most likely to live in the most disadvantaged, dangerous neighborhoods.

Experience of bullying in school also was not related to violence. The indicator available for bullying was limited (yes or no report of bullying before and after age 12), which may account for the findings. It also may be that bullying is not a key influence on older girls, that girls do not often respond to bullying with physical aggression, that violence other than bullying in school is most relevant to counterviolence by girls, or that the finding is due to girls' decreased violence in school as they get older, which was documented by Gottfredson, Gottfredson, and Payne (2005).

Consistent with prior research, completion of more grades in school was predictive of low numbers of assaults. Also consistent, a higher level of parental monitoring throughout adolescence was related to no or few assaults in late adolescence.

Further quantitative research is needed on the connection of girls' violence to some probable influences on girls' violence that were not available in the NLSY97 data. As already noted, a likely predictor is sexual abuse (Cottrell & Monk, 2004; Ryder, 2007). Another is exposure to and victimization by other forms of violence (e.g., Artz, 2004; Ness, 2004; Hunt & Laidler, 2001; Miller, 2001: 49; Song, Singer, & Anglin, 1998; Herrera &

McCloskey, 2001; Becker & McCloskey, 2002; Blum, Ireland, & Blum, 2003).
As is common with available data, the advantages of a large, representative,
longitudinal data set that included many girls are partly counterbalanced by
the disadvantage in the particular measures available for the analysis.

Findings from predictive positivist research need to be interpreted in
relation to and supplemented by findings from qualitative research that can
present a more detailed picture of girls' characteristics and situations and
their violent actions. Despite the need to draw on additional research and
theory to more fully understand girls' violence at the point they are about
to transition out of adolescence, the analysis of the NLSY97 does have some
implications for the range and form of interventions that would be relevant
to the small number of girls who do engage in violence at age 16 or 17.

IMPLICATIONS FOR INTERVENTIONS

At the least, the NLSY97-based findings raise questions about a focus on
dedicating resources to such things as medical screening and help with
coping directed at early puberty girls in bad neighborhoods. Until there is
further replication of the finding about early menarche and complementary
qualitative research to explain whether and how it promotes girls' violence,
the focus is not warranted. There is more compelling evidence of the need
to improve neighborhoods or change housing assistance to ensure that
more girls live in safe neighborhoods, and to provide substantial help for
girls who run away, including long-term help for girls at a young age and
with permanently "empty" families that cannot meet their daughters' needs
(Schaffner, 2006).

One intervention that would logically flow from the NLSY97 and
other reviewed findings is to improve the most disadvantaged, crime-ridden
neighborhoods. Beginning in 2000, the conservative Bush administration
deemphasized community development and urban policy, leaving states
and central cities with the most serious urban blight struggling financially
to address the needs of poor urban communities (Vidal & Keating, 2004).
In the current federal policy environment, communities are encouraged to
prevent delinquency by engaging internal leadership and institutions in an
assessment of community needs and the selection of research-verified effective practices (Caliber Associates, 2002). Given that 75% of communities
receive less than $52,000 to do this, and because community-level services
for youth are very fragmented (Bishop & Decker, 2006), it is difficult to
understand how the most crime-ridden and disadvantaged communities can
meaningfully build up or use resources to address delinquency in general,
and girls' violence in particular.

An alternative intervention is to help families move out of the most
disadvantaged neighborhoods. An evaluation of a U.S. Department of Housing
and Urban Development project, which was a Clinton-era initiative, showed

that this strategy ultimately resulted in less violence (and property offending) by girls (Kling, Ludwig, & Katz, 2005). Families in Baltimore, Boston, Chicago, Los Angeles, and New York City were provided with vouchers that allowed them to move out of housing projects or other very disadvantaged communities. Compared to an experimentally formed group that did not move, girls who moved did better in school, more often expected to attend college, and were arrested less often. Like neighborhood development, housing policies enabling families to escape dangerous neighborhoods are not currently in vogue. The predominant political preference and related government interventions emphasize individual-level control and punishment and interventions focused on reducing particular risk factors within family, peer, and community systems (Bishop & Decker, 2006).

A consideration of the NLSY97 findings regarding runaways and the state of current programming to support runaway girls is troubling. Based on their review of literature identifying risk and protective factors that contribute to girls' serious delinquency, Mullis, Cornille, Mullis, and Huber (2004) recommended a gender-specific continuum of care that would include prevention and early intervention. Such a continuum would be responsive to early runaway behavior and the contexts that promote it. In contrast to the need for intensive programming to assist runaways, there is very limited literature on effective programs for runaways, and none specific to girls (Slesnick & Prestonnik, 2005). There also is a dearth of useful programs. A 2001 national assessment by the American Bar Association and the National Bar Association concluded that most programs for runaway girls "have focused on control rather than the provision of effective support for girls to become successful and to grow beyond the trauma that often drives their runaway behavior" (12).

Existing programs that target improving girls' progress in school and training parents to better monitor their children are consistent with the NLSY97-based findings. There are problems, however, with a sole concentration on these approaches, to the exclusion of addressing the broader context that promotes girls' violence. First, it is unclear that limited-focus interventions can counteract the influences they ignore, and dangerous neighborhoods can be a powerful influence on youth. Recommendations for a more multifaceted set of interventions in what are called wraparound services that address multiple needs (Covington & Bloom, 2003:. 1; Reed & Leavitt, 1998) are a rejection of narrowly focused, time-limited interventions. Also, because of parental substance abuse, mental illness, and other stressors, some girls will never be able to rely on their families to provide adequate parenting, protection, and material and emotional support (Schaffner, 2006). As noted in discussion of the literature on runaways, sometimes families perpetrate violence against girls. Very few programs address the range of special circumstances and problems of girls who break the law (Girls Incorporated, 1996), and existing programs for girls typically address an outcome or symptom of girls' distress, rather than underlying causes (Ms. Foundation for Women, 1993; Greene, Peters, & Associates, 1998). Yet, the analysis we have presented coupled with the findings of prior qualitative and quantitative research suggests that broader neighborhood changes and a wider range of services, available at a young age and continuously over time, would have most influence in reducing older girls' assaults.

NOTE

1. The software, STATA 8, was used for the weighting and the analysis.

REFERENCES

Acoca, L., & Dedel, K. (1998). *No place to hide: Understanding and meeting the needs of girls in the juvenile justice system.* San Francisco, CA: National Council on Crime and Delinquency.

American Bar Association & National Bar Association. (2001). *Justice by gender: The lack of appropriate prevention, diversion and treatment alternatives for girls in the justice system.* Washington, DC: American Bar Association and the National Bar Association.

Artz, S. (2004). Revisiting the moral domain: Using social interdependence theory to understand adolescent girls' perspectives on the use of violence. In M. Moretti, C. Odgers, and J. Jackson (eds.), *Girls and Aggression: Contributing Factors and Intervention Principles* (101–113). New York: Kluwer Academic/Plenum Publishers.

Baier, C. J., & Wright, B. R. E. (2001). If you love me, keep my commandments: A meta-analysis of the effect of religion on crime. *Journal of Research in Crime and Delinquency* 38: 3–21.

Baldry, A. C. (2003). Bullying in schools and exposure to domestic violence. *Child Abuse & Neglect* 27: 713–732.

Baumrind, D. (1996). The discipline controversy. *Family Relations: Journal of Applied Family and Child Studies* 45(4): 405–414.

Becker, K. B., & McCloskey, L. A. (2002). Attention and conduct problems in children exposed to family violence. *American Journal of Orthopsychiatry* 72: 83–91.

Benson, M. L., Greer, L. F., DeMaris, A., & Van Wyk, J. (2003). Neighborhood disadvantage, individual economic distress and violence against women in intimate relationships. *Journal of Quantitative Criminology* 19: 207–235.

Bishop, D. M., & Decker, S. H. (2006). Punishment and control: Juvenile Justice Reform in the USA. In J. Junger-Tas & S. H. Decker (eds.), *International Handbook of Juvenile Justice* (3–35). Dordrecht: Springer.

Bjerregaard, B., & Smith, C. (1993). Gender differences in gang participation, delinquency, and substance use. *Journal of Quantitative Criminology* 4: 329–355.

Blum, J., Ireland, M., & Blum, R. W. (2003). Gender differences in juvenile violence: A report from Add Health. *Journal of Adolescent Health* 32(3): 234–240.

Bottcher, J. (1995). Gender as social control: A qualitative study of incarcerated youths and their siblings in Greater Sacramento. *Justice Quarterly* 12(1): 33–57.

Broidy, L. (1995). Direct supervision and delinquency: Assessing the adequacy of structural proxies. *Journal of Criminal Justice* 23: 541–554.

Brooks-Gunn, J., Duncan, G. J., Klebanov, P. K., & Sealand, N. (1993). Do neighborhoods influence child and adolescent development? *American Journal of Sociology* 99: 353–395.

Brown, L. M. (1998). *Raising their voices: The politics of girls' anger*. Cambridge: Harvard University Press.

Browne, K. D., & Hamilton, C. E. (1998). Physical violence between young adults and their parents: Associations with a history of child maltreatment. *Journal of Family Violence* 13(1): 59–79.

Caliber Associates. (2002). *2002 Report to Congress: Title V Community Prevention Grants Program*. NCJ 202019. Washington, DC: U.S. Department of Justice, Office of Justice Programs, Office of Juvenile Justice and Delinquency Prevention.

Campbell, A. (1991). *The girls in the gang*. Cambridge, MA: Basil Blackwell.

Caspi, A., Lynam, D., Moffit, T., & Silva, P. (1993). Unraveling girls' delinquency: Biological, dispositional, and contextual contributions to adolescent misbehavior. *Developmental Psychology* 29: 19–30.

Cernkovich, S. A., & Giordano, P. C. (1987). Family relationships and delinquency. *Criminology* 25: 295–321.

Chamberlain, P. (2003). *Treating chronic juvenile offenders: Advances made through the Oregon Multidimensional Treatment Foster Care Model*. Washington, DC: American Psychological Association.

Chen, X., Tyler, K. A., Whitbeck, L. B., & Hoyt, D. R. (2004). Early sex abuse, street adversity, and drug use among female homeless and runaway adolescents in the Midwest. *Journal of Drug Issues* 34: 1–21.

Clear, T. R. (2007) *Imprisoning communities: How mass incarceration makes disadvantaged neighborhoods worse*. Oxford; New York: Oxford University Press.

Cottrell, B., & Monk, P. (2004). Adolescent-to-parent abuse. *Journal of Family Issues* 25(8): 1072–1095.

Covington, S., & Bloom, B. (2003). Gendered justice: Women in the criminal justice system. In B. E. Bloom (ed.), *Gendered justice: Addressing female offenders* (1–20). Durham, NC: Center for Gender and Justice.

Dallaire, D. H. (2007). Incarcerated mothers and fathers: A comparison of risks for children and families. *Family Relations* 56 (5): 440–453.

Dietrich, L. C. (1998). *Chicana Adolescents: Bitches, 'Ho's, and Schoolgirls*. Westport, CT: Praeger.

DuRant, R. H., Cadenhead, C., Pendergrast, R. A., Slavens, G., & Linder, C. W. (1994). Factors associated with the use of violence among urban black adolescents. *American Journal of Public Health* 84 (4): 612–617.

Elliot, D. S., Huizinga, D., & Menard, S. (1989). *Multiple problem youth: Delinquency, substance use, and mental health problems*. New York: Spinger-Verlag.

Esbensen, F., & Winfree, L. T. (1998). Race and gender differences between gang and non-gang youth: Results from a multi-site survey. *Justice Quarterly* 15: 505–525.

Fagan, J. (1990). Social processes of delinquency and drug use among urban gangs. In C. R. Huff (ed.), *Gangs in America* (183–219). Newbury Park, CA: Sage Publications.

Farrington, D. P. (1993). Understanding and preventing bullying. *Crime and Justice* 17: 381–458.

Farrington, D. P. (2002). Families and crime. In J. Q. Wilson & J. Petersilia (eds.), *Crime: Public Policies for Crime Control* (129–148). Oakland, CA: Institute for Contemporary Studies Press.

Ge, X., Brody, H. Simons, R. L., Murry, V. M. 2002. Contextual amplification of pubertal transition effects on deviant peer affiliation and externalizing behavior among African American children. *Developmental Psychology* 38: 42–54.

Girls Incorporated. (1996). *Prevention and parity: Girls in juvenile justice.* Indianapolis: Girls Incorporated National Resource Center.

Gottfredson, G. D., Gottfredson, D. C., & Payne, A. A. (2005). School climate predictors of school disorder: Results from a national study of delinquency prevention in schools. *Journal of Research in Crime and Delinquency* 42(4): 412–444.

Grant, L. (1984). Black females "place" in the desegregated classrooms. *Sociology of Education* 57(2): 98–111.

Greene, Peters, & Associates. (1998). *Guiding Principles for Promising Female Programming: An Inventory of Best Practices.* Washington, DC: Office of Juvenile Justice and Delinquency Prevention, U.S. Department of Justice.

Hamalainen, M., & Pulkkinen, L. (1995). Aggressive and non-prosocial behavior as precursors of criminality. *Studies on Crime and Crime Prevention* 4: 6–21.

Haynie, D. (2003). Contexts of risk? Explaining the link between girls' pubertal development and their delinquency involvement. *Social Forces* 82(1): 355–397.

Haynie, D. L., Nansel, T., Eithel, P., Crump, A. D., Saylor, K., Yu, K., & Simons-Morton, B. (2001). Bullies, victims, and bully/victims: Distinct groups of at-risk youth. *Journal of Early Adolescence* 21(1): 29–49.

Herrera, V. M., & McCloskey, L. A. (2001). Gender differences in the risk for delinquency among youth exposed to family violence. *Child Abuse and Neglect* 25: 1037–1052.

Ingoldsby, E. M., & Shaw, D. S. (2002). The role of neighborhood contextual factors on early-starting antisocial behavior. *Clinical Child and Family Psychology Review* 6: 21–65.

Jang, S. J., & Johnson, B. R. (2003). Strain, negative emotions, and deviant coping among African Americans: A test of general strain theory. *Journal of Quantitative Criminology* 19: 79–105.

Jang, S. J., & Johnson, B. R. (2004). Explaining religious effects on distress among African Americans. *Journal for the Scientific Study of Religion* 43: 239–260.

Jang, S. J., & Johnson, B. R. (2005). Gender, religiosity, and reactions to strain among African Americans. *Sociological Quarterly* 46: 323–357.

Joe, K. A., & Chesney-Lind, M. (1995). Just every mother's angel: An analysis of gender and ethnic variations in youth gang membership. *Gender and Society* 9(4): 408–430.

Joe, K. A., & Chesney-Lind, M. (1999). Just every mother's angel: An analysis of gender and ethnic variations in youth gang membership. In M. Chesney-Lind and J. Hagedorn (eds.), *Female Gangs in America: Essays on Girls, Gangs and Gender* (210–231). Chicago: Lakeview Press.

Johnson, B. R., Jang, S. J., De Li, S., & Larson, D. (2000). The 'invisible institution' and Black youth crime: The church as an agency of local social control. *Journal of Youth and Adolescence* 29: 479–498.

Juvonen, J., Graham, S., & Schuster, M. (2003). Bullying among young adolescents: The strong, the weak, and the troubled. *Pediatrics* 112(6): 1231–1237.

Kling, J. R., Ludwig, J., & Katz, L. F. (2005). Neighborhood effects on crime for female and male youth: Evidence from a randomized housing voucher experiment. *Quarterly Journal of Economics* 120(1): 87–130.

Laidler, K. J., & Hunt, G. (2001). Accomplishing femininity among the girls in the gang. *British Journal of Criminology* 41: 656–678.

Leitz, L. (2003). Girl fights: Exploring females' resistance to educational structures. *International Journal of Sociology and Social Policy* 23(11): 15–43.

Lindsey, W. E., Kurtz, P. D., Jarvis, S., Williams, R. N., & Nackerud, L. (2000). How runaway and homeless youth navigate troubled waters: Personal strengths and resources. *Child and Adolescent Social Work Journal* 17(2): 115–141.

Lipsey, M. W., & Derzon, J. H. (1998). Predictors of violent or serious delinquency in adolescence and early adulthood. In R. Loeber and D. P. Farrington (eds.), *Serious and Violent Juvenile Offenders: Risk Factors and Successful Interventions* (86–105). Thousand Oaks, CA: Sage.

Long, J. S. (1997) Regression models for categorical and limited dependent variables. Thousand Oaks, CA: Sage Publications.

Long, J. S., & Freese, J. (2003). *Regression Models for Categorical Dependent Variables Using STATA.* College Station, TX: Stata Corporation.

McCormack, A., Janus, M. D., & Burgess, A. W. (1986). Runaway youths and sexual victimization: Gender differences in an adolescent runaway population. *Child Abuse & Neglect* 10: 387–395.

McCurley, C., & Snyder, H. N. (2004). Victims of violent juvenile crime. Washington, DC: Juvenile Justice Bulletin, Office of Juvenile Justice and Delinquency Prevention. National Institute of Justice.

Maguire, K., & Pastore, A. L. (eds.). (1997). *Sourcebook of criminal justice statistics 1996.* Washington, DC: U.S. Bureau of Justice Statistics.

Miller, J., & Decker, S. (1999). Women and gang homicide. Unpublished Manuscript. (Cited in J. Miller, 2001, *One of the Guys: Girls, Gangs, and Gender.* New York: Oxford University Press, 123.)

Miller, J. (2001). *One of the guys: Girls, gangs, and gender.* New York: Oxford University Press.

Miranda, M. K. (2003). *Homegirl in the public sphere.* Austin: University of Texas Press.

Molnar, B. E., Browne, A., Cerda, M., & Buka, S. (2005). Violent behavior by girls reporting violent victimization: A prospective study. *Archives of Pediatrics and Adolescent Medicine* 159(8): 731–739.

Molnar, B. E., Miller, M. J., Azrael, D., Buka, S. L (2004). Neighborhood predictors of concealed firearm carrying among children and adolescents: Results from the project on human development in Chicago neighborhoods. *Archives of Pediatrics & Adolescent Medicine* 158: 657–664.

Molnar, B. E., Shade, B. S., Kral, H. A., Booth, E. R., & Watters, K. J. (1998). Suicidal behavior and sexual/physical abuse among street youth. *Child Abuse and Neglect* 22: 213–222.

Ms. Foundation for Women, National Girls Initiative. (1993). *Programmed neglect, not seen, not heard: Report on girls programming in the United States.* New York: Ms. Foundation for Women.

Mullis, R. L., Cornille, T. A., Mullis, A. K., & Huber, J. (2004). Female juvenile offending: A review of characteristics and contexts. *Journal of Child and Family Studies* 13: 205–218.

Murray, J., Janson, C., & Farrington, D. (2007). Crime in adult offspring of prisoners: A cross-national comparison of two longitudinal samples. *Criminal Justice and Behavior* 34: 133–149.

Nansel, T. R., Overpeck, M. D., Haynie, D. L., Ruan, W. J., & Scheidt, P. C. (2003). Relationship between bullying and violence among U.S. Youth. *Archives of Pediatric & Adolescent Medicine* 157: 348–353.

Ness, C. D. (2004). Why girls fight: Female youth violence in the Inner City. *Annals of the American Academy of Political and Social Science* 595: 32–48.

Obeidallah, D., Brennan, R. T., Brooks-Gunn, J., & Felton, E. (2004). Links between pubertal timing and neighborhood contexts: Implications for girls' violent behavior. *Journal of the American Academy of Child and Adolescent Psychiatry* 43(12): 1460–1468.

Odgers, C. L., & Moretti, M. M. (2002). Aggressive and antisocial girls: Research update and challenges. *International Journal of Forensic Mental Health* 1(2): 103–119.

Osgood, D. W., Johnston, L. D., O'Malley, P. M., & Bacherman, J. G. (1988). The generality of deviance in late adolescence and early adulthood. *American Sociological Review* 53(1): 81–93.

Pattillo-McCoy, M. (1998). Church culture as a strategy of action in the black community. *American Sociological Review* 63: 767–784.

Phillips, S. D., Erkanli, A., Keeler, G. P., Costello, E. J., & Angold, A. (2006). Disentangling the risks: Parent criminal justice involvement and children's exposure to family risks. *Criminology & Public Policy* 5: 677–702.

Portillos, E. L. (1999). Women, men and gangs: The social construction of gender in the Barrio. In M. Chesney-Lind and J. Hagadorn (eds.), *Female Gangs in America*. Chicago: Lake View Press.

Reed, B. G., & Leavitt, M. (1998, September). Modified wraparound and women offenders: A community corrections continuum. Paper presented at the International Community Corrections Annual Research Conference, Arlington, VA.

Regnerus, M. D., & Elder, G. H. (2003). Religion and vulnerability among low-risk adolescents. *Social Science Research* 32: 633–658.

Ryder, J. A. (2007). "I wasn't really bonded with my family": Attachment, loss and violence among adolescent female offenders. *Critical Criminology* 15: 19–40.

Sampson, R. J., & Morenoff, J. D. (1999). Beyond social capital: Spatial dynamics of collective efficacy for children. *American Sociological Review* 64: 633–660.

Saner, H., & Ellickson, P. (1996). Concurrent risk factors for adolescent violence. *Journal of Adolescent Health* 19: 94–103.

Sampson, R. J., Morenoff, J. D., & Raudenbush, S. (2005). Social anatomy of racial and ethnic disparities in violence. *American Journal of Public Health* 95(2): 224–232.

Schaffner, L. (2006) Girls in trouble with the law. New Brunswick, NJ: Rutgers University Press.

Silverthorn, P., & Frick, P. (1999). Developmental pathways to antisocial behavior: The delayed-onset pathway in girls. *Development and Psychopathology* 11: 101–126.

Slesnick, N., & Prestonnik, J. L. (2005). Ecologically based family therapy outcomes with substance abusing runaway adolescents. *Journal of Adolescence* 28: 277–298.

Snyder, H., & Sickmund, M (1999). Juvenile offenders and victims: 1999 National report. Office of Juvenile Justice and Delinquency Prevention: National Center for Juvenile Justice.

Song, L., Singer, M., & Anglin, T. (1998). Violence exposure and emotional trauma as contributors to adolescents' violent behaviors. *Archives of Pediatric and Adolescent Medicine* 152: 531–536.

Steinberg, L., Mounts, N. S., Lamborn, S. D., & Dornbusch, S. M. (1991). Authoritative parenting and adolescent adjustment across varied ecological niches. *Journal of Research on Adolescence* 1: 19–36.

Sullivan, M. L. (1989). "Getting paid": Youth crime and work in the inner city. Ithaca: Cornell University Press.

Sullivan, P. M. & Knutson, J. F. (2000). Maltreatment and disabilities: A population-based epidemiological study, *Child Abuse & Neglect* 24: 1257–1274.

Tyler, A. K., & Cauce, M. R. (2002). Perpetrators of early physical and sexual abuse among homeless and runaway adolescents. *Child Abuse and Neglect* 26: 1261–1274.

Tyler, K. A., Hoyt, D. R., Whitbeck, L. B., & Cauce, A. M. (2001). The impact of childhood sexual abuse on later sexual victimization among runaway youth. *Journal of Research on Adolescence* 11: 151–176.

Vidal, A. C. & Keating, W. D. (2004). Community development: Current issues and emerging challenges. *Journal of Urban Affairs* 26(2): 125–137.

Wilson, W. J. (1987) *The truly disadvantaged: The inner city, the underclass, and public policy.* Chicago: University of Chicago Press.

Wolfgang, M. E., Thornberry, T. P., & Figlio, R. M. (1987). *From boy to man: From delinquency to crime.* Chicago: University of Chicago Press.

EPILOGUE

MORAL PANICS, VIOLENCE,
AND THE POLICING OF GIRLS

Reasserting Patriarchal Control in the New Millennium

Walter S. DeKeseredy

Ten years ago, Meda Chesney-Lind (1999) observed that many academics, journalists, politicians, and members of the general public were accessing "one of the oldest traditions within criminology—sensationalizing women's violent crimes" (1). This statement still holds true in North America today and there is ample evidence that "things are set to get worse" (Silvestri & Crowther-Dowey, 2008: 106). Ironically, at a time when crime discussion is dominated by calls for more prisons, more executions, and "what about the victim," a market remains for belittling female crime victims (DeKeseredy, 2009; Schwartz & DeKeseredy, 1994). Growing numbers of conservative fathers' rights groups, academics, politicians, and others intent on rolling back the achievements of the women's movement fervently challenge research showing high rates of male-to-female beatings, sexual assaults, and other highly injurious forms of female victimization that occur behind closed doors (DeKeseredy & Dragiewicz, 2007; Stanko, 2006). Moreover, while many people, especially men, are quick to point out human rights violations in totalitarian countries, they simultaneously whitewash or ignore the victimization of women in their own so-called democratic societies (Kallen, 2004; Silvestri & Crowther-Dowey, 2008). And, it is not surprising that despite scores of journal articles and studies showing that men are more violent than are women in heterosexual relationships, we continue to hear the highly injurious mantra "But women do it too." Of course, no commentary on the antifeminist backlash is complete without mentioning government cuts to women's programs, which is another prime example of "patriarchy reasserted" (Dragiewicz, 2008).

There is an important battle being waged over the nature of women's violence and aggression. Similarly, as pointed out throughout this book, there is, in typical U.S. style, a "war on girls" (DeKeseredy, 2000). Some well-known and widely used weapons in this war are "condemnatory media images" of teenage girls, such as those involving relational aggression in Hollywood movies like *Mean Girls* (Chesney-Lind & Irwin, 2008; Schissel, 1997). Such films, statistically rare cases of brutal female violence reported by the media, and untrue claims of a major surge in female youth violence like that offered in James Garbarino's (2006) controversial trade book *See Jane Hit* fuel moral panics about girls deemed to be in conflict with the law or who use various means of rebelling against patriarchal dominance in schools, dance halls, at home, and elsewhere.

The concept of the moral panic was developed by Stanley Cohen (1980) to describe a situation in which a condition, episode, person, or a group of persons come to be defined as a threat to society. The objects of moral panics are usually people. Certainly, the media, together with some social scientists, lawyers, agents of social control, and other "experts," have jumped on the bandwagon to transform girls who violate a myriad of patriarchal gender norms in the United States, Canada, and other parts of the world into folk devils. A folk devil is "a socially constructed, stereotypical carrier of significant social harm" (Ellis, 1987: 199). As vividly pointed out by contributors to this volume, many girls are labeled as being made up of "sugar and spice and everything evil" (Schissel, 1997: 51).

The chapters in this volume stress what may seem painfully obvious, but worth stating again nonetheless: the criminal justice system helps reassert patriarchy. As Mike Males reminds us, there are no convincing data to support the ubiquitous media images about girls' violence. That said, these media constructions do fulfill another purpose; they encourage a social understanding of female violence that supports what Meda Chesney-Lind (1997: 152) calls "equality with a vengeance—the dark side of the equity or parity model of justice that emphasizes the need to treat women offenders as though they were 'equal' to male offenders." Nevertheless, those favoring getting tough on girls' violence obviously aren't interested in using more punitive means of dealing with young men who sexually assault female dating partners and acquaintances "in numbers that would numb the mind of Einstein" (Stephen Lewis cited in Vallee, 2007: 22).Consider that large- and small-scale surveys consistently show that approximately 25% of female undergraduates experience some variation of this crime on an annual basis (DeKeseredy & Flack, 2007).

A burglary or robbery rate this high would turn a high school or college campus upside down, but when the crime is the sexual victimization of women and girls, there is less concern. There are many reasons for this, but the more important are gender politics and powerful interest groups with stakes in demonizing girls and denying the extent of sexual assaults to reassert patriarchy (DeKeseredy & Dragiewicz, 2007). For example, in March 2006, psychologist William F. Flack Jr. and I met with a lawyer at a small private university in the United States to discuss sexual assault on his campus and its immediate surroundings. He stated that a recent study of unwanted sex among students at his school is flawed and, at best, reveals a high rate of "regretted sex." When I told him that unless his institution of higher learning developed an effective prevention plan, there was a strong likelihood that victims' parents would sue, this lawyer replied that he was more worried about lawsuits filed by "alleged perpetrators." Such a response presumes that false allegations of sexual assault are more significant problems than true ones. However, less than 2% of campus rapes reported to the police are false allegations (DeKeseredy & Flack, 2007).

Elliott Currie (2004) found that many white, middle-class youth are on a "road to whatever." "Whatever" is a world that many of his respondents and other teenagers use to describe how they felt before committing dangerous or self-destructive acts. It is, according to Currie, "an emotional place in which they no longer cared about what happened to them and that made trouble not only possible but likely" (14). What motivates them to start and continue this journey? The conservative knee-jerk response to this question is leniency, inadequate discipline, the ethos of self-expression, and other symptoms of "liberalism." Currie's research and this collection show that nothing can be further from the truth. Since the 1990s, lawmakers in the United States, Canada, and other advanced industrial nations have passed draconian laws aimed at regulating youth deviance, and zero-tolerance polices are now common approaches to dealing with relatively minor female transgressions and incivilities in schools across North America. This collection of readings, then, makes explicit that mainstream methods of dealing with girls' "misbehavior" are definitely not informed by feminism or symbolic interactionist Edwin Schur's (1973) call for radical nonintervention. It should also be stated in passing that until relatively recently the United States belonged to a small group of countries that executes people for crimes they committed as juveniles.

Not everyone is at equal risk of being the victim of violence and some victims get more attention than do others (Currie, 2008). Eve Buzawa and David Hirschel support this point. Their analysis of National Incident-Based Reporting System (NIBRS) data shows that compared to adult males, adult females, and juvenile males, juvenile female victims of non-intimate partner domestic violence were the least likely targets of assault to have this harm result in arrest. Moreover, juvenile females were the most likely group to be arrested for simple and aggravated assault, and the second most likely, after juvenile males, to be arrested for intimidation offenses. Many girls, then, are being punished from all directions because they are the targets of both increased criminalization and victimization, an issue also addressed in chapter 3 in this volume by Meda Chesney-Lind. Consider, too, that at a June 2008 National Institute of Justice Sexual Assault Workshop, most of the world's leading experts in the field stated that rates of male-to-female sexual assault have increased in the last few decades. Thus, swift and severe punishment does little, if anything, to improve girls' quality of life.

In badly divided countries like Canada and the United States where politics and media-induced moral panics too often overrule logic, money tends to flow to the issues *du jour*, rather than the most important problems. Barry Glassner (1999) asks whether we as a people are afraid of the wrong things. The media and the populace following behind are afraid of whatever is being newly hyped: terrorist attacks, road rage attackers, methamphetamine, rape drugs, school shootings, "girls gone wild," and other events that are statistically relatively rare. Meanwhile, statistically frequent problems are ignored: homelessness, the lack of proper medical care, particularly among pregnant women (leading to a truly embarrassingly large infant mortality rate) and children, malnourishment of children, extraordinarily low literacy rates, and the alarming number of girls who are beaten, raped, and abused in a myriad of other ways (Schwartz & DeKeseredy, 2008; Stark, 2007). I couldn't agree more with Buzawa and Hirschel's claim that "there should be considerable concern regarding the extent to which we are criminalizing youth and failing to protect them when victimized."

Moral panics about girls have been around for decades, but like U.S. swimmer Michael Phelps' performances at the 2008 Summer Olympics in Beijing, they are, as Mike Males puts it, now "setting records for ferocity." He offers more evidence of the selective inattention given to the harsh realities many girls face today. What is especially disturbing, as Males observes, is that on top of trivializing violence and other harms inflicted on girls, some journalists, academics, and others profit politically, socially, and economically from belittling or demonizing girls' many legitimate achievements. True, the world is not a great place for many young women, but, as Males observes, if we actively listen to girls, a different picture emerges than that painted by academics such as Garbarino (2006). Certainly, today's North American "typical girl" is not like Lindsay Lohan or Paris Hilton. Rather, Males presents reputable survey data showing that most girls today are happy, having fun, and are not on the path to becoming "unruly women" (Faith, 1993).

Listening to girls' voices is deemed radical by most North Americans and the politicians who "represent" them because Canadian and U.S. laws still view children as powerless and as parents' personal property. However, arguments similar to Males' are made by progressive child activists and highly respected scholars around the world, including those who do not identify themselves as feminists. Moreover, child participation in the creating and implementation of the policies and laws that affect them is a key ingredient of the United Nations (UN) Convention on the Rights of the Child (UNCRC), which was adopted by the UN General Assembly in 1989 and came into effect 2 September 1990. Approximately 191 countries have ratified the UNCRC, but Somalia and the United States want no part of it (Olsson, 2003). No wonder there continues to be a war on youth in the United States., and Canada is not much better.

Perhaps large groups of people are reluctant to listen to adolescents for other reasons. For example, Currie's (2004) interviews with boys and girls sensitize us to the role of modern social Darwinist culture. The aforementioned road to whatever starts in youths' families, "which often embody the 'sink or swim' ethos of the larger culture—a neglectful and punitive individualism that sets adolescents up for feelings of failure, worthlessness, and heedlessness that can erode their capacity to care about themselves and others" (14). Darwinism also guides techniques helping professionals and teachers use to treat troubled teenagers, and Currie found that "there is no help out there" for many delinquent youth raised in Darwinian households. In fact, teachers and therapists driven by Darwinian thought exacerbated his interviewees' problems.

If "there is no help out there" for many non-incarcerated female youths, the same can be said about girls in penal institutions. Data presented in chapter 3 by Meda Chesney-Lind strengthen Liz Kelly's (1987) claim that sexual violence exists on a continuum ranging from nonphysical acts such as threats of violence to actual rapes. This is certainly the case for large groups of girls in U.S. juvenile facilities. Although the idea of a continuum is often used to portray moving from the least serious to the most serious, all of these behaviors are serious. Chesney-Lind's analysis of gender and training schools compels us not to create a hierarchy of abuse or violence because many abused girls are drawn into a web of long-term terror at home and in penal institutions through a barrage of events that many people might regard as minor (Kirkwood, 1993). Furthermore, there is a large literature showing that many battered girls and women, regardless of whether they are behind bars, state that the emotional and psychological attacks they endured were worse than the physical pain (DeKeseredy & Schwartz, 2001).

On top of raising awareness about incarcerated girls being abused in ways few of us could imagine, Chesney-Lind correctly points out that police statistics can make a problem look much worse than it actually is. This is certainly the case with girls' violence. More reliable means of measuring this behavior are victimization and self-report surveys, which routinely show that girls are not getting "worse." Still, no other U.S. data set receives more popular attention than arrest data, especially from the media. Perhaps, then, we need more survey researchers with data that challenge sexist moral panics and we need to engage in "newsmaking criminology." This approach is defined as the "conscious efforts of criminologists and others to participate in the presentation of 'newsworthy' items about crime and justice" (Barak, 1988: 565).

Since newspapers, television shows, and magazines reach large audiences, progressive scholars and activists should take every opportunity to disseminate their data and views to the media, creating a situation where they are "seen and heard, not after the fact, but proactively" (Renzetti, 1999: 1236). To achieve this goal, scholars with an alternative perspective on girls' violence and societal reactions to it should volunteer to appear on talk shows, invite the media and call press conferences about special events, new studies, book launches, and so on. That feminist articles and letters are periodically published by the mainstream press and that some of the contributors to this volume have been on television serves as evidence that the media do not totally dismiss or ignore struggles against patriarchal, capitalist, and racist oppression (Caringella-MacDonald & Humphries, 1998; DeKeseredy et al., 2003).

Melissa Dichter, Julie Cederbaum, and Anne Teitelman (see chapter 4) are among the growing number of researchers and government agencies (e.g., Centers for Disease Control and Prevention) that contend that violence against women is multidimensional in nature and that definitions and research should recognize that many women's lives rest on a "continuum of violent actions" (National Institute of Justice, Bureau of Justice Statistics, 1996). Indeed, as Dichter and her colleagues note, violence can also be psychological, and such abuse can be more painful than physical and sexual violence. There are also quantitative and qualitative data sets showing that many abused women simultaneously experience different types of abuse (e.g., DeKeseredy et al., 2006).

To support the erroneous contention that girls are as violent as boys and women are as violent as men, conservative academics (e.g., Dutton, 2006) and fathers' rights groups artificially narrow the definition of violence between intimates to obscure injurious behaviors that display marked sexual asymmetry, such as sexual assault. Dichter et al. reveal that rather than an unacceptable or hysterical broadening of the definition of violence, sexual assault is commonly part of the experiences of abused women and girls (cf., DeKeseredy & Dragiewicz, 2007). They also identify the pitfalls of relying on crude counts of behavior. The gendered context of violence in intimate relationships needs to be taken seriously and this involves moving beyond simply counting slaps, hits, and punches, an issue that has repeatedly been raised in a variety of academic and political settings. Sexually symmetrical data generated by various renditions of the Conflict Tactics Scale (CTS) tell us little, if anything, about why boys and girls or women and men use violence in intimate relationships and the consequences of their behaviors. Nevertheless, these findings have had devastating effects on abused women and girls and their struggles for effective social support services (Dasgupta, 2001; DeKeseredy & Schwartz, 2003; Saunders, 2002). As Dichter et al. state, "The evidence compels us to incorporate an understanding and awareness of sex and gender differences when considering partner violence—its etiology, pathways, and most importantly, its potential consequences."

"Let's Put It into Context" is the title of Stephen Lab's (2003) commentary on public housing violence research done by Ireland, Thornberry, and Loeber (2003). It is also something strongly recommended in chapter 5 by Meda Chesney-Lind, Merry Morash, and Katherine Irwin. They reviewed the extant literature on relational aggression with a critical eye and found that girls' relational aggression is not equivalent to physical violence, aggression, or bullying. Further, boys also commit acts of relational aggression, but are not targeted as much for doing so by journalists and others who contribute to moral panics about girls' violence. Yet, again, as Chesney-Lind et al. observe, we see the draconian effects of net-widening policies and it is typically the girls who suffer most. As stated previously, relatively new domestic violence laws and zero-tolerance school policies have exacerbated the policing of girlhood. Moreover, limited funds that could be used to prevent more serious forms of aggression are diverted to curb behaviors that do not pose major threats to the social, political, or economic order of the United States. It is often said that feminists need to develop a sophisticated theory of girls' aggression and violence that carefully addresses the broader contexts of these behaviors. In chapter 6, Judith Ryder answers this call and uses a version of attachment theory to frame girls' perspectives and use of violence. In addition to offering an empirically informed, novel way of understanding girls' violence, her research reminds us that to effectively help girls in conflict with the law, we need to focus on their significant others' abusive and neglectful behaviors, especially hurtful things done by adults responsible for their health, development, and well-being. Ryder's work, like many other studies, shows that reducing caregiver violence is one of the most important steps we can take to reduce violence outside domestic/household settings.

Although they study different topics and are guided by different theoretical perspectives, criminologist Elliott Currie and the Canadian authors of chapter 7 (Sibylle Artz and Diana Nicholson) have at least one thing in common. They recognize that supportive schools and teachers lower the risk of girls' involvement in aggression and violence. Sound research shows that developing what Currie (2004) defines as a "culture of support," such as inclusive schools and offering troubled teenagers places to go when they leave or are thrown out of their homes, enhances adolescents' health and well-being. Such policy proposals make many people uncomfortable, given the extreme punitiveness of the United States and that large groups of Canadians support laws and policies that mirror authoritarian and gender-blind approaches advanced by U.S. neoconservative politicians, researchers, activists, and practitioners (DeKeseredy, 2009; Grabb & Curtis, 2005). However, Artz and Nicholson found that an inclusive school climate influences girls' assessments of their school experiences, and as argued by social support theorists and proponents of other theoretical perspectives, buffers them from the stress or strains related to past victimization and other injurious symptoms of patriarchy.

The importance of understanding the contexts of girls' lives is, and rightfully so, repeated throughout this book. Contrary to what neoconservative criminologists assert, violence is not a property of the individual. Rather, as Marion Brown points out in chapter 8, violence is spawned by people's conditions and circumstances. She also adds to the large body of research showing that "therapeutic" or "rehabilitative" contexts, such as group homes, may actually promote the harmful behaviors they were designed to curb. Recall that one of Brown's group home respondents stated, "I swear to God this place is just making me worse." An earlier Canadian study of a different topic uncovered similar results. For example, based on her participant observations of homeless women in a hostel, Harman (1989: 106) found that

> The hostel has come to replace home for them. Women who become dependent upon hostels learn that they may exist, in perpetuity, without money or resources of any kind. The hostels replace traditional female roles by being modeled after homes and requiring women to do daily housekeeping chores, and by subjecting them to the rules and regulations of a larger structure that makes the decisions and has disciplinary power. In other words, they teach, foster, and reward domesticity.

Brown's research confirms the well-founded fears of feminists who are hesitant to recommend criminal justice system intervention of any sort. Many women and girls find their experiences with agents of social control—particularly their emphasis on blaming, punishing, individual responsibility, and taking the details of their behaviors out of the context of the lives of those involved—alienating and disempowering. Often, then, mainstream policies mirror the factors that promote violence and victimization.

Brown used qualitative methods to examine ways in which girls who use violence negotiate the living space of the group home. Similarly, in chapter 9, Nikki Jones presents some of the results of her ethnographic research on how girls negotiate conflict and violence in inner-city neighborhoods. Jones' contribution speaks to me on many levels, but one key feature of her work that stands out the most is the importance of examining how broader social forces shape socially and economically excluded urban girls' use of violence. A large social scientific literature shows that chronic urban poverty and an exclusionary labor market are major symptoms of "turbo-charged capitalism" (Lutwak, 1995; Young, 1999), which in turn spawns violent crimes committed by men in public housing estates and other poor metropolitan areas (DeKeseredy et al., 2003). However, much of this work is gender-blind because it ignores girls and women in conflict with the law. Such scholarly selective inattention leaves the door wide open for some journalists, politicians, academics, among others, to, as Jones puts it, "pathologize" young women (especially those of color) and dismiss or ignore the broader political, economic, and social contexts in which girls use violence. Thus, Jones helps fill a major research gap.

In chapter 10, Merry Morash, Suyeon Park, and Jung Mi Kim echo Nikki Jones' emphasis on developing a rich sociological understanding of neighborhood context and its influence on girls' violence. What is especially important is their quantitative research on girls who are violent in late adolescence. Much more theoretical and empirical work on these young women is needed, and the excuse that there are "too few to count" is partially responsible for the selective inattention identified by Morash et al. Consistent with the other contributors to this book, these scholars enhance our understanding of gender and crime by focusing on some key unexamined dimensions of girls' experiences (Adelberg & Currie, 1987).

In addition to suggesting other progressive policies, Morash et al. call for improving the socially and economically excluded, crime-ridden neighborhoods and briefly document the devastating effects of neoconservative Bush administration policies. Such right-wing initiatives too numerous to describe here are not limited to the United States. For example, from the mid-1990s to the start of this new millennium, former Ontario premier Mike Harris and his successor Ernie Eves contributed to the social and physical disorder, which they alleged directly causes crime (DeKeseredy, 2009). While they and their fellow Progressive Conservative Members of Provincial Parliament denounced crime and promised safer streets and communities, their massive cuts to healthcare, welfare, and employment insurance tossed many mentally ill people, homeless families and individuals, and unemployed youths into city streets, where they and many of their behaviors scared local residents (DeKeseredy et al., 2003; National Council of Welfare, 2000). These cuts constitute another example of "Learning from Uncle Sam" (Jones & Newburn, 2002: 97) about how to deal with what Marxist scholar Stephen Spitzer (2008: 72) refers to as "social junk" or people who fail to, are unable to, or who refuse to "participate in the roles supportive of capitalist society."

Chesney-Lind's (2007: 212) commentary on the shift from welfare state to penal state in the United States is also relevant to Canada: "Along with this shift, of course, comes public attitudes about crime issues and criminals that reinforce prison as a viable 'solution' to the many social problems associated with this nation's long struggle with racial justice and income inequality." Although the Canadian homicide rate dropped by 10% in 2006 compared to 2005 (Li, 2007), one of the Harper federal government's new slogans is "Serious Crime = Serious Time," and its omnibus Tackling Violent Crime Act became law on 28 February 2008, parts of which "mimic failed U.S. methods" (Travers, 2007), such as a variation of the "three-strikes, you're out" sentencing law.[2]

Twenty-six U.S. states and the U.S. federal government now have three-strikes laws (Jones & Newburn, 2002), and the Canadian government's similar legislation came into effect shortly after Toronto was designated as "Canada's poverty capital" (Monsebraaten & Daly, 2007). There, close to 30% of families (about 93,000 households raising children) live in poverty, which is a 16% increase since 1990 (United Way of Greater Toronto, 2007). It is likely that a sizeable portion of Toronto's poor girls will soon end up in correctional settings in response to their use of violence and drugs to cope with the stress of daily life-events caused by social and economic exclusion (DeKeseredy et al., 2003; Young, 1999).

In an epilogue to another progressive volume, Meda Chesney Lind (2007: 218) urges readers "to get beyond the traditional way of doing criminology." One way of doing this is to carefully read the works collected here because they give voice to a vital part of our society that is routinely subject to moral panics and a myriad of sexist techniques of social control. Moving beyond traditional criminology also requires a constant struggle to eliminate sexism in all aspects of women's lives, and there are reasons to be optimistic. For example, although Canada and the United States are patriarchal countries, every major social institution, such as the family, the workplace, the university community, and so on has been affected by laws and other means of eliminating patriarchal practices and discourse. Further, public opinion polls reveal that most North Americans support gender equality in most parts of social life (DeKeseredy, Ellis, & Alvi, 2005; Renzetti & Curran, 2002).

Still, in this current political economic climate, is it correct to assume that more progressive leaders would create more liberal policies and laws and terminate neoconservative ones? This empirical question can only be answered empirically. Nevertheless, there is evidence strongly suggesting that it is erroneous to presume that progressive policies would be implemented if a Democrat is elected U.S. president or if a Liberal or New Democratic Party member is elected Canadian prime minister.

At the time of writing this chapter, in the United States, we are already witnessing many Democrats adopting an approach Currie (1992: 93) defined 16 years ago as "progressive retreatism." This involves embracing parts of conservative policies to win elections. This is not a new Democrat strategy. For example, when Bill Clinton ran for president in 1992, "No Republican was going to 'out-tough' him on crime" (Chesney-Lind, 2007: 212). Recall that he interrupted his New Hampshire campaign to preside over the execution of Rickey Ray Rector in Arkansas (Sherrill, 2001). It appears, too, that as of fall 2007, Stephan Dion, Canadian Liberal Leader of the Official Opposition, also did not want to be "out-toughed" on crime.

At that time, Stephen Harper led a minority government, which could have easily fallen had Dion called for a parliamentary nonconfidence vote on the Tackling Violent Crime Act. However, he lacked confidence about going into a fall 2007 election and did not want to "trigger one by defeating the populist law-and-order agenda of the Conservatives" (Hebert, 2007: A17). Another thing that worries me and many others is that few, if any, politicians in Canada and the United States are providing answers to one question of central importance to the contributors to this volume: "What about the girls?"

NOTES

1. Stephen Lewis is cofounder and codirector of AIDS-Free World, a new international AIDS advocacy organization, based in the United States. He was also Canada's Ambassador to the United Nations from 1984 to 1988.

2. The Tackling Violent Crime Act includes revisions to the Canadian Criminal Code, such as: mandatory minimum sentences for firearms offenses; reverse onus on bail for firearms offenses; making it easier for police to investigate and for prosecutors to prosecute people for impaired driving; raising the legal age of sexual consent to 16 from 14; and making it easier to prosecute and indefinitely incarcerate "dangerous offenders" (MacCharles, 2007: A17; Monroe, 2008).

REFERENCES

Adelberg, E., & Currie, C. (1987). Introduction. In E. Adelberg & C. Currie (eds.), *Too Few to Count: Canadian Women in Conflict with the Law* (11–22). Vancouver, BC: Press Gang Publishers.

Barak, G. (1988). Newsmaking criminology: Reflections on the media, intellectuals, and crime. *Justice Quarterly* 5: 565–588.

Caringella-MacDonald, S., & Humphries, D. (1998). Guest editors' introduction. *Violence Against Women* 4: 3–9.

Chesney-Lind, M. (1997). *The female offender: Girls, women, and crime.* Thousand Oaks, CA: Sage.

Chesney-Lind, M. (1999). Review of Patricia Pearson's *When she was bad: Violent women and the myth of innocence. Women & Criminal Justice* 10: 114–118.

Chesney-Lind, M. (2007). Epilogue: Criminal justice, gender and diversity: A call for passion and public criminology. In S. L. Miller (ed.), *Criminal Justice Research and Practice: Diverse Voices from the Field* (210–220). Boston: Northeastern University Press.

Chesney-Lind, M., & Irwin, K. (2008). *Beyond bad girls: Gender, violence and hype.* New York: Routledge.

Cohen, S. (1980). *Folk devils and moral panics.* Oxford: Basil Blackwell.

Currie, E. (1992). Retreatism, minimalism, realism: Three styles of reasoning on crime and drugs in the United States. In J. Lowman & B. D. MacLean (eds.), *Realist Criminology: Crime Control and Policing in the 1990s* (88–97). Toronto: University of Toronto Press.

Currie, E. (2004). *The road to whatever: Middle-class culture and the crisis of adolescence.* New York: Metropolitan Books.

Currie, E. (2008). Pulling apart: Notes on the widening gap in the risks of violence. *Criminal Justice Matters* 70: 37–38.

Dasgupta, S. D. (2001). Towards an understanding of women's use of non-lethal violence in intimate heterosexual relationships http://www.vawnet.org/VNL/library/general/AR_womviol.html. (accessed 3 March 2008).

DeKeseredy, W. S. (2000). *Women, crime and the Canadian criminal justice system.* Cincinnati: Anderson.

DeKeseredy, W. S. (2009). Canadian crime control in the new millennium: The influence of neo-conservative U.S. policies and practices. *Police Practice and Research* 10: 1–12.

DeKeseredy, W. S., Alvi, S. Schwartz, M. D., & Tomaszewski, E. A. (2003). *Under siege: Poverty and crime in a public housing community.* Lanham, MD: Lexington Books.

DeKeseredy, W. S., & Dragiewicz, M. (2007). Understanding the complexities of feminist perspectives on woman abuse: A commentary on Donald G. Dutton's *Rethinking domestic violence. Violence Against Women,* 13, 874–884.

DeKeseredy, W. S., & Flack, W. F. Jr. (2007). Sexual assault in colleges and universities. In G. Barak (ed.), *Battleground Criminal Justice* (693–696). Westport, CT: Greenwood.

DeKeseredy, W. S., & Schwartz, M. D. (2001). Definitional issues. In C. M. Renzetti, J. L. Edleson, & R. K. Bergen (eds.), *Sourcebook on Violence against Women* (23–34). Thousand Oaks, CA: Sage.

DeKeseredy, W. S. and Schwartz, M. D. (2003). Backlash and whiplash: A critique of Statistics Canada's 1999 General Social Survey on victimization." *Online Journal of Justice Studies* [Online]. Available: http://ojjs.icaap.org/.

DeKeseredy, W. S., Schwartz, M. D., Fagen, D., & Hall, M. (2006). Separation/divorce sexual assault: The contribution of male peer support. *Feminist Criminology* 1: 228–250.

Dragiewicz, M. (2008). Patriarchy reasserted: Fathers' rights and anti-VAWA activism. *Feminist Criminology* 3: 121–144.

Dutton, D. G. (2006). *Rethinking domestic violence.* Vancouver, BC: University of British Columbia Press.

Ellis, D. (1987). *The wrong stuff: An introduction to the sociological study of deviance.* Toronto: Macmillan.

Faith, K. (1993). *Unruly women: The politics of confinement and resistance.* Vancouver: Press Gang.

Garbarino, J. (2006). *See Jane hit: Why girls are growing more violent and what we can do about it.* New York: Penguin Press.

Glassner, B. (1999). *The culture of fear: Why Americans are afraid of the wrong things.* New York: Basic Books.

Grabb, E., & Curtis, J. (2005). *Regions apart: The four societies of Canada and the United States.* Toronto: Oxford University Press.

Harman, L. D. (1989). *When a hostel becomes a home: Experiences of women.* Toronto: Garamond.

Hebert, C. (2007, October 19). Dion now looks down the barrel. *Toronto Star,* A17.

Ireland, T. O., Thornberry, T. P., & Loeber, R. (2003). Violence among adolescents living in public housing: A two site analysis. *Criminology & Public Policy* 3: 3–38.

Jones, T., & Newburn, T. (2002). Learning from Uncle Sam? Exploring U.S. influences on British crime control policy. *Governance* 15: 97–119.

Kallen, E. (2004). Social inequality and social injustice: A human rights perspective. Basingstoke, UK: Palgrave Macmillan.

Kelly, L. (1987). The continuum of sexual violence. In J. Hanmer & M. Maynard (eds.), *Women, Violence and Social Control* (46–60). Atlantic Highlands, NJ: Humanities Press International.

Kirkwood, C. (1993). *Leaving abusive partners.* Newbury Park, CA: Sage.

Lab, S. P. (2003). Let's put it into context. *Criminology & Public Policy* 3: 39–44.

Li, G. (2007). Homicide in Canada, 2006. *Juristat: Canadian Centre for Justice Statistics* 27: 1–19.

Luttwak, E. (1995, November). Turbo-charged capitalism and its consequences. *London Review of Books*, 6–7.

MacCharles, T. (2007, October 19). Government warns opposition not to hold up anti-crime bill: "Three strikes'" rule that includes indefinite sentences becomes sticking point. *Toronto Star*, A17.

Monroe, S. (2008, February 29). Tackling violent crime act. http:/wwwcanadaonline. about.com/od/bills/p/violentcrime.htm (accessed 29 February 2008).

Monsebraaten, L., & Daly, R. (2007, November 26). Canada's poverty capital. *Toronto Star*, A1, A6–A7.

National Council of Welfare. (2000). *Justice and the poor.* Ottawa: National Council of Welfare.

National Institute of Justice. (1996). *Domestic and sexual violence data collection: A report to Congress under the Violence Against Women Act.* Washington, DC: Government Printing Office.

Olsson, P. (2003). *Legal ideals and normative realities: A case study of children's rights and child labor activity in Paraguay.* Lund, Sweden: Lund Studies in Sociology of Law, Lund University.

Renzetti, C. M. (1999). Editor's introduction. *Violence Against Women* 5: 1235–1237.

Renzetti, C. M., & Curran, D. J. (2002). *Women, men, and society.* Boston: Allyn & Bacon.

Saunders, D. G. (2002). Are physical assaults by wives and girlfriends a major social problem? A review of the literature. *Violence Against Women* 8: 1424–1448.

Schissel, B. (1997). *Blaming children: Youth crime, moral panics and the politics of hate.* Halifax: Fernwood.

Schur, E. M. (1973). *Radical nonintervention.* Englewood Cliffs, NJ: Spectrum.

Schwartz, M. D., & DeKeseredy, W. S. (1994). People without data attacking rape: The Gilbertizing of Mary Koss. *Violence Update* 5(5): 8, 11.

Schwartz, M. D., & DeKeseredy, W. S. (2008). Interpersonal violence against women: The role of men. *Journal of Contemporary Criminal Justice* 24: 178–185.

Sherrill, R. (2001, January 8). Death trip: The American way of execution. *Nation.* http://www.thenation.com/doc/20010108/sherrill (accessed 3 March 2008).

Silvestri, M., & Crowther-Dowey, C. (2008). *Gender & crime.* London: Sage.

Spitzer, S. (2008). The production of deviance in capitalist societies. In E. J. Clarke (ed.), *Deviant behavior: A text-reader in the sociology of deviance*, Seventh Edition (67–74). New York: Worth.

Stanko, E. A. (2006). Theorizing about violence: Observations from the Economic and Social Research Council's Violence Research Program. *Violence Against Women* 12: 543–555.

Stark, E. (2007). Coercive control: How men entrap women in personal life. New York: Oxford University Press.

Travers, J. (2007, October 23). On crime issue, facts don't matter. *Toronto Star*, A18.

United Way of Greater Toronto. (2007). *Losing ground: The persistent growth of family poverty in Canada's largest city*. Toronto: Author.

Vallee, B. (2007). *The war on women*. Toronto: Key Porter.

Young, J. (1999). *The exclusive society*. London: Sage.

ABOUT THE CONTRIBUTORS

Sibylle Artz, is Full Professor in Child and Youth Care at the University of Victoria. Her research focuses on children and youth who use aggression and violence, particularly girls who use violence. After first working in frontline child and youth care for more than 20 years, she became an academic in the 1990s and has since published more than 50 refereed articles, written two books, *Feeling as a Way of Knowing* (1994) and *Sex, Power and the Violent School Girl* (1997), and coedited a third book, *Working Relationally with Girls* (2004), with Dr. Marie Hoskins. She was chosen in 1998 as Academic of the Year by the Confederation of University Faculty Associations of British Columbia, and in 2004, received the Award of Distinction for Research from the McCreary Youth Foundation of Vancouver. In 2008, she was selected for a Leadership Victoria Award for her many years of community-based research.

Marion Brown, PhD, is Assistant Professor and Field Education Research Faculty at the Dalhousie University School of Social Work in Nova Scotia, Canada. Her research in the area of critical girlhood studies focuses on the construction of the female subject, with recent research on the use of violence by girls living in institutional settings.

Eve S. Buzawa is Professor and Chairperson of the Department of Criminal Justice at the University of Massachusetts-Lowell. She received her bachelor's degree from the University of Rochester, and her master's and doctoral degrees from the School of Criminal Justice, Michigan State University. Dr. Buzawa's research interests and publications encompass a wide range of issues pertaining to policing, violence, and domestic violence. She has authored and edited numerous books and monographs. Her most recently published book, *Domestic Violence: The Criminal Justice Response*, will be coming out in its fourth edition shortly. In addition, she is coeditor with Evan Stark of a four-volume set, *Violence Against Women in Families and Relationships: Making and Breaking Connections*, published in 2009 with Praeger/Greenwood.

She has served as a principal investigator on several federally funded research projects that involved working closely with numerous police agencies throughout the country, as well as other criminal justice and community agencies. She is experienced at working with police, criminal history, and survey data. In addition, she has administered and been involved in a variety of police training projects.

She is past president of the Society of Police and Criminal Psychology, past president of the Northeast Association of Criminal Justice Sciences, and past board member for the Academy of Criminal Justice Sciences.

Julie A. Cederbaum is Assistant Professor in the School of Social Work at the University of Southern California. Her research interests include primary and secondary HIV prevention; social work and public health practice with families; and interventions with families and youth. Her most recent work examined mother-daughter communication about abstinence and safer sex. Specifically, she targeted understanding the differences in mother communication and daughter HIV-risk behaviors between HIV-positive and HIV-negative mother-daughter dyads. Dr. Cederbaum received her PhD from the University of Pennsylvania, her MPH from the University of Pennsylvania, her MSW from UCLA, and her BA from Drew University.

Meda Chesney-Lind, PhD, is Professor of Women's Studies at the University of Hawaii at Manoa. Nationally recognized for her work on women and crime, she is the author of *Girls, Delinquency and Juvenile Justice, The Female Offender: Girls, Women and Crime, Female Gangs in America, Invisible Punishment*, and *Girls, Women and Crime*, published in 2004. She has just finished a book on trends in girls' violence, entitled *Beyond Bad Girls: Gender, Violence and Hype*. She received the Bruce Smith, Sr. Award "for outstanding contributions to Criminal Justice" from the Academy of Criminal Justice Sciences in April 2001. She was named a fellow of the American Society of Criminology in 1996 and has also received the Herbert Block Award for service to the society and the profession from the American Society of Criminology. She has also received the Donald Cressey Award from the National Council on Crime and Delinquency for "outstanding contributions to the field of criminology," the Founders award of the Western Society of Criminology for "significant improvement of the quality of justice," and the University of Hawaii Board of Regent's Medal for "Excellence in Research."

Finally, Chesney-Lind has been included among the scholars working with the Office of Juvenile Justice and Delinquency Prevention's Girls Study Group. In Hawaii, she has worked with the Family Court, First Circuit, advising them on the recently formed Girls Court as well as helping improve the situation of girls in detention.

Walter S. DeKeseredy is Professor of Criminology, Justice, and Policy Studies at the University of Ontario Institute of Technology (UOIT). Author of 13 books and over 70 journal articles, he has received major awards for his scholarship from two divisions of the American Society of Criminology and the Institute on Violence, Abuse, and Trauma.

Melissa E. Dichter is Post-Doctoral Research Fellow at the VA Center for Health Equity Research and Promotion (CHERP) at the Philadelphia VA Medical Center where she studies the impacts of partner violence and associated trauma on women's health, health care, and well-being. Her research interests focus on intimate partner violence among adults and adolescents and the intersections of the healthcare, criminal legal, and social services systems in responding to intimate partner violence. Dr. Dichter is also a research affiliate of the Evelyn Jacobs Ortner Center on Family Violence at the University of Pennsylvania. Dr. Dichter received her PhD in Social Welfare and MSW in Clinical Social Work from the University of Pennsylvania, and her BA in Child Development from Tufts University.

David Hirschel is Professor of Criminal Justice at the University of Massachusetts-Lowell and Professor Emeritus of Criminal Justice at the University of North Carolina at Charlotte. Dr. Hirschel's primary research interests are in victims of crime, particularly spouse abuse, international criminal justice, and legal issues in criminal justice. He has conducted funded research and published books, book chapters, and articles on a wide variety of criminal justice topics.

Katherine Irwin, PhD, is Associate Professor of Sociology at the University of Hawaii, Manoa. Her research focuses on youth culture, youth violence, and the construction of violent girls. Her work has appeared in *Qualitative Sociology, Youth Violence and Juvenile Justice, Sociological Spectrum, Critical Criminology,* and *Youth and Society.* She has just published a book (with Meda Chesney-Lind) exploring girls' violence, titled *Beyond Bad Girls: Gender, Violence, and Hype.*

Nikki Jones earned her PhD in Sociology and Criminology from the University of Pennsylvania in 2004. She is an associate professor in the Department of Sociology at the University of California, Santa Barbara. Her areas of expertise include urban ethnography, race and ethnic relations, gender studies, and criminology and criminal justice, with a special emphasis on the intersection of race, gender, and justice. She is the author of *Between Good and Ghetto: African American Girls and Inner City Violence.*

Jung-mi Kim holds an MS in Criminal Justice from the School of Criminal Justice, Michigan State University. Her master's thesis focused on general strain theory and the school experiences of South Korean youth.

Mike Males has a PhD in social ecology from the University of California, Irvine, and currently is senior researcher for the Center on Juvenile and Criminal Justice, San Francisco, and YouthFacts.org, an online information service. His books include *Framing Youth: Ten Myths about the Next Generation* and *The Scapegoat Generation*, along with numerous articles, op-eds, research papers, and presentations on youth issues. He worked with youth in community and wilderness programs for 10 years.

Merry Morash, PhD, is Professor in the School of Criminal Justice, Michigan State University. Her focus is on gender and crime causation, victimization, and the justice system response. Current work includes analysis of wife abuse connected to migration for marriage. She is author of *Understanding Gender, Crime, and Justice*, published by Sage; and *Women on Probation and Parole: A Feminist Critique of Community Services and Programs* (New England University Presses).

Diana Nicholson has been engaged in research related to supporting at-risk youth for the past decade. She possesses a general interest in various aspects of effective practice with children and youth, and has a special interest in inquiry- and relationally based educational initiatives. Her recently completed dissertation research focused on exploring conceptions of "knowledge" with youth with the intent to inform how teachers embody knowledge in teaching-learning encounters with youth.

Suyeon Park is a PhD candidate in the School of Criminal Justice at Michigan State University. She received a master's degree in Political Science from Ewha Women's University. Her major interests include immigration, crime, and victimization and violence against women. Her dissertation focuses on Vietnamese women who migrated to South Korea to marry, and the patterns of these women's help-seeking when victimized by wife abuse.

Judith A. Ryder, PhD, is Assistant Professor, Sociology & Anthropology Department, at St. John's University in Queens, New York. She specializes in gender and family violence, corrections and juvenile delinquency, and has directed several federally funded research grants investigating issues of violence, maltreatment, and substance abuse. Her current book project explores links between childhood traumatic experiences and violent offending among teenage girls.

Anne M. Teitelman is Assistant Professor in the Center for Health Disparities Research at the University of Pennsylvania, School of Nursing. Dr. Teitelman's research focuses on promoting equity and sexual health for adolescent girls and young women. Her work is informed by a developmental and gender perspective. Her early qualitative and quantitative research explored family and partner influence on girls' sexual health. This led to her current studies on HIV prevention among adolescent girls and understanding how partner relationship dynamics, including violence and abuse, contribute to girls' vulnerability to HIV and other sexually transmitted infections. She is currently PI on an NIH-funded study to develop and evaluate an HIV and partner abuse prevention intervention for African American adolescent girls. Dr. Teitelman is also co-investigator for a CDC-funded study examining assets and stressors in relation to youth violence. She is also co-PI on a pilot study exploring young women's attitudes and barriers to the human papillomavirus (HPV) vaccine. Her prior research was funded by the Michigan Department of Community Health. She publishes her work in journals representing a variety of disciplines and presents at national and international research meetings. Dr. Teitelman is a member of the Center for AIDS Research at Penn, the Philadelphia Community Violence Prevention Collaborative, a Senior Fellow in the Leonard Davis Institute of Health Economics, and Affiliated Faculty with the Ortner-Unity Center on Family Violence. She received her PhD from the University of Michigan, her MSN from Yale University, and her BA from Vassar College.

INDEX